Fighting for Acceptance

Fighting for Acceptance

✦

Mixed Martial Artists and Violence in American Society

David T. Mayeda, PH.D.
David E. Ching

iUniverse, Inc.
New York Lincoln Shanghai

Fighting for Acceptance
Mixed Martial Artists and Violence in American Society

iUniverse books may be ordered through booksellers or by contacting:

iUniverse
2021 Pine Lake Road, Suite 100
Lincoln, NE 68512
www.iuniverse.com
1-800-Authors (1-800-288-4677)

Because of the dynamic nature of the Internet, any Web addresses or links contained in this book may have changed since publication and may no longer be valid.

The views expressed in this work are solely those of the author and do not necessarily reflect the views of the publisher, and the publisher hereby disclaims any responsibility for them.

Photographer: Stephen Mayeda

ISBN: 978-0-595-47891-0 (pbk)
ISBN: 978-0-595-71395-0 (cloth)
ISBN: 978-0-595-60048-9 (ebk)

Printed in the United States of America

Contents

FOREWORD

BY JASON "MAYHEM" MILLER

When Dr. Mayeda asked me to write a foreword for *Fighting for Acceptance* I said, "Yes, of course I'll write a forward!" But then I asked myself, "What the hell is a foreword?" After a quick internet search I realized that I was presented with the daunting task of placing words on a page that would be read by millions of eyeballs, and I had a mini-panic attack. It's rare for me to feel that emotion.

I was sweatin', but then that I switched on MayheM-mode and realized that I strip down to my skivvees and punch, kick, and choke other grown men for the enjoyment of thousands of bloodthirsty fans, who shout out their enjoyment at every violent act that I commit with a chorus of blood-curling shrieks, like the speaking of tongues at a Pentecostal church. The image of two warriors battling in an enclosed cage sparks images of Roman times, as gladiator slaves fought each other to the death for the enjoyment of the crowd, who eventually tired of the spectacle, and upped the stakes by placing the wretches of society to do battle with lions and tigers.

To the untrained eye (read: ignorant) we aren't too far from that point. All that we would need is George W. Bush wearing a laurel giving the thumbs up or down on the life or death of a competitor. But again that is simple minded ignorance, to be redundant. The simplicity of our sport is also its beauty. The rules are so basic and unrestrictive that they lend themselves to some of the most beautiful exchanges and most heart wrenching stories that could take place over the course of a few five minute rounds. Once you learn what is going on between the ropes, or within the confines of the rubber coated fencing, barbarism quickly shifts to science. Savagery to strategy. Brutality to the pureness of sport.

I didn't get into this sport for the chance to beat someone up without going jail. I entered into this sport for the skill, for the challenge and brains it takes to succeed in the arena of combat. The allure of playing the now clichéd "Ultimate Game of Chess" was much too strong for me to pass up. If boxing is the "sweet science," then mixed martial arts must be considered quantum physics. This book also includes some powerful suggestions to help push the sport forward. I'm a pessimist, so I don't have the greatest feelings about the suggestions coming to fruition, but I'm glad that Dave has the gusto to press forward. In fact, I can't think of someone better qualified to write such a book. Rarely do you run into a scholar with such a passion for mixed martial arts. Also being an athlete himself lends a special perspective that a normal bookworm couldn't begin to ascertain.

For the next few hundred or so pages, David Mayeda should take you through the sport's long journey, through its inception as a violent spectacle to its current stage, now considered the fastest growing sport in America. During that journey, you will get to hear from some of the sport's biggest stars, many of whom have walked down the long and twisted road that is mixed martial arts, often stumbling, and at times crawling, but now standing tall and proud as a staple in mainstream American culture.

PART I

THE MIXED MARTIAL ARTS PHENOMENON

Frank "Twinkle Toes" Trigg (left) trading blows with "Ruthless" Robbie Lawler (Honolulu, Hawaii).

1

INTRODUCTION—THE MIXED MARTIAL ARTS PHENOMENON

BY DAVID MAYEDA

UFC, the early years, when there was no rules…. Groin shots were okay, and I used to think that's so barbaric. I remember I had this sick knot in my stomach when I saw an episode of *Inside Edition*. They had this exposé story, "Is this human cock-fighting?" or something like that, and they showed a clip of some guy just taking free shots to this guy's groin. I had this horrible, I felt like throwing up. I was thinking, I would never be able to stomach watching this, ever.

—Interview with Nolan Hong

Some people just can't see stuff when it's right in front of them, and if you are in the media and you're covering the Indy 500 or the NHL playoffs, and you are not covering Chuck Liddell and "Rampage" Jackson, you are a dinosaur, and you are a rotary phone in a cell phone world. Today is the day in America MMA went mainstream. You may not like it, but young people do.

—ESPN Sports Radio Host, Colin Cowherd on "The Herd," May 25, 2007

When people hear the words "mixed martial arts" (MMA), "ultimate fighting," or "cage fighting," the first thing that often enters their mind is an image of two heavily muscled, enraged men trying to beat each other into oblivion within the confines of a steel cage. They are ensconced by uncontrolled and bloodthirsty fans, who demand violence, who crave to hear the brutal collision of knuckles meeting skull, and who are on edge of fighting themselves. It is an event reserved almost entirely for men, who attempt to assert their masculine superiority via the vicious domination of another man. In some cases, especially in the early 1990s, such a description may not be too far from reality. As described in this book's opening quote, the level of uninhibited violence that characterized MMA in its early days caused interviewee Nolan Hong to literally feel nauseous. Wouldn't you? Or maybe you'd love it.

As for me, in the mid-1990s, I had seen a few MMA matches on video, but I never really gave them a second thought. Nor did I consider following the violent craze. But in 2005, I started watching the Ultimate Fighting Championship's (UFC) reality show, *The Ultimate Fighter*, and like many other mainstream sports fans, I got hooked. There was something that drew me to it, and it wasn't the typical drama that emits from virtually all reality shows. Flat out, it was the mix of athleticism and violence. A former high school wrestler myself, each week I wanted to watch ex-collegiate wrestling standout, Josh Koscheck, run roughshod through the other competitors, whose fighting styles were grounded more in jiu-jitsu, boxing, or kickboxing. Koscheck did not win the reality show, but he has since become a marquee UFC star. That's not really the point. The point is, as someone who holds a Ph.D. and who enjoys work in violence prevention, I had to ask myself, why was I drawn so powerfully to this violent sport? And more importantly, how might the growing popularity of MMA affect street violence in America?

Eventually, the co-author for this book, Dave Ching, gave me a call. He had been nudging me for years to give MMA a try, which I always declined. Dave asked me if I thought it would be interesting to carry out a study on MMA and its possible effects on society. I told him that since I'd been hooked on watching *The Ultimate Fighter*, I had been thinking the same thing. Shortly thereafter, we began kicking around ideas, and soon enough we were scheduling our first interview. So if you have ever wondered who these "ultimate fighters" are, what goes on in their heads, what kinds of upbringings they had, and how they see themselves fitting into today's society, then this book is for you. From an academic standpoint, it is a book for college classes in sociology, sports psychology, American Studies, and gender studies. At the same time, it is also a book for sports fans and critics that are curious about this growing MMA phenomenon. And of course, it is a book for MMA fans, fighters, coaches, and others involved in the MMA industry.

When we began this project, we had a few goals. We wanted to put out a product that informed readers about this growing sports phenomenon, through the lens of mixed martial artists themselves. However, it took us the better part of two years to carry out all research phases. As time passed, we continuously became more educated on the MMA game, and our goals expanded. In reading through this work, we hope you walk away with a greater awareness of how diverse those in the MMA industry are, and see that like many other athletes, they are forced to pummel their way through exploitation, structural barriers, and stereotypes. Conversely, we also hope you will see how the MMA industry (and other sporting industries) can be reformed, not only to protect the athletes, but also to heighten their responsibility in promoting a civil, egalitarian, and nonviolent society. In short, we hope as a reader, you use the criticism raised by interviewees and through our analyses constructively—to put political pressure on MMA organizations to make improvements, while simultaneously accounting for the political concerns weighing on mixed martial artists.

As you read on, you'll see that one of the joys that came with working on this project was the privilege of learning from the individuals we interviewed. Any seasoned teacher can relate—we learn as much from our students as they learn from us. One of the first MMA competitors we met, Jason "MayheM" Miller, was quick to point out that he was not highly educated, and truthfully, he is self-admittedly a little "bananas." But anyone who spends five minutes with the guy will realize how innately intelligent and well read he is. Miller told us fanatical stories about driving from Atlanta to California to pursue his MMA dream with only $600 to his name, and at age nineteen nonetheless! So far it's worked out for Miller. He probably has a lot more than $600 in the bank these days.

Then we met people like Yoji Matsuo, who holds a masters degree in civil engineering from the University of California at Berkeley, and Colin Oyama, who holds a law degree and passed the bar exam in California, both of whom now make their livings in the MMA industry. As we continued on this journey, we were more and more intrigued by the diverse range of people who competed, coached, and trained in this controversial and highly violent sport. We even noticed that there were interviewees who had moral issues with their participation in MMA, like hobbyist Terrance (pseudonym) who said of his MMA involvement:

> I do a lot more thinking about what it is that draws me … it's natural for me because I've wrestled my whole life with my brothers and this and that. But you know, it's like an addiction to go to the gym and train mixed martial arts, and I do think about why I do it so much. I'm always hurt, something's always hurt. And more specifically I wonder why fighting is such a natural thing for people to do outside of the gym, not just for a sport but for a way to settle confrontations or get mad at each other and do that. And I spend a lot more time thinking about that sort of thing, and I don't know if I've learned any

answers to those questions but I have become more aware of it in my own life and tried to separate myself from any sort of violence except for in the gym.

It was these and other types of moral conundrums which Terrance raised that we try to address in this book, and as you grapple through the chapters, you will confront a variety of issues raised by forty mixed martial artists, trainers, and hobbyists. You will hear their voices, feel their pain, and consider their opinions while learning about this sport and its inner most intricacies.

Chapter Two of this book outlines a history of violence and injuries in American sports, demonstrating that sporting violence is hardly unique to MMA. Chapter Three will briefly explain the methodology utilized for this project and introduce the forty mixed martial artists we interviewed. From there, you will hear more substantially from the men we interviewed. Chapters Four and Five will examine the interviewees at an individual level, identifying patterns with regard to their upbringing, how they got into the MMA game, and some of the personal issues they deal with as mixed martial artists. In Chapters Six, Seven, and Eight, we examine the sport's growth at a more social and political level, as the interviewees offer their opinions on how this violent sport of MMA might influence violence in American society, how MMA fits in with traditional notions of martial arts, and how they feel protected (or endangered) as participants in this combat sport. In Chapter Nine, we compare MMA to boxing, offering tangible suggestions for protecting fighters. In Chapter Ten, we summarize interviewees' viewpoints on how they feel stigmatized in society as they fight for acceptance. Finally, Chapter Eleven summarizes our final thoughts on the MMA game.

While carrying out this project, there were a few times when Dave and I seriously had to consider whether or not the MMA phenomenon was big enough to merit such a project. But as the months went by, we found ourselves riding a bullet train that just didn't seem to slow down, and at times it was very difficult to keep up. Let's look at how fast this train is moving. In the past decade or so, MMA has changed dramatically. It is currently considered the fastest growing sport in America. As ESPN sports radio host, Colin Cowherd states at the beginning of this chapter, MMA burst onto the American mainstream sports world with a vengeance on May 25, 2007. Despite mainstream media's general reluctance to cover the sport, MMA's growing popularity among young men was simply too large to ignore. On this date, MMA stories were featured prominently in *The Los Angeles Times* (Pugmire, 2007), *The New York Times* (Sandomir, 2007), the *Orange County Register* (Karas, 2007), *USA Today* (Velin, 2007) and surely numerous other major newspapers nation-wide. In addition to this, that same week MMA stars graced the covers of *Sports Illustrated* (Wertheim, 2007) and *ESPN the Magazine* (Glock, 2007), while ESPN provided extensive coverage of MMA on cable television.

The stimulus for this media explosion was the pre-fight hype of then UFC Light Heavyweight Champion Chuck "The Iceman" Liddell and the man who defeated Liddell for the title the following night on May 26, Quinton "Rampage" Jackson. Currently, the UFC is MMA's most dominant organization. Yet even before the media blitz that surrounded the Jackson-Liddell competition, MMA's popularity could not be completely ignored. *Newsweek* magazine covered the sport in October 2006 (Scelfo, 2006), and on December 10, 2006, the popular news show, *60 Minutes*, featured a story carried out by investigative reporter Scott Pelley titled, "Mixed Martial Arts: A New Kind of Fight," illustrating the sport's intricacies that make it so much more complex than a typical bar room brawl.

Furthermore, the financial numbers simply cannot be denied. According to the Associated Press, revenues in 2006 for the UFC's ten pay-per-view events exceeded $205 million—some reports saying just under $223 million (Karas, 2007). In comparison, professional wrestling's World Wrestling Entertainment held sixteen pay-per-view events, garnering about $200 million, while boxing on HBO held eleven events, earning $177 million (Goldman, 2007; Sandomir, 2007). In fact, due to MMA's rapidly growing popularity, a mild rivalry has emerged with boxing, in which promoters and competitors have thrown verbal jabs at one another, debating whether or not MMA is taking over boxing as America's premier combat sport (Pugmire, 2007; Stapleton, 2007). Nobody could have forecasted the sport's unbelievably hasty growth.

The UFC's popularity increased even more on September 8, 2007, again with Quinton "Rampage" Jackson taking center stage. On this date, "Rampage" unified the UFC and Pride Fighting Championship (Pride FC) Light Heavyweight titles by defeating Dan Henderson in an extremely competitive five-round match between two close friends. The Jackson-Henderson match, which took place in London, England, was a ratings triumph for the UFC, being the most widely viewed MMA match of all time in North America. As posted on the UFC's official website, this event was watched by more male sports fans than any other sporting event that day within the 18–49 age group:

> The first ever UFC title fight on Spike TV drew a staggering 4.7 million viewers on Saturday, September 8 (9:00pm-12:11am) making it the most watched UFC event ever and the most watched mixed martial arts event ever in North America. The "UFC 75" telecast emanating from the O2 Arena in London, England peaked at 5.6 million for the bout between UFC light heavyweight

champion Quinton "Rampage" Jackson and PRIDE champ Dan Henderson. The fight card drew more Men 18–34 and Men 18–49 than anything else on television, broadcast or cable on September 8, including heavy sports competition from college football on ABC and ESPN, NASCAR on ABC, and the U.S. Open Women's Final on CBS. (UFC.com, 2007).

Toppling other mainstreamed sports in the television ratings department, MMA continued to prove its media value. And the UFC's media successes continued. Predicted UFC President, Dana White, of the recent December 2007 fight between Chuck Liddell and Pride FC legend "The Axe Murderer" Wanderlei Silva, "They've wanted to fight each other for years, and now it's finally happening. It's going to be the biggest moment in this sport's history" (Rosen, 2007a). Within the MMA community, Liddell's victory of Silva was a mammoth moment.

Although television has been the primary form of media through which MMA has risen (Downey, 2006), as MMA star and interviewee for this book Jason "MayheM" Miller states, "The sport thrives on the internet." Widely read internet pages such as Sherdog.com and MMAWeekly.com dedicate themselves to covering the latest news and rumors within the world of MMA. MMA organizations have their own websites (e.g., UFC.com; IFL.tv; Pridefc.com; Bodogfight.com; Wec.tv; Totalfighting.net; EliteXC.com). Hence, as with so many other industries, the internet highway has become a critical vehicle for MMA organizations to propagate their sport. In any Borders or Barnes & Noble bookstore, magazines dedicated to MMA are readily stocked, such as *Ultimate Grappling*, *Tapout Magazine*, *Gladiator Magazine*, and *MMA Worldwide*. These magazines cover competition results, provide training and diet tips, include interviews, and not surprisingly often feature "ring girls." To deny the impact that MMA is having in American sporting culture would be remiss to say the least.

What is "Mixed Martial Arts?"

Like many readers, I never had a real clue into the MMA concept until the industry caught me in its web in 2005. To the casual American sports fan and those not terribly interested in sports, MMA is still likely an enigma associated with grotesque barbarism. The idea of pitting two men in a ring (often times a caged ring) to fight one another can, no doubt, evoke images of reckless abandon and unmitigated machismo, where pride outweighs the chance of sustaining or inflicting critical injury. And as will be discussed shortly, there was a time in America when MMA stood far closer to the above description than it does now.

MMA is a combative style of competition between two opponents in which a variety of fighting disciplines are utilized in a highly strategic manner. Within sporting circles, there are specific sports known as "combat sports" that set two opponents against each other in one-on-one fashion with physical contact being paramount to the competition. In other words, although singles tennis is a one-on-one sport, it is not a combat sport. Some of the more common combat sports include jiu-jitsu, boxing, kickboxing, karate, tae kwon do, judo, and wrestling. It is important to note that a number of these sports are Olympic sports—amateur boxing, tae kwon do, judo, and two forms of wrestling (freestyle and Greco-Roman). In fact, wrestling is widely acknowledged as the world's oldest competitive sport.

The UFC defines MMA as "… an intense and evolving combat sport in which competitors use interdisciplinary forms of fighting that include jiu-jitsu, judo, karate, boxing, kickboxing, wrestling and others to their strategic and tactical advantage in a supervised match …" (The New UFC Fact Sheet, 2007). The UFC is not the only MMA organization or league. In fact, many others exist and have been rising and falling as MMA has evolved over the years. Currently, the International Fight League (IFL) stands as one of the UFC's chief competitors. In describing MMA, the IFL states, "The roots of MMA date back to the ancient Greeks and the early Olympic sport of Pankration, in which combatants faced each other with very few rules" (IFL Website, 2007).

The famous martial arts practitioner and movie star Bruce Lee actually advocated for a "mixed" version of various martial arts disciplines, hoping to identify the most effective aspects of each martial art when utilized in actual combat, as opposed to in practice sessions. Said UFC Hall of Fame star and former multiple time Heavyweight Champion, Randy Couture, in one of our interviews:

> … I think a lot of the martial arts schools across the country are moving away from the traditional martial arts programs to more of a mixed martial arts curriculum. I think Bruce Lee would be very proud of the movement and what's happening. It's kind of all about what's effective and not getting caught up in one particular style or another.

As Couture suggests and as will be described throughout this book, today's MMA practitioners have come to realize that they must know at least a little bit of each of these disciplines, while also mastering an expertise in at least one to be a truly successful mixed martial artist. Another interviewee for this book, Steven Saito, credited Bruce Lee as the original MMA practitioner:

Bruce Lee practiced and promoted his philosophy of MMA thirty-five years ago. His revolutionary ideas and practice methods continue to have a significant impact in the martial arts world today. If you were to study his training regimen, you would see how amazingly similar his workouts are to those of MMA practitioners today.… Bruce Lee took what was useful from his classical Gung fu style and refined his techniques based on his individuality. Bruce was very much a pragmatist and scientist. He firmly believed in the method of trial and error—of correction and refinement. He discarded what did not work for him and refined what was useful.

In short, one of America's greatest sports icons, and easily the most widely known martial arts icon, imparted onto us a tradition of MMA utilized unknowingly by many mixed martial artists and MMA organizations.

Contrary to much public opinion, today's MMA organizations are also characterized by enforcing a wide range of rules. Okay, well, there are not tons of rules, but there are rules, and they are very significant. There are structured weight classes, rounds with time limits, protective gloves, judges, and a referee who holds substantial power to quickly end competitions. These types of rules will be detailed more extensively in Chapter Seven, which addresses safety issues. At sanctioned MMA competitions, medical doctors are present, and competitors are *usually* provided with medical insurance that covers potential injuries acquired during competition. Finally, MMA rules prohibit a wide variety of physical tactics that could be used in a street fight. For instance, attacks to the eyes, throat and groin are off limits. Head butts (butting an opponent's head with one's own head) and strikes to the back of the head are illegal (MMAWeekly.com, 2006). The establishment of these rules has played a large role in pushing MMA's recent popularity (Graham, 2007).

As far as the competitive setting is concerned, MMA competitions take place in two different types of structures. In some organizations, a caged structure is used. The UFC, for example, utilizes the "octagon," a raised canvas shaped with eight sides, surrounded by a fence. Other organizations such as the now defunct Pride FC and the IFL use a ring that is essentially the same as a boxing ring—four sides surrounded by ropes with no cage. These different competitive structures provide for differing fighting styles and offer a different visual perspective for fans.

Although a few female mixed martial artists have gained some notoriety (e.g., Megumi Fujii, Roxy "Balboa" Richardson, Erin Toughill), MMA, like so many other sports, is dominated by male athletes. Recently *MMA Worldwide* featured two articles on female MMA competitors Tara LaRosa (Norbeck, 2007) and

Amanda Buckner (Gentry, 2007). An article in *Ultimate Grappling* on Gina Carano titled, "One Hot Fighter," seemed to celebrate her sex appeal as much as her athleticism (Dhoot, 2007); notably, the successful and athletic fighter Carano also landed a slot as a trainer in the reality show *Fight Girls*, aired on the cable television station designated for women, Oxygen. Carano is currently being marketed as the face of women's MMA, and is now a permanent cast member on the 2008 version of *American Gladiators*. Although women are making quick progress in the sport (Gregory, 2007), it is still only on occasion that nationally televised MMA cards will have a match involving female competitors. This is hardly surprising, given America's history that discourages women from participating in sports that involve greater levels of physical contact (Cahn, 1994). Likewise, it is not surprising that MMA as an industry is laden with sexist imagery. As in boxing, most MMA competitions have scantily clad "ring girls" carrying ring cards in between rounds to predominantly male audiences, while advertising companies draw on provocative female images' allure to men at MMA events and on television shows.

This manipulative use of sexist female imagery is hardly endemic to MMA. The world of sports, especially male-dominated sports (e.g., American football), is saturated with misogynistic representations and metaphors (Messner, 2002; Nelson, 1995). It is not uncommon for a MMA competitor (or even a commentator) to denigrate an opponent by describing him in feminized terms (e.g., bitch, pussy), a phenomenon that happens in many other sporting venues, thereby perpetuating the idea that women are inherently inferior to men (Katz, 1996). Thus in this manner, MMA as a sport has evolved in ways that follow the conventional American sporting storyline where women are distinguished as substandard objects, peripheral to the male center (Bass, 1996).

This notwithstanding, a substantially larger proportion of MMA fans are female than one would initially assume. And the MMA female fan-base is not there merely to watch athletic men stripped down to their shorts compete against one another. Kailua, Oahu, Hawaii resident Chelsie Castillo is a recent MMA fan, who told us of her interest in MMA:

> I never thought I would like MMA. I figured it was just a bunch of moke (*i.e.*, thuggish) guys beating each other up. Before I went to my first fight I was nervous.... It turned out to really be about more than just fighting. I really started to get into it when I started watching *The Ultimate Fighter*. I got to learn about the hard work that goes into being a fighter. I got to learn the stories behind the fighters and they became real people to me. I could get behind them and become a real fan. I started watching *Fight Girls* and that inspired

me to learn muay Thai. I was so excited to see Gina Carano fight at Elite XC, and I knew then that night I had become a real fan of MMA. Then when I saw Chris Leben fight, it was even better. I knew him. I saw how hard he worked for his KO. You can't half ass the sport. If you do it'll eat you alive—the fans and the opponent. I love being a fan of MMA because it's something real in this superficial world.

Sounds like a typical sports fan to me. The marketing of MMA stars, the personal stories behind their professional lives, and reality shows such as *The Ultimate Fighter* and *Fight Girls* have clearly captured the interest of an unlikely demographic.

A Brief History of Mixed Martial Arts

MMA began creeping into the sports world long before 2007. Most MMA aficionados look to November 12, 1993 as the date that it was conceived in the United States. At this time, the UFC was run by Robert Meyrowitz, Arthur Davie and Rorion Gracie, who founded WOW Productions in Colorado. WOW was backed financially by the Semaphore Entertainment Group, who enabled the UFC to stage its first tournament in Denver, Colorado. Clyde Gentry's book, *No Holds Barred: Ultimate Fighting and the Martial Arts Revolution*, probably provides the most complete historical account of the UFC's origin. In this tournament style competition, experts in various fighting disciplines/arts were matched up to see which fighting style was truly superior. At the very first UFC, among other competitors, there was a Samoan sumo wrestler, a Dutch Karate Champion, an American boxer, a kickboxer, professional wrester and pancrase competitor Ken Shamrock, and the eventual tournament winner, Brazilian jiu-jitsu star, Royce Gracie (Gentry, 2001).

At this time, the competitors were not proficient in MMA as they are today. Again, this "challenge" was more of a spectacle to determine which practitioner, who had expertise in one specific fighting discipline, was the most effective fighter. Physically, Royce Gracie was the smallest competitor in the tournament. Thus, by winning in relatively easy fashion, he proved jiu-jitsu was clearly the dominant style. Of note, Gentry (2001) describes the limited set of rules at this first UFC challenge:

> … six-ounce boxing gloves were required if the fighter's usual art employed closed-fist strikes to the head; otherwise, bare knuckles were permitted. Everything else was allowed with the exception of eye gouging, biting and groin

strikes. There would be five rounds of five minutes, divided by one-minute breaks. There would be no judges ... (p. 52).

Moreover, there were no weight classes. Winners were determined by way of knockout, submission, or the opponent's cornermen throwing in the towel—a sign of submission when the competitor does not choose to or cannot quit. Royce Gracie also went on to win UFC 2 and 4, then retiring from the UFC after fighting Ken Shamrock to a draw in UFC 5. Gracie eventually returned to the UFC to face off against then UFC Welterweight Champion Matt Hughes in 2006.

With the limited number of rules, there was obviously resistance to holding future UFC events across the country. UFC I was held in Denver largely because Colorado "had no boxing commission and thus no legal way to regulate prize-fighting" (Downey, 2007, p. 201). In subsequent cities where UFC events (or "fight cards") were held, political resistance was common and frequently quite powerful. Nevertheless, UFC tournaments managed to take place wherever they could, frequently canceling and changing venues, leading Arizona Senator John McCain to write Wyoming Governor Jim Geringer, "The 'Ultimate Fighting Championship' is a disturbing and bloody competition which places contestants at great risk for serious injury or even death, and it should not be allowed to take place anywhere in the United States" (quoted in Gentry, 2001, p. 122). The next year in 1996, McCain referred to the UFC as "human cockfighting" on the Senate floor, a phrase still widely known today among MMA enthusiasts and critics.

McCain was not alone in heavily criticizing the sport and making the comparison to "human cockfighting." The medical community also took a strong stance against MMA (then known predominantly as "ultimate fighting"). Dr. Lonnie Bristow, former President of the American Medical Association, argued, "Far from being legitimate sports events, ultimate fighting contests are little more than human cock fights.... The rules are designed to increase the danger to fighters and to promote injury rather than prevent it" (quoted in Gentry, 2001, p. 112). And in the *Journal of the American Medical Association*, Dr. George Lundberg wrote the following in hopes of banning "ultimate fighting":

> It is literally a fight to the finish—be that death, incapacitation, or surrender. The more violent, destructive, and dangerous the events are, the more the promoters and some spectators seem to like it.... The more blood the better—on opponents, on ring officials, and on ringside spectators. This is one completely repulsive activity.... Just as they do not now telecast "underground" dogfights from Georgia or cockfights from Arkansas, legal bullfights from Juarez, Mex-

ico, or human executions from prisons, they should not telecast these human fights. (Lundberg, 1996, p. 1685).

The UFC was clearly in a fight of its own—a political one.

Making Reform and Bringing in a New Era

Over the years, the UFC continued to marginally persevere and hold fight events. Through the 1990s, stars emerged, such as Royce Gracie and Ken Shamrock. With no professional venue to capitalize from their athletic training, ex-college and Olympic wrestlers also began testing their athletic skills in the UFC. Dan "The Beast" Severn was one of these amateur wrestlers who came onto the scene, winning two eight man tournaments and the Ultimate Ultimate 1996 tournament, eventually becoming one of only four men who is now inducted into the UFC Hall of Fame (along with Gracie, Shamrock, and Couture). Despite the overall level of athleticism rising among UFC contestants, the competition was still viewed and marketed as a kind of blood sport. In reference to the moniker "human cockfighting" being assigned to MMA, one of our interviewees, Derek Stadler, stated, "Well in the beginning … that's what they (were) marketing.… They didn't really know what MMA was too." Dan Henderson echoed Stadler's point in another of our interviews: "… when the sport first came out, it was marketed as a barbaric spectacle, you know, two guys go into the cage, and one guy comes out type of thing.… That's not exactly how it was … it's drastically changed since then." Let's hope so.

Tank Abbott was one of those fighters who quenched the thirst expressed by bloodthirsty UFC fans. According to Gentry (2001), Abbott would thrive on beating opponents with his overwhelming size and immense knockout power, sometimes grinning to both his screaming supporters and detractors alike through the octagon's cage while methodically punishing his foes. Abbott's fame among UFC fans became infamy among UFC critics. With all the criticism, the UFC was cut from cable television 1997, as well as from some home video and pay-per-view distributors (Gold, 2007a). Notably in this same year, a rival MMA organization emerged in Japan—Pride FC, which would soon become the UFC's primary international rival.

This brought UFC promoters to begin changing their marketing strategies, moving away from total *vale tudo* ("anything goes" in Portuguese), and incorporating more rules designed to protect fighters and gain public acceptance. In 2000, New Jersey legally sanctioned MMA matches, becoming the first state to do so. But it was not until January 9, 2001, that the UFC acquired major financial backing. On this date, Las Vegas casino owners Lorenzo and Frank Fertitta purchased the UFC under the company name Zuffa, LLC ("Zuffa" means "fight" in Italian), partnering with their friend and then boxing manager, Dana White, who would be named UFC President. Things were not easy financially for White and the Fertitta brothers as they took over the UFC reigns.

> … the casino-mogul brothers Frank and Lorenzo Fertitta bought the UFC for $2 million. The UFC built on the reform efforts. Soon there were weight divisions and professional judges. But it seemed as if it had all come too late. The UFC was hemorrhaging money—the White-Fertitta partnership had lost $44 million by 2003—and was surviving almost entirely through a rabid Internet-based fan base. (Gold, 2007a, p. A27).

Financial challenges notwithstanding, the UFC pushed on, building new stars, reclaiming access to cable television, and meticulously acquiring legally sanctioned status state-by-state across the country. Presently, twenty-three states and the District of Columbia sanction MMA matches (Sandomir, 2007), largely a result of the increased rules and mainstreamed marketing approaches, and the UFC is pushing aggressively to get MMA legalized in all fifty states (Brodesser-Akner, 2007). With regard to the reform in rules, UFC President Dana White was recently quoted in *Sports Illustrated* as saying, "If it wasn't for Senator McCain, we wouldn't be where we are today" (Syken, 2005, p. 30). One of our interviewees, Paul Halme, agrees with White. In referencing Senator McCain, Halme said, "He probably was a big influence on the sport making the turn where it's at…. You know I'm happier about the sport the way it is now. It's more accepted because of the changes."

Hitting the Mainstream and the Pursuit for Sporting Legitimacy

Following the reality show craze currently permeating network and cable television, the UFC created its own reality show on Spike TV, which proclaimed itself to be a station reserved exclusively for men. Dubbed *The Ultimate Fighter*, like many other "reality" shows, this one was far from reality, lodging sixteen aspiring mixed martial artists in one house with no televisions or phones, where they would compete week by week for the chance to attain a lucrative financial contract with the UFC. Not surprisingly, the reality show was an instant hit with males in the eighteen to thirty-four year old demographic.

In the meantime, Pride FC in Japan had already made a huge name for itself. Even before the UFC was starting to lure in the American mainstream, Pride FC was selling out 50,000-plus seat arenas in Japan for their fight cards. And while the UFC drew its fighters primarily from the United States and Brazil, Pride FC had a much more international list of competitors. Obviously since Pride FC was based in Japan, it had a large number of Japanese competitors. Additionally, Pride FC boasted numerous fighters from Brazil, Holland, Cameroon, South Korea, the United States, England, Russia, Croatia and so on. Had it not been for *The Ultimate Fighter* reality show, Pride FC may have remained the dominant MMA organization in the world.

However, *The Ultimate Fighter* provided a visual setting that pulled in a much wider range of male sports fans. The show made stars out of these up and coming young mixed martial artists and their coaches (Navarro, 2006), while also providing viewers with a peek into some of the training regiments and psychological and physical issues they deal with. About to enter its seventh season, *The Ultimate Fighter* is essentially an outreach tool where the UFC advertises upcoming pay-per-views and other major fight cards to be aired on Spike TV, also creating storylines that can culminate into enticing MMA match-ups. In hindsight, the UFC reality show was likely the primary catalyst that pushed MMA into becoming truly mainstreamed. How mainstreamed you may ask? *The Ultimate Fighter* reality show "often outdraws NBA and baseball games among the coveted 18- to 34-year-old male demographic" (*USA Today*, 2006, p. 01D). As some of our interviewees will mention, the show gave MMA the necessary exposure it had always needed. However, a number of our interviewees also cautioned that the show reaffirmed too many negative stereotypes about mixed martial artists.

As the UFC and MMA in general began exploding in popularity in 2005, a number of new phenomena occurred. To begin with, more MMA competitors began training as true professional athletes. Although this still happens very frequently today, it was far more common in the past that mixed martial artists were forced to train while also holding down a primary job to make ends meet. With more money flowing into the sport, a greater proportion of fighters' salaries (or purses) increased so that they could focus only on training and competition, more similar to an athlete competing in the National Football League or National Basketball Association (though mixed martial artists' purses are still miniscule in comparison). "Fighting used to be a side activity for most fighters, with only the top-of-the-line guys being able to train full time. That gave those fighters an advantage against up-and-coming fighters who needed to train on the side while working full-time jobs" (Martin, 2007). Now there are more than just a handful of stars who train full time, thereby increasing the pool of elite mixed martial artists in all weight classes.

UFC promoters (namely Dana White) also were quick to point out that with the professionalization of MMA, a fairly large number of mixed martial artists had emerged as highly positive role models. Although such statements were surely tied to revamping the sport's image, it was difficult to ignore the numbers. In the past, a successful college wrestler had no way to utilize his athletic talents occupationally after college. If one earned All-Conference honors in football at the N.C.A.A. Division I level, he would at least get a tryout with an NFL team, and possibly be drafted. But for wrestlers (like most women's collegiate sports), there was no professional equivalent, even for All-Americans. Hence, earning a college degree was more important for wrestlers than athletes who could move on to revenue-producing sports, should they be that talented.

Dana White was quoted as saying in the *USA Today* that youth posting fight videos over the internet would "be better off going to college, like most of our fighters" (*USA Today*, 2006, p. 01D), although no research has stated exactly what percentage of mixed martial artists have actually earned college degrees. According to this same article, MMA has appealed to such a wide variety of fans because so many mixed martial artists are more like everyday people that fans can identify with, as opposed to flamboyant, self-centered athletes that make headlines in many other sports. Professor Michael Masucci was quoted in the *Los Angeles Times* saying of mixed martial artists, "These guys are trained at the highest level using the latest technology. They're not just putting their beer down and walloping on people" (Arritt, 2006, p. D10).

Clearly, the UFC worked (and is still working) extensively to present itself as a legitimate sport with quality citizens. Perhaps no mixed martial artist portrays this image more than former UFC Heavyweight Champion, Randy Couture. Regaining the Heavyweight Title at age forty-three, middle-aged men could identify with this Hall of Famer. But in addition to his age, Couture has always been noted as well-spoken, highly educated, and a most gracious sportsperson. Of course there were and are mixed martial artists who embody an opposing persona, as noted by another highly regarded mixed martial artist interviewed for this book, Dan Henderson: "I mean we have our share of arrogant fighters as well. But for the most part, they're pretty humble cause I think deep down they know that they're the cream of crop as far as martial arts go." With athletes like Couture and Henderson, the UFC has found it easier to negotiate the popular and political terrain—maintaining its edgy extreme sporting image that would draw in younger viewers, while also spotlighting its socially celebrated role models who satisfied political conservatives and attracted a more diverse socio-economic fan-base.

The Rise of New Mixed Martial Arts Organizations

With the UFC's rapidly growing popularity and Pride FC already holding such popularity in Japan, other organizations in the United States began sprouting. Within the past two years, World Extreme Cagefighting (owned by the UFC), Bodog Fight, Elite Extreme Combat, and the IFL all emerged as major players in the MMA world. Dallas Mavericks owner Mark Cuban is also throwing himself into the mix, creating his own MMA league, and his league should become a major player given Cuban's wealth and experience in sports ownership. Said Cuban of his upcoming league and his desire to model MMA after his National Basketball Association team, "The key to the future of MMA in my opinion is creating a foundation for young fighters to turn professional with confidence they can make a living and take care of their families" (Gross, 2007a). The IFL has taken its own twist in attempting to find a unique MMA niche by making itself team oriented where twelve city-based teams face off in dual meets. Teams earn points when individuals within the team win matches. The league has playoffs, and each season culminates with a final team earning the championship. As noted previously, these organizations have their own websites. They often times hold their own pay-per-view events, and IFL matches are shown weekly on Fox Sports Net (McCarthy, 2007).

In addition to new organizations emerging, older MMA organizations benefited from the new and rising interest in MMA. In Hawaii for example, Icon Sport stands as a MMA organization that consistently draws large audiences. Icon Sport—previously known as Super Brawl and recently bought out by Elite Extreme Combat—actually drew almost 8,000 fans for a fight card in 1999, illustrating the organization's longevity in the industry (Morinaga, 2006). And as will be discussed more extensively in this book, smaller organizations are constantly popping up all over the country, trying to capitalize on MMA's increasing popularity, sometimes putting mixed martial artists at risk since these less established organizations cannot as easily provide adequate safety measures.

Even gyms that provide training in MMA are becoming more apparent. In the past, gyms tended to focus more on traditional martial arts (e.g., karate, judo) or boxing. Now sporting gyms have jumped on the MMA bandwagon and are providing classes in MMA as its own discipline. Randy Couture describes this evolution: "Where once the karate or Brazilian jiu-jitsu black belt, Olympic wrestler, or McDojo specialist was out to prove his style's supremacy, now stood a full-fledged mixed martial artist, adept at all facets of the sport" (Couture, 2006, p. 13). Many mixed martial artists have opened their own gyms as a way to promote their sport and insure a livelihood, knowing their athletic longevity may not be especially long. Some of the mixed martial artists and/or trainers interviewed for this book who have taken this route include Dan Henderson, Randy Couture, Chris Reilly, Antonio McKee, Guy Mezger, and Travis Lutter.

The UFC Takes Control and goes Global

In March 2007, the UFC cemented its status as the premier MMA organization in the world when Lorenzo and Frank Fertitta purchased Pride FC reportedly for $70 million (Wertheim, 2007, p. 60). The two organizations had been fierce competitors over the years. MMA fans constantly debated over the internet as to which organization had superior fighters—if a UFC champion in a certain weight class fought Pride FC's counterpart champion, who would win? With the UFC's acquisition of Pride FC, such questions are now being answered.

In a conference call involving Lorenzo Fertitta, Dana White, and Nobuyuki Sakakibara (then Pride FC CEO), Lorenzo Fertitta stated of the merger/purchase:

> What we've created here is a global platform. The UFC is, obviously, very successful in North America. We're venturing out to Europe, to the U.K. where we haven't even had our fight, yet, and we've had a tremendous amount of success based on the initial ticket sales. The buzz is happening there. Now, by combining and bringing Pride in, which is a dominant player in Asia, it's really given us a true global platform. (Arias, 2007).

To date, it appears that the UFC is signing former Pride FC athletes on an individual basis with the Pride FC organization falling completely defunct. However, what is most noteworthy for the purposes of this text is the astonishing growth and organizational changes that have occurred within the MMA industry over the past fourteen years, especially within the past two years. And the UFC has made known its plans to expand beyond the United States. Dana White was quoted in *Television Week* as saying:

> Our strategy right now is global ... we are now in 150 countries with a powerful product that everyone understands. What we want to do now is take our events to these markets and create the first global pay-per-view with people from all over the world buying the fight. (Pursell, 2007, p. 3).

Travis Lutter agreed with White, telling us in our interview, "Man, it's got a world market. It's literally got a world market." Given the UFC's ambitions and these incredible changes in the MMA industry as a whole, we felt it was impor-tant to interview a variety of MMA competitors and attain their personal views on how they see themselves within this constantly evolving industry, as well as how they feel MMA may or may not impact society at large in the years to come.

Project Overview

We first decided to tackle this project late in 2005. From day one, we felt that it would be important to interview a diverse group of mixed martial artists. This book was never envisioned to be about interviewing the most famous or popular MMA practitioners. We simply wanted to talk with young men who were just getting started, and those who had been in the business for quite some time, to get their varying viewpoints on how MMA had affected their lives and how they felt MMA may affect their social surroundings.

However, as we got to know more and more MMA competitors, and as the industry changed so fast in the midst of our project, the project turned and twisted in so many ways. As MMA trainer and co-owner of Legends Gym in Hollywood, CA, Chris Reilly, said to us in his interview:

> … just look at how much things have changed since the first time we met. It's amazing how much the sport has changed. And I'm sure by the time you get this done and this gets out to anyone, it will be a completely new scene after that. And so it's a really exciting, it's really an amazing time.

We started interviewing MMA competitors in February 2006. Consequently, many of the questions we asked became moot. For instance, questions about the MMA industry's growth potential were answered to a large degree on May 25, 2007, when MMA made headlines across the American mainstream media (though we still do not know what will happen globally).

In addition, we never anticipated being able to interview some of the top names in the business, but through snowball sampling (primarily via Jason "May-heM" Miller), we were able to interview the likes of Randy "The Natural" Cou-ture, Quinton "Rampage" Jackson, and "Dangerous" Dan Henderson—all of whom currently or recently held MMA titles in the UFC or Pride FC (ostensibly, Henderson still holds a Pride FC title, despite the company's apparent closure). Likewise, when we approached a number of MMA veterans for interviews who had made a name for themselves over the years—Antonio McKee, Guy Mezger, Frank Trigg, Travis Lutter, Allan Goes, Tony Fryklund, and Chris and Mike

Onzuka—we were welcomed into their gyms, despite us being complete strangers, and they even allowed us to interview MMA fighters who they were training.

Obtaining the interviews was not an easy task (see Chapter Three for a description of the methodology); we were blown off, rejected and "stood up" by quite a few other MMA competitors with whom we wanted to speak. At the same time, we were equally amazed at the hospitality displayed by so many of the individuals we interviewed. We became close friends with some of our interviewees, worked out regularly with some, and admittedly lost the complete objectivity that is so sternly demanded in many academic circles.

Our very first interview was with Nolan Hong, co-owner of a small business that sells MMA products and who has only had one MMA competition. Towards the end of the interview, he commented on the MMA community by making the following statement:

> It's like a whole 'nother world in there. You guys will see that when you start interviewing more people. And for the most part, the majority of the people involved are very passionate. I think that will be the common denominator that you will see, that they are all very passionate about it. Then you're going to have a lot of varying opinions, tons of stories, good and bad, regarding the sport, but ... I think the thing is you're going to become, more attached ...

In all respects, he couldn't have been more correct.

2

AMERICAN ACCEPTANCE OF SPORTS INJURIES AND VIOLENCE

BY DAVID MAYEDA

It seems people want to think that here in America, we live in a peaceful, warm and fuzzy society. We don't start wars over religion or xenophobic idiosyncrasies, or oil for that matter. I mean come on, we're the protectors of the world! (Wait, what happened in Rwanda in 1994, and what's happening in Darfur and Kenya now?) Our police departments would never abuse ethnic minorities. It's bad enough that Michael Vick admitted to bank rolling wicked dog fights in Virginia, but our authorities would never sic police dogs on humans, or spray them down with fire hoses as they fought peacefully for their civil rights. We would never imprison American citizens based purely on their race and then have them fight for us in battalions that would later have the highest casualty rates in American war history. And we would never take people's land, damn near exterminate them through war and disease, only to atone for our little mishaps by oh so generously giving them little plots of land in North America and the Pacific. And likewise in the United States, we would never have ritualistic competitions that actually put people's health at risk simply to entertain the masses. We're not that primitive, are we?

The fact of the matter is, fighting and violence have always been accepted in various circles of American society. If you think MMA is bad, sit tight and read on. Fighting as an informal but institutionalized practice was far more common than one might realize long before sports gripped the American consciousness as they do today. During the sixteenth and seventeenth centuries, in states such as Virginia, Kentucky, Mississippi, Alabama, and Georgia, "rough-and-tumbling" was a widespread form of fighting that males used to settle disputes and acquire a respected reputation. Rough-and-tumbling was essentially an all out, no-holds-barred form of fighting between two men with the only prohibition being the use of weaponry. Occasionally today, people refer to MMA as "no-holds-barred" competition. But what is really meant by "no-holds-barred?" Biting, choking, hair pulling, striking and tearing off of testicles were all accepted fighting techniques in rough-and-tumbling. Onlookers would surround the two fighters, cheering them on until one man quit or was incapacitated. Two men would engage in rough-and-tumble matches to uphold their honor, and the level of violence in these matches was extreme to say the least.

According to Gorn (1995), severing an opponent's body part would earn high praise, with eye gouging yielding the most respected adulations:

> Amid the general mayhem … gouging out an opponent's eye became the sine quo non of rough-and-tumble fighting, much like the knockout punch in modern boxing. The best gougers, of course, were adept at other fighting skills. Some allegedly filed their teeth to bite off an enemy's appendages more efficiently. Still, liberating an eyeball quickly became a fighter's surest route to victory and his most prestigious accomplishment. (p. 38).

Obviously, this brutality was not celebrated amongst all social groups. However, among men whose lives were characterized by fear of the unknown, such excessive violence was highly distinguished and not seen as terribly abnormal. "Violent sports, heavy drinking, and impulsive pleasure seeking were appropriate for men whose lives were hard, whose futures were unpredictable, and whose opportunities were limited" (Gorn, 1995, p. 45). In short, depending largely on the cultural environment, violence—either in or out of sport—can be interpreted and accepted on vastly different levels (Lance, 2005).

Thus, returning to an examination of violence in MMA and sports in general, it is critical to remember that violence in socially accepted arenas has a long standing place in American society, and as we situate the MMA phenomenon within a broad American historical context, the levels of violence occurring in MMA should not be especially shocking. Hey let's not kid ourselves, sporting violence and physical injuries were phenomena our society accepted, and often times glamorized, long before MMA entered the sporting scene in 1993. This notwithstanding, the greatest criticisms directed towards MMA competitions have revolved around the issue of safety, and there is no question, MMA is a violent sport—one that puts athletes at risk of sustaining serious injury. However, sporting violence is hardly something unique to MMA.

Much of our society already accepts violence and injury in a wide variety of sports, for many age groups and both sexes. Sports can be divided into three categories, based on the level of physical contact involved:

- High-contact/collision sports (e.g., American football, rugby, hockey, boxing)

- Incidental contact sports (e.g., basketball, soccer)

- Non-contact sports (e.g., track & field, swimming, volleyball)

Obviously, MMA is a high-contact/collision sport. MMA participants often pull opponents into their grasp, strike one another with kicks and punches, and manipulate body parts to earn submission victories. To the reader unfamiliar with a diverse understanding of athletic activities and American sports history, this may sound gruesome, barbaric, and completely uncivilized. But as noted above, violence and injury in sports are essentially par for the course.

Boxing and Professional Football

Boxing (or prizefighting) has struggled to become part of the American fabric for centuries. In the early days, boxing was commonly known as bare-knuckle fighting since gloves were not used. Weight classes (like the early days of the UFC) were non-existent, or divided into only two categories. Illustrating its most extreme levels, Sammons (1990) notes that in 1887, a "… fight went on for three hours and thirty-nine minutes before officials called it a draw" (p. 8), and that another fight which took place in over one hundred degree weather during the Summer of 1889 lasted seventy-five rounds (p. 10). The brutality that characterized boxing's early days raised questions as to whether or not the sport should actually be deemed a crime. Thus, like MMA, boxing went through a series of reforms in order to gain acceptance in American mainstream society.

Today, boxing remains under heavy scrutiny. Like MMA, boxing is "one of the only major sports where direct harm to an opponent's head is an objective of the sport, and where victory is proclaimed when the opponent is rendered senseless" (Toth, McNeil, & Feasby, 2005, p. 693). In other sports (e.g., American football and hockey), obviously head injuries can happen, but they are not a direct athletic goal. A report from the 1999 Annual Meeting of the American Medical Association (American Medical Association, 1999) notes the following:

> Boxing-induced acute brain injury can cause death, although acute mortality from boxing is rare. A subpopulation of professional boxers suffers from chronic neurological injury, the severity of which in later life correlates in some studies with the frequency of exposure (number of bouts), and possibly

severity of head trauma as measured by the occurrence of technical or concussive knockout. (p. 6).

In other words, boxing often causes brain damage, period. Dementia pugilistica (chronic traumatic brain injury) is more commonly referred to as being "punch drunk." Approximately 17 percent of all retired boxers suffer from the punch drunk syndrome (Lewis, 2006), symptoms of which include short-term memory, short attention span, slow muscular movement, and difficulty processing information. Ever listened to a middle-aged boxer speak and notice a lisp, or how much slower he speaks in comparison to when he was just getting started in his early twenties? You got it, that's the punch drunk syndrome. With regard to less long-term injuries, simple facial cuts are the most common injuries in boxing (Bledsoe, Li, & Levy, 2005). And finally, boxing deaths cannot be ignored. "Since 1970, about 50 professional boxers have died in the ring" (Newfield, 2001, p. 15).

Boxing, however, is not the only sport that puts athletes at risk of serious injury. As early as 1983, scholars who advocated for a ban on boxing were comparing its level of risk with American football (Annas, 1983). A number of studies have been conducted which document the variety of serious injuries that occur in American football. It is commonly known among football coaches and players that defensive players who tackle ball carriers are at greatest risk for spinal and/or head injury, especially when they use their helmet as a weapon, and that this tackling practice (intentionally going helmet-to-helmet) is illegal. This notwithstanding, medical practitioners still express their concern that football players are at high risk for concussions and spinal injuries (Pelletier, 2006; Torg, Guille, & Jaffe, 2002). The recent spinal injury sustained by Buffalo Bills tight end, Kevin Everett, is a sobering reminder of this grave injury that can happen in football (Wawrow, 2007). With regard to knee injuries, one study on the National Football League (NFL) found that between 1998 and 2002, thirty-three injuries to the anterior cruciate ligament (ACL) occurred to either running backs or wide receivers, seven of which impaired athletes from returning to competition (Carey et al., 2006).

And then there is the problem of concussions. NFL football fans who remember the brutal hit sustained by then Kansas City Chiefs quarterback Trent Green at the beginning of the 2006 football season surely also recall watching his helmet bounce violently off the ground. That concussion kept him out of the first half of the 2006 season. Then in 2007 when playing for the Miami Dolphins, Green suffered another grade three concussion (the most severe) during a game against the Houston Texans, causing concern about Green's football future (Battista, 2007). A recent study conducted by the University of North Carolina's Center for the Study of Retired Athletes found that among retired NFL football players, the number of concussions sustained correlated positively with rates of diagnosed clinical depression (Schwarz, 2007a). In other words, the more concussions a football player sustained as a pro, the more likely he was to be depressed for no apparent reasons in mid-adulthood. Not surprisingly, the NFL reportedly attempted to downplay the study's findings (Schwarz, 2007b).

College and High School Athletics

Between 1989 and 2002, there was an average of about fifteen catastrophic spine injuries to high school or college football players. Statistically, these numbers are extremely low, provided that in a given year approximately one million high school students and 75,000 college students play football. For example, between 1989 and 2002, only about one in every 192,000 high school or college football players fell victim to quadriplegia as a result of a football injury (Boden et al., 2006, p. 1231; see also Mueller, 2001).

The more common concern is concussions. At the college level when comparing various sports, football players tend to be at highest risk of suffering a concussion. It is estimated that about 9 percent of all college football players suffered from a concussion between 1997 and 2000. Other sports in which players were at high risk for sustaining a concussion were ice hockey, wrestling, men's and women's soccer, and men's and women's lacrosse (Covassin, Swanik, & Sachs, 2003, p. 20; Brophy et al., 2007). Without having a particular focus on age, one study compared football with ice hockey and soccer stating that, "Likely at least in part because of its large number of participants, football accounted for the largest total number of head injuries, concussions, and combined concussions/ skull fractures/internal head injuries presenting to (emergency departments) from 1990 to 1999" (Delaney, 2004, p. 82).

Our society also seems to have accepted that certain women's and girls' sports place participants at high risk for serious knee injury. In particular, a great deal of research has spotlighted the risk that women take of sustaining an ACL tear when playing basketball or soccer. ACL injury rates for women are double those for men when it comes to college soccer, and triple for college basketball (Arendt, Agel, & Dick, 1999); a higher number of these injuries occurs for females during athletic movements that do not involve contact with other athletes (Agel, Arendt, & Bershadsky, 2005) due to sudden stops or landing from a jump (Chappell et al., 2005). *Sports Illustrated* pointed out in 1995 that among six major college athletic conferences, eighty-seven female basketball players had been sidelined from ACL injuries versus only twenty-six male basketball players. The article was subtitled, "Women's basketball is making great strides, but it is suffering an epidemic of torn knee ligaments along they way" (McCallum & Gelin, 1995, p. 44).

In addition to basketball and soccer, women and girls are more likely to tear an ACL in skiing, gymnastics, and volleyball (Baker, 1998). Because athletes can frequently return to competitive athletic form after an ACL tear, these injuries may not seem extremely serious at first. However, the long-term effects of an ACL injury can be. "Blowing out an ACL can end a girl's sports career, but doctors have also suspected that the injury sets the stage for osteo-arthritis, a degenerative joint disease that typically strikes older people" (Fackelmann, 2004, p. 9D).

Returning to high school sports, during the 2005–06 school year, 4.2 million high school students participated in at least one of the following nine sports: football, wrestling, boys' and girls' soccer, boys' and girls' basketball, volleyball, baseball, and softball. During this year, 1,442,533 injuries occurred, with football having the highest incidence rate, though girls' basketball and wrestling had higher proportions of athletes who endured injuries resulting in seven-or-more days lost due to the injury (Comstock et al., 2006, p. 2673). Just ask the photographer for this book how he tore his ACL as a high school freshman—football.

Despite the low occurrence of severe or fatal injuries in football, the sport remains a dangerous one. Ramirez and colleagues (2006) worked with eighty-six high school football teams in California in 2001 and 2002 to determine the range of injuries players endured. Their study reports an injury rate of 25.5 per 100 players. Sprains and strains composed 46.1 percent of all injury types, followed by skin contusions, abrasions or lacerations (16.9 percent), and concussions (10.8 percent). About 7 percent of injuries were factures, and 5 percent were dislocations or subluxations (p. 1152). With regard to absolute numbers, the study recorded 204 concussions, 118 fractures (mostly to the wrist, hand, or finger), and 79 dislocations/subluxations (mostly to the shoulder).

Clearly, concussions in high school football are a serious issue. A self-report study carried out during the 1996–97 school year in Ohio and Pennsylvania found that 47.2 percent of all high school football players had experienced at least one concussion as a result of playing football. Moreover, of those athletes who received a concussion, 73.6 percent reported having had multiple concussions (Langburt et al., 2001, p. 84). Although these rates seem unusually high, high school football players seldom report concussions to coaches, athletic trainers, or doctors because (1) they do not know the signs or severity of concussions, (2) they fear losing playing time, and/or (3) they fear being labeled weak by coaches and teammates (Schwarz, 2007c). This is not surprising, given that their NFL role models behave accordingly in underreporting concussions (Schwarz, 2007d). Female high school athletes also suffer from concussions, especially in basketball and soccer, at rates that greatly exceed their male counterparts in those same sports; like males, many female athletes also fear reporting possible concussions to coaches (Schwarz, 2007e). And that's just high school.

Youth Sports

In a given year in the United States, about "3.5 million children under age 14 receive medical care for a sports injury." In 2003, over 205,000 children between the ages of five and fourteen were sent to an emergency department for an injury sustained while playing basketball and over 185,000 for an injury sustained while playing football (*Hospitals and Health Networks*, 2006, p. 22). In a study of 678 youth football players (fourth-eighth grade), 259 reported sustaining an injury, 13 percent of which were considered major injuries (Malina et al., 2006). Additional research on youth football states that quarterbacks and running backs are at greatest risk for injury, and that the most likely body part to be injured is the knee (Adickes & Stuart, 2004). Although these knee injuries among youth do not normally involve torn ligaments, the ongoing occurrence of these injuries exemplifies our society's general acceptance of a sport that puts young people at physical risk.

Turning to hockey, on a yearly basis, between 10 and 12 percent of all youth hockey players, ages nine through seventeen sustain a head injury, frequently concussive in nature (Toth, McNeil, & Feasby, 2005, p. 702). A study conducted in Canada found that among hockey players ages nine through sixteen, approximately thirty injuries occurred for every one hundred players in a given season (Roberts, 2007). Thus, the scientific literature shows that although injuries in youth sports are relatively low, injuries to children still occur. We as a society have always seemed to place more value on children's athletic participation than the emotional, physical, and financial costs that youth injuries can incur. Hmm, maybe we do attach value to violence.

Injuries in Mixed Martial Arts

Okay, let's not forget MMA, for it is also a violent and injurious sport. Unfortunately, with the sport being so young, very little research has been conducted that covers MMA injury rates. Kachhar and colleagues (2004) studied four MMA maneuvers (judo hip toss, suplex, souplesse, and guillotine drop). Through video analysis, they studied the impact MMA athletes sustained while enduring these maneuvers. Results from the study conclude that some of these moves can cause whiplash and compression injuries to the cervical spine. It should be noted, however, that the moves described in this study are extraordinarily rare and difficult to execute in an actual match. In a study of kickboxers, research found that repeated head trauma had a cumulative effect, resulting in pituitary dysfunction (Tanriverdi et al., 2007). The pituitary gland is located at the base of the brain and controls the functions of other endocrine glands.

Bledsoe and colleagues (2006) probably conducted the best synopsis of injuries among MMA competitors by analyzing injuries reported in every MMA match held in Nevada from September 2001 to December 2004. According to this prevalence study, a total of 171 MMA matches transpired during this time period, resulting in ninety-six injuries to seventy-eight competitors (p. 138). Now those are some high rates! Similar to boxing, the most common type of injury was "facial laceration," accounting for 47.9 percent of all injuries. Hand injuries were next at 13.5 percent, with nose injuries being the third most common, accounting for 10.4 percent of all injuries (p. 137). This study also found that the likelihood of injury increased with the age of a competitor, as well as with the length of time a match lasted. Finally, a study published in 2002 argued that at that time, medical insurance was rarely provided in MMA or other martial arts competitions (Young, 2002).

Celebrated Violence in Sports

Now let's turn to the real issue. Can we really hate on MMA when our culture craves and compensates for sporting violence? The most exciting parts of sporting events often times seem to be when fights break out. When fights happen during those sports that have historically been most popular in the United States (football, baseball, basketball, and hockey), fans seem to be the most engaged. Fights between players in these sports garner extensive media attention and in many cases, sports media glorifies fighting (Kerr, 2002). It would just be remiss to deny that our society had accepted and even celebrated violence expressed through sport long before MMA emerged.

Between 1995 and 1999, there were 542 league punishments dealt by the NFL, Major League Baseball, the National Basketball Association (NBA), and the National Hockey League (NHL). Of these 542 punishments, 249 (46 percent) were for fighting (Nagel, Southall, & O'Toole, 2004, p. 20). In hockey, fighting is actually a revered ritual. In a 2007 edition of the *Sporting News*, Steve Greenberg wrote of the NHL, "The time has come for commissioner Gary Bettman and the rest of this dying league to drop the kid gloves and fight. Enough already with giving peace a chance. All they need is love … of ice-reddening violence" (p. 7). And in response to a vicious, premeditated attack that occurred during a hockey game, former NHL player Dave Shultz blamed the incident on the NHL for not allowing fighting to the same degree as in years past and went on to write, "As far as I'm concerned, fighting is one of the more celebrated traditions of hockey. It is what keeps things civil, on a basic human level of understanding and respect in competition" (Shultz, 2004, p. 9). In essence, Shultz argued that in the NHL a more "subdued" form of fighting would help prevent highly malicious, premeditated attacks, rather than argue players should simply learn to stop their violent aggression all together. In fact, one study on hockey players found that as players increased in age and competitive level, they were more likely to legitimize aggression and violence as a professional aspect of their sport (Visek & Watson, 2005).

Turning to the NBA, it is fairly easy to recall recent brawls between various teams and individual players. Who can forget the fan-induced brawl that erupted between former Indiana Pacers players Ron Artest, Stephen Jackson, and a number of Detroit Pistons fans (Carter, 2007; McCallum, 2004)? True, Artest and Jackson were penalized heavily by the NBA, but can American fans deny their fascination in witnessing the fighting with fans in the stands and on the court, aired over and over on sports television shows?

And the celebrated violence is not just related to fighting. *New York Times* columnist William Rhoden (2007) comments on the permitted violent injuries that can characterize the NFL:

> What can you do about concussions in a sport whose popularity is rooted in violent collisions? Bizarre as it sounds, boxing has an effective method of dealing with concussions: A fighter who sustains one is not allowed to fight for at least a month. In contrast, a football player who sustains a concussion can return to the game. (p. D1).

And the media capitalizes off our yearning for violence in football, knowing that the most vicious hits occurring in NFL games are what sells and attracts a greater fan base (McCarthy, 2005). Not to mention, television commercials aired during major sporting events are often times muddled in heavy violence (Tamburro et al., 2004; Anderson, 1997).

The point of this chapter is not necessarily to point out that one demographic group of athletes in one sport sustains more serious injuries than others. Nor is it the point of this chapter to argue that because serious sporting injuries are prevalent among young women and children that injuries in MMA should be acceptable. Rather, the literature summarized above showcases how much our society already accepts the possibility of injury as an inevitable aspect of athletics in a wide variety of demographic groups. Our society heralds sporting achievement to such a high degree that possible sporting injuries are simply viewed as being a normal part of the game. In an article titled "Sports Injuries in Children," the authors write, "Physical injury is an inherent risk in sports participation and, to a certain extent, must be considered an inevitable cost of athletic training and competition" (Sharma, Luscombe, & Maffulli, 2003, p. 255). Could our acceptance be verified any more bluntly?

Thus, it is a bit surprising that members of our society have become so outraged over health risks within the sport of MMA. So many adults already encourage children to play sports, even those sports that involve heavy levels of physical contact (soccer, basketball), and those that require physical collisions (hockey and football). We do not seriously question the high numbers of concussions that happen each year in high school, college, and professional football and hockey. Nor do we seriously question the growing number of ACL tears that happen in football, women's/girls' basketball, and women's/girls' soccer. All these injuries can have long-term negative consequences and could very well be considered a public health risk (Waddington, 2004).

Boxing and MMA are unique, in that for these sports, blows to the head and the physical harm of an opponent are actual sporting objectives; *intent* to harm is present. Whereas in sports like hockey and football, blows to the head occur unintentionally (well, hopefully unintentionally) and with protective headgear. What differentiates MMA from boxing is the variety of methods one may employ to win a competition and the ability to "tap out" (or quit). Wrestling, for instance, is a sport/discipline built into MMA, and its injury rate (though higher than some sports) can be relatively low—about one in every one hundred amateur wrestlers sustains an injury in either practice or competition (Jarret, Orwin, & Dick, 1998). As will be detailed in Chapter Seven, MMA competitors interviewed for this project argued extensively that MMA was far safer than the general public perceived it to be due to the large variety of methods to win and lose a match.

Finally, sporting culture in general is violent. More to the point, it celebrates violence, and it did so long before MMA reached its current level of popularity. This is not to say that a majority of amateur and professional athletes are violent themselves. Such statements would be stereotypical and most of the time false. However, there are definitely pockets within sporting cultures that reproduce violence, and the mainstream sporting media does little (if anything) to quell these violent cultural images. Likewise, MMA organizations are often promoting and selling violence. Downey's (2007) thought provoking article states of MMA:

> Promoters encourage fighters to use striking strategies because they are per-ceived to be more popular with fans. A public relations executive at Zuffa explained to me that, if a fighter put on a "good show"—he was aggressive and exciting to watch—he would be invited back even if he lost (p. 216).

Sure, no doubt, MMA is violent and dangerous and has some serious issues for consideration. But if anything, MMA is simply adding to what is already a vio-lent sporting culture. Or wait, let's get it straight. MMA is adding to an already violent American culture.

3

METHODOLOGICAL NOTES AND THE INTERVIEWEES

BY DAVID MAYEDA

Interview Settings and Topics

As noted at the end of Chapter One, we decided to carry out this project during the latter part of 2005. David Ching had been a MMA fan for many years, really since the beginning in 1993. In addition to following the UFC, he had also followed Pride FC, K-1, King of the Cage, and a few other MMA organizations throughout the years. Already mentioned in Chapter One, I did not become fascinated with MMA until 2005. As we all got engrossed in this project, we became more attached emotionally to the sport. The reality is—and it is best to make this point upfront—all three contributors to this book (the third contributor being photographer, Stephen Mayeda) now follow the MMA industry very closely and are in varying degrees fans. We became close friends with some interviewees, trained jiu-jitsu a little bit with them, spent time together watching MMA pay-per-views, and just hung out as normal friends would. Even photographer Stephen Mayeda still gets caught up spending a little too much time checking out MMA matches on YouTube, and I even decided to partake in a few amateur submission grappling and sport pankration competitions in November 2007.

Sam Sheridan's (2007) *A Fighter's Heart* provides an especially rich, ethnographic perspective into different MMA and combat sport communities. Sheridan spent a great deal of time training extensively in muay Thai kickboxing in Thailand, with the Miletich Fighting System in Iowa, in Brazil with the Brazilian Top Team, boxing with world class boxers, and so on. We're not kidding ourselves, none of us trained anywhere near as much as Sheridan. At most we partook in a few jiu-jitsu seminars and did a bunch of conditioning workouts with a small proportion of those we interviewed. Sheridan states that by training at length with MMA competitors, it helped him to acquire a deeper friendship with them, and in turn, gather better information for his ethnography. Conversely, at times when he was injured and unable to train, it damaged his data gathering process. Speaking of a time when he was injured, Sheridan wrote:

> It wasn't only that I couldn't train; it affected everything about me, about how the friendships went. Fighters will talk very differently to someone who works out with them, to someone they've been sparring and struggling with. There is an instant intimacy; fighters are friends after they fight because they have tested and know each other. As males, their respective status is known. Without a chance to prove myself as at least a willing beginner, I was a perennial outsider, tolerated instead of welcomed. (p. 105, 106).

Unlike Sheridan, we had neither the time nor the willingness to fully train MMA with those we interviewed and endure the physical beatings we surely would have taken. Hence, our approach was different on a few levels. We bounced around, speaking one-on-one in more formalized interviews with mixed martial artists, normally only spending that short window of time with them. Also, our approach was more political than Sheridan's, and this is reflected in the topics we addressed. All in all however, the process was simply different. Again, we feel those we spoke with were quite open and welcoming, knowing we were simultaneously critical scholars and fans.

From my personal perspective as an avid sports fan and former athlete, I tend to love sports in general. But I also know that sports contribute to a great deal of social ills. Come on now, let's not kid ourselves—within sporting contexts, there are coaches and parents that go way overboard in youth sporting contests (Gervis & Dunn, 2004; Wingert & Lauerman, 2000), media that normalize discrimination against women, girls, and homosexuals (Daddario, 1998; Davis, 1997; Sabo, 1994), excessive injury rates (see Chapter Two), and cultural values that perpetuate racism (Mayeda, 2001; Mayeda, 1999; Miller, 1998; Birrell, 1989). Cities will even invest literally hundreds of millions of dollars into sporting stadiums while nearby dilapidated low-income housing communities stagnate in poverty and police departments remain understaffed (Websdale, 2001). So like all institutions and industries, sporting ones have their major problems.

My love-hate relationship with athletics is ultimately one where the love outweighs the hate, and consequently, my academic hobby in sports sociology hopes to reform sporting institutions for the better. Thus, as we became more attached to this project and feared losing our critical objectivity, we maintained a strong critical outlook by reminding ourselves that constructive criticism makes things better. Furthermore, as Chris and Mike Onzuka reminded us during a photo shoot, if a sport is legitimate, it will stand up to the criticism.

We conducted this project in four geographic sites:

- Honolulu, Hawaii

- Los Angeles/Orange County, California

- Dallas, Texas

- Las Vegas, Nevada

Honolulu was chosen for obvious reasons, as the two authors reside there. However, Hawaii has also been a MMA hotbed for many years (Morinaga, 2006). Admittedly, we were disappointed in our inability to interview certain MMA practitioners from Hawaii who have attained international recognition, such as B.J. Penn, Faleniko Vitale, Wesley Corriea and more recently, Kendall Grove. Los Angeles and Orange County, California were chosen because of MMA's enormous popularity in Southern California. As Michael Frison stated when we interviewed him:

> Man, it's (MMA) exploding, especially in California. I mean California right now is basically the hub of martial arts in the world. You know, you won't find more talented, and credentialed individuals I think anywhere in the world than you will in California right now.

Dallas was selected because Texas is a state with a burgeoning MMA community. The UFC recently held a major fight card in Houston that was covered extensively in *Sports Illustrated* (Wertheim, 2007). Plus, some prominent MMA practitioners who agreed to be interviewed (Guy Mezger and Travis Lutter) reside and work in the Dallas area, and Mark Cuban's new MMA organization is based in Dallas. Finally, Las Vegas, Nevada was chosen because of its distinct association with MMA, it being the home of the UFC and most of the major UFC events. Unfortunately, the smallest number of interviewees for this project came from Las Vegas. We also interviewed one MMA hobbyist who lived in Oregon but was vacationing in Hawaii (this was also the sole interviewee who requested his identity be kept confidential).

Interviews were conducted in a variety of settings—in MMA gyms, gym offices, the back of MMA gyms, weight rooms, restaurants, coffee shops, hotel lobbies, and fighters' homes. We were able to interview fighters through a snowball sampling process in which interviewees would refer us to their friends and training partners. Once again, we need to give some extra credit to Jason "MayheM" Miller in this department. He hooked us up with Randy Couture, Dan Henderson, and Quinton Jackson, three of the biggest and most successful MMA stars. In all likelihood, we would not have been able to land such interviews without Miller's help.

In a few cases, mixed martial artists who owned gyms and trained others, such as Antonio McKee, Travis Lutter, Tony Fryklund, and Guy Mezger, would refer us to their protégés. Hence, all interviews, with the exception of one, were conducted in person. The sole interview that was not conducted in person was with Randy Couture, and it was conducted over the phone. Although we had hoped to conduct all interviews in person, we made this sole exception for Couture due to his status in and importance to the MMA community. We were fortunate to meet Couture later during a promotional event in Honolulu.

Generally speaking, it was not too difficult to schedule interviews. However, as with any major research project, we did have our maddening moments. There were a few times when potential interviewees would agree to meet us for interviews only to cancel at the last minute or simply not show up. Sometimes MMA fighters would politely give us their e-mail addresses or phone numbers to set up interviews but not respond after we contacted them. And when these types of mishaps occurred, it could be quite frustrating. But in retrospect, this did not occur too often, and interviews tended to transpire very smoothly.

Interview questions were developed after consulting the academic and popular literature in sports sociology, much of which surrounds the combat sport of boxing. Broadly speaking, questions revolved around two very extensive topical areas. The first major topical area focused on fighters themselves, for example their individual backgrounds and families, and what they deal with on a personal level emotionally, physically, and politically. The second major topical area focused more on societal issues, including how interviewees felt the sport has evolved over the years with regard to safety, whether or not the sport would increase or decrease street violence, and if they felt the MMA community had a social responsibility in curbing street violence.

The mixed martial artists we spoke with gave an amazingly wide variety of answers and opinions that will be presented throughout Chapters Four through Ten. Of the forty men we interviewed, thirty-two were interviewed individually.

Four interviews were held in pairs due to time constraints—JJ Ambrose & Savant Young; Jesse Juarez & Emanuel Newton; Chris & Mike Onzuka; and Guy Mezger & Chris Bowles. Interviews ranged in time from twenty-five to one hundred and fifteen minutes depending on how much interviewees had to say, and every interview was transcribed verbatim. In all, the interview transcriptions totaled 561 pages (an average of about fourteen pages per interviewee). They were typed in Times New Roman 12-font with 1.25 inch margins, single spaced. No, transcribing the interviews was not fun.

We informed all interviewees that they could conceal their identities if they desired. A few interviewees asked to make that decision after the interview was completed. In the end, thirty-nine of the forty interviewees preferred their names were made known. There were a few topical areas in which interviewees asked that their identities remain hidden, namely when we were discussing injuries. Essentially, some fighters did not want us to disclose injuries they had sustained either in MMA or other sports since divulging such information would also be exposing a personal weakness for future opponents to see and take advantage of. All interviewees were given a consent form to read and sign that explained our project and gave us approval to hold the interview. Finally, interviewees were offered $35.00 as compensation for their time and contributions, though some interviewees declined and agreed to do the interview for free.

Our choice not to make interviewees' identities confidential is a methodological concern that merits some discussion, as it precluded interviewees from divulging incriminating information. For example, if an interviewee had used performance-enhancing drugs in his past, he would have been far more likely to admit it if we guaranteed confidentiality. Nevertheless, our goal was not to implicate fighters in past or present wrong doings. It is common in qualitative research projects that researchers ask interviewees not to disclose personal information and instead, to describe their observations of a community setting in order to make educated policy suggestions. In taking this approach, we feel interviewees were open and honest regarding the topics addressed in this study despite their identities being made public.

Thirty-three of the interviewees with whom we spoke were professional MMA competitors (past or present); many of these competitors also trained other MMA athletes. The range of professional competitions these thirty-three interviewees had varied immensely. Some were seasoned veterans of the sport (e.g., Guy Mezger has had forty-four MMA competitions), while others only had a few (e.g., Cleyburn Walker only had one at the time of his interview). In order to attain a more diverse range of opinions and perspectives we also interviewed four people who trained others in MMA but did not compete professionally, and three people who only trained in MMA as hobbyists but did not compete professionally or train others.

Like the interview transcribing, conducting our analyses of the interviews was equally tiresome. Once most of the transcriptions were completed, we read through them and categorized the various themes that we had provoked through our questions along with themes that interviewees raised themselves. Initially, we came up with seventeen major themes that emerged from the interviews. Realizing that this was too many for a cohesive book, we discussed and debated over which of those seventeen themes to dismiss or coalesce with other themes. Eventually we agreed upon seven major themes that are represented in Chapters Four through Ten.

Presented below are the individuals we interviewed and a brief description of each person's background, listed in order of interview date. When possible and applicable, interviewees' professional MMA records are provided, as listed on Sherdog.com (we acknowledge that Sherdog.com may not capture every professional competition for each interviewee; therefore, Sherdog.com records have been adjusted when requested by interviewees).

The Interviewees
Nolan Hong

Interview date: February 13, 2006

Interview location: Honolulu, Hawaii

Nolan Hong frequently jokes that he is an undefeated MMA competitor with a record of 1-0. Hong's interest in the MMA community lies more in his role as co-owner of a small business called Fighter's Corner, which sells MMA products in Honolulu, Hawaii. He was twenty-five years old at the time we interviewed him. In addition to managing his store, Hong enjoys working in Hawaii's acting community and can do a great impersonation of just about any MMA competitor.

Derek Stadler

Interview date: March 1, 2006

Interview location: Honolulu, Hawaii

Derek Stadler is a young fighter from Hilo, Hawaii who was twenty-one when we interviewed him. He grew up learning judo from his father and wrestling in high school before starting a professional career in MMA. Stadler was one of the most mild mannered and polite mixed martial artists we spoke with. With a strength in jiu-jitsu, Stadler has built up a 3-1 professional MMA record.

Jason "MayheM" Miller

Interview date: March 2, 2006

Interview location: Honolulu, Hawaii (Miller also resides in Hollywood, CA)

"MayheM" is one of the most entertaining and enigmatic MMA competitors in the industry. He has fought in numerous MMA organizations, including the UFC, Icon Sport, the World Fighting Alliance, and World Extreme Cagefighting. He recently signed to compete with Mark Cuban's HDNet Fights. As an adolescent, "MayheM" knew he had a few talents. In reference to his father, Miller said, "He had me on a self-help book that made me write out my goals, and write out what I was good at. And a few things [were] entertaining people, and fighting." There's no question, "MayheM" knows how to entertain. *Ultimate Grappling* describes Miller's fight entrances: "… it's a guarantee that there will be no seats left and everyone in attendance will be standing, waiting for his extravagant ring entrances to begin" (Monroe, 2007, p. 89). But Miller is also an accomplished mixed martial artist. It was in Hawaii where "MayheM" really started making his name, eventually winning the Icon Sport 185-lb. title in September 2006 with a submission victory over Robbie Lawler. He was twenty-five years old at the time of our interview and currently holds a 19-5 MMA professional record.

Chris & Mike Onzuka

Interview date: April 11, 2006

Interview location: Honolulu, Hawaii

Chris and Mike Onzuka are twin brothers who grew up in Honolulu, Hawaii. They have taught jiu-jitsu for many years now and are heavily involved in Hawaii's MMA scene. They attended the very first UFC in 1993 and have both competed at the World Jiu-jitsu championships in Brazil. They own "O2 Martial Arts Academy" in Aiea, Hawaii where they teach jiu-jitsu classes and also offer classes in escrima, kickboxing, submission grappling and self defense. In addition to running their gym, Chris holds a bachelors degree from the University of Hawaii with a double major earned in real estate and finance and a minor in economics, and now works for Bank of Hawaii in the appropriations department. Also highly educated, Mike holds a bachelors degree in mechanical engineering and works for a fire protection firm. On March 31, 2007, they were given the Lifetime Achievement Award by Icon Sport for their longtime support of and contributions to MMA in Hawaii.

Yoji Matsuo

Interview date: July 5, 2006

Interview location: Honolulu, Hawaii (Matsuo resides in Irvine, California)

Yoji Matsuo was born and raised in Tokyo, Japan; he and his family moved to Irvine, CA when he was thirteen years old. Matsuo graduated with honors from the University of California, Irvine before moving on to the University of California, Berkeley, where he attained his masters degree in civil engineering. After graduating from Berkeley, Matsuo moved back to Irvine and worked in civil engineering for ten years, and recently, as an expert witness in legal cases that had civil engineering matters. Matsuo got involved in MMA as a fitness goal and it soon became one of his major hobbies. He has competed in amateur submission grappling tournaments and is now a trainer at Bear Essential Combat in Fountain Valley, California. There he is also co-owner of the Bear Essential Combat store. He was thirty-five years old at the time of interview.

Tony "The Freak" Fryklund

Interview date: July 8, 2006

Interview location: Las Vegas, Nevada

Tony Fryklund owns and manages his gym, "Fight Club," in Las Vegas Nevada. He is a long time MMA veteran who made his professional MMA debut at UFC 14 in 1997. Before that, however, Fryklund built an extensive background in karate, boxing, kickboxing, and jiu-jitsu. While managing and instructing in his gym, Fryklund also trains and continues to compete in MMA. An advocate for the traditional aspects of martial arts, Fryklund has trained with some of the top MMA individuals and groups in the business, including the Miletich Fighting System. When meeting Fryklund, he gave us one of his business cards, which has a picture of him enraged in fury with blood streaming down his face after a MMA competition in Canada. Fryklund had been cut above his eyes possibly impairing his vision, so the referee stopped the fight even though Fryklund was not hurt. Sam Sheridan (2007) quoted Fryklund regarding this picture in his book *A Fighter's Heart*:

> "I could fight fine" Tony said, "If I had trouble seeing, that was my problem, you know? It was cosmetic, a scratch on the hood. You don't throw away the car just because a windshield wiper is busted.... I was so emotional that now I can understand a temporary insanity plea" (p. 52, 53).

A classic quote. Fryklund was thirty-five years old when we interviewed him.

Robert Otani

Interview date: July 8, 2006

Interview location: Las Vegas, Nevada

Of half Japanese, half Caucasian descent, Robert Otani is a young MMA competitor who was twenty-three years old when interviewed. Originally from Oxnard, California, Otani moved to Las Vegas after finishing college to make his way into the MMA business. He had only been training and competing in MMA for about seven months at the time of our interview and only had one professional fight under his belt. A highly accomplished athlete, Otani grew up learning judo from his father, also dabbling in wrestling and playing football in high school. Perhaps most impressive, Otani played football as a linebacker for the University of Southern California where he won two N.C.A.A. Division I national championships and earned his bachelors degree in sociology.

Quinton "Rampage" Jackson

Interview date: September 24, 2006

Interview location: Irvine, California

Before Quinton "Rampage" Jackson entered the UFC, he had already made a huge name for himself in Japan through Pride FC. Just before coming to the UFC, he was competing in the World Fighting Alliance (WFA). To understand Jackson's stardom, know that Dana White and the UFC purchased an entire organization just to get "Rampage." Said White, "The purchase of the WFA was for one reason and one reason only. And that was to get Quinton Jackson in the UFC" (Davidson, 2007). In doing so, Jackson became the only man to defeat Chuck "The Iceman" Liddell twice, thereby winning the UFC Light Heavyweight Championship on May 26, 2007. When describing Jackson, his good friend Jason Miller said, "Big, strong black guy … you don't wanna be standin' there in front of his punches.… Cause if you stand in front, you're gonna be, "Boom!" Your block is rocked." Charismatic, comical, and spiritual, "Rampage" is heavily profiled in MMA magazines and internet pages. On September 8, 2007, Jackson sealed his legacy in the sport by winning a competitive and historically significant five round decision over another good friend, Dan Henderson, to unify the UFC and Pride FC Light Heavyweight Championships. Jackson was twenty-eight years old at the time of interview, and he currently holds a 28-6 professional MMA record.

Toby "Tiger Heart" Grear

Interview date: September 25, 2006

Interview location: Hollywood, California

Toby Grear grew up in a middle-class community in Ohio. In high school, he swam and played football before playing water polo for a few years at the University of Dayton. Grear graduated from the University of Dayton with a degree in business administration and marketing and a minor in psychology. While in college, Grear took up muay Thai kickboxing and fell in love with it, but after graduation he moved to Southern California to pursue a career in advertising. Eventually, Grear began teaching kickboxing classes and decided to establish a MMA career. Holding a professional MMA record of 4-4, Grear won the Total Fighting Alliance Lightweight Title on April 28, 2007. He and his girlfriend, Roxy "Balboa" Richardson (also a mixed martial artist) were featured on a front page story of *The Los Angeles Times* (Gold, 2007b).

Randy "The Natural" Couture

Interview date: September 26, 2006

Interview location: Hollywood, California (by telephone)

Considered a MMA legend and one of the best strategists in the game, Randy Couture is one of only four men inducted into the UFC Hall of Fame. With a decorated collegiate and Greco-Roman wrestling background behind him, Couture entered the octagon for the first time at UFC 13 on May 30, 1997; he was thirty-three years old at that time. Just over two years later, Couture won his first UFC Heavyweight Title by defeating Maurice Smith on December 21, 1999. After taking some time off, Couture captured the UFC Heavyweight Title again in November 2000 by defeating Kevin Randleman. Couture made history, however, when he dropped down to the light heavyweight division and defeated Tito Ortiz for that title in 2003, becoming the first person to win championships in two separate weight classes (Krauss, 2004, p. 60–77). At the time of our interview, Couture was retired. Amazingly, Couture made another comeback and won the Heavyweight Title for a third time by defeating Tim Sylvia on March 23, 2007 at the "young" age of forty-three. In addition to this, Couture holds a bachelor's degree from Oklahoma State University in German (Wall, 2005) and frequently served as a UFC commentator. Couture recently tendered his resignation from the UFC while still champion, stating that he felt unappreciated, given how he has served as an ambassador for the UFC for eleven years and also that he was disappointed the UFC had not signed former Pride FC fighter Fedor Emelianenko, who Couture saw as his only remaining challenge. Couture, however, did not define his resignation as a retirement (Cain, 2007a).

Colin Oyama

Interview date: November 7, 2006

Interview location: Irvine, California

Colin Oyama was born and raised in Hawaii, growing up in Wailua on Oahu's North Shore. Oyama now resides in Irvine, California. Oyama played football for Whittier College where he earned his bachelor's in political science and shortly thereafter attained his law degree from Loyola Marymount University. Oddly enough, it was during law school that Oyama began learning and competing in muay Thai competitions. Describing law school, Oyama said, "… it gets crazy sometimes so, you need an outlet you know. I started doing muay Thai fights (laughs). Go to class, black eye, you know. But it was a good outlet for me, at least to get through school." Now Oyama is a full time MMA instructor and co-owner of No Limits Gym located in Irvine, California.

Bao Quach

Interview date: November 7, 2006

Interview location: Irvine, California

Bao Quach grew up in Orange County, California and was twenty-seven years old at the time of interview. Quach graduated from California State University, Fullerton with a degree in kinesiology. Currently competing at 145 lbs., Quach has built up a professional MMA record of 10-8-1. Among other organizations, he has competed in King of the Cage, World Extreme Cagefighting, Gladiator Challenge, and the International Fighting Organization. For a living, Quach teaches classes in MMA and competes professionally. With regard to his long term goals, Quach says, "down the line … I want to be able to open up my own school, have my own set of fighters. Train people. Train people that don't want to fight (professionally), you know. Open up the martial arts to everybody."

Bear St. Clair

Interview date: November 17, 2006

Interview location: Costa Mesa, California

Bear St. Clair grew up in Costa Mesa, California. He still resides and works in Orange County, California as a MMA trainer. St. Clair probably sustained more injuries than any other person we interviewed as a result of training in the combat sports. In his "synopsis" of injuries, St. Clair said he had broken every knuckle in both hands, had multiple hamstring and calf tears, torn knee cartilage, torn his Achilles, chipped two vertebrate, detached bicep tendons, had two shoulder surgeries, broken two ribs, had a crushed trachea, a cracked sternum, and he actually went on listing more. St. Clair was twenty-seven years old at the time of interview. He is also owner of Bear Essential Combat, a MMA gym located in Fountain Valley, California.

Michael Frison

Interview date: November 18, 2006

Interview location: Irvine, California

Michael Frison was born and raised in Washington State, about 30 minutes south of Seattle. Though not into high school sports, Frison enjoyed studying the traditional martial arts at the time. Said Frison, "I grew up watching Bruce Lee and Chuck Norris and everything like that …" He earned his bachelor's degree in psychology with an emphasis in sports psychology from Western Washington University and is three courses shy of completing a second bachelor's in bio-kinetics and kinesiology, something he says he is doing "just for fun." Frison works full time as a manager and trainer at Orange County Kickboxing, but has no plans to engage in a professional MMA career. Frison was thirty years old at the time of interview.

Dustin Phan

Interview date: November 18, 2006

Interview location: Irvine, California

Dustin Phan is an undergraduate student at the University of California, Irvine, majoring in math. He grew up in Fountain Valley, California. Phan played a little lacrosse in high school, but was influenced more by a traditional martial arts background as a youth. At the time of interview, Phan was a jiu-jitsu instructor at Orange County Kickboxing and competing in amateur jiu-jitsu tournaments. However, he did not have any plans to pursue a professional MMA career. Phan was nineteen years old at the time of interview.

JJ Ambrose

Interview date: November 20, 2006

Interview location: Lakewood, California

JJ Ambrose grew up in Bullhead City, Arizona, where he enjoyed boxing and wrestling as a youth. Said Ambrose of his transition from boxing to wrestling, "I did amateur boxing. When I was fifteen, I went to the nationals and took third, and I decided my arms were too short to be boxing, so I turned to wrestling." He placed third in the Arizona State Wrestling Championships his senior year of high school and then moved to southern California to continue wrestling at the junior college level. Instead, Ambrose moved into MMA, and he recently won the World Fighting Alliance Welterweight title on April 28, 2007. Ambrose currently has a 5-1 MMA professional record and was nineteen years old at the time of interview.

Jason Bress

Interview date: November 20, 2006

Interview location: Aliso Viejo, California

We held a short, impromptu interview with Jason Bress and were very fortunate to do so. Bress grew up in Hemet, California before moving to Orange, California for high school. Bress competed in wrestling at the junior college level where he earned All-American honors. Afterwards however, Bress became heavily interested in muay Thai kickboxing and competed in various parts of Asia. Although we did not get to spend an adequate amount of time with Bress, he offered some extremely important suggestions on safety measures and general life planning for mixed martial artists that are presented in Part Two of this book. Bress currently works in Aliso Viejo, California teaching various aspects of the combat sports at LA Boxing.

Allan Goes

Interview date: November 20, 2006

Interview location: Aliso Viejo, California

Allan Goes was born in Brazil and came to the United States as a young man in hopes of establishing a MMA career. He is a MMA veteran having competed in the sport since 1995. He has had MMA competitions in the UFC, Pride FC, and Rumble on the Rock, and currently competes in the IFL for Maurice Smith's Seattle Tiger Sharks. Over the years, Goes has amassed a MMA record of 10-5-2. In addition to competing in the IFL, Goes is married with children and operates his own martial arts system in Mission Viejo, California. Goes was thirty-five years old when we interviewed him.

Jesse Juarez

Interview date: November 20, 2006

Interview location: Lakewood, California

Jesse Juarez grew up in Torrance, California. Juarez had a stellar athletic career at North Torrance High School where he played football, wrestling, and track, earning All-American honors in wrestling. Juarez then wrestled at Golden West Community College before transferring to Montana State University-Northern, where he won the NAIA nationals in 2005 at 184 pounds. In addition to competing as a professional mixed martial artist under the tutelage of Antonio McKee, Juarez works in the real estate market through his father's company. Juarez is of French, Italian, and Tongan descent and was twenty-four years old at the time of interview, with a 2-1 professional MMA record. On July 21, 2007, Juarez won his first MMA title at a card called "Invincible 4," held in Ontario, California; he also is an alternate for the IFL's Tokyo Sabres.

Emanuel Newton

Interview date: November 20, 2006

Interview location: Lakewood, California

Emanuel Newton also grew up in Torrance, California. Said Newton of his parents, "… pretty crazy. I lost, my mom died when I was pretty young too. I lost both my parents pretty early. So I was on my own when I was sixteen." Newton is a fulltime professional mixed martial artist and also works security at a night club. Said Newton of his strengths as a fighter, "I got a hard head. I can take a punch." Additionally, Newton holds a strong wrestling background, having competed for Cerritos Community College. Newton was twenty-two years old at the time of interview and currently holds an 8-3-1 professional MMA record, competing in the light heavyweight division. He has competed in King of the Cage, Gladiator Challenge, and in a few organizations in Mexico, and recently began competing in the IFL.

Savant Young

Interview date: November 20, 2006

Interview location: Lakewood, California

Savant Young was raised in South Central Los Angeles and was another inter-viewee who grew up learning traditional martial arts. Young's athletic success, smile, and upbeat, polite personality have made him a major star in the IFL, where he competes for the Tokyo Sabres along side Antonio McKee. Young is a crafty boxer who holds an 8-6 professional MMA record. Along with his wife, Young is the father of a son and daughter. Speaking of his family and their per-spectives on his MMA profession, Young began laughing as he said, "… my wife likes it. She supports the sport. My kids, they like it. They get a kick out of telling their teachers, you know, their dad beats people up for a living." Previously, Young worked in post-production at a video editing company, but he now makes MMA his full time career. Young was thirty years old at the time of interview.

Antonio McKee

Interview date: November 21, 2006

Interview location: Lakewood, California

Antonio McKee is one of the most athletic and successful mixed martial artists we spoke with, boasting a professional MMA record of 48-3-1. In addition to this, McKee is a former Junior College National Champion in wrestling. McKee com-peted in the IFL for the Tokyo Sabres along side some of his protégés who train under him at his gym in Lakewood, California, "The Bodyshop Fitness." McKee is extremely confident, intelligent, and outspoken and was not shy about express-ing his opinions on societal concerns within the MMA world, including race and class-based discrimination. He was thirty-six years old when interviewed.

Jamie Yager

Interview date: November 21, 2006

Interview location: Lakewood, California

Jamie Yager grew up in Pasadena, California and is another of Antonio McKee's protégés. He was a multi-sport high school athlete, playing football, wrestling, and baseball, making it to the California state meet in wrestling as a senior, as well as the California Hall of Fame Game in football. Yager initially chose to advance his football career, playing as a free safety with a university in Kansas for two years. After the birth of his son, Yager returned to southern California, where he now works as a personal trainer and at a health foods store. At the time of interview, Yager had not yet had a professional MMA competition, but was in the process of preparing for one. He was one week away from his twenty-third birthday at the time of interview.

Dan Henderson ("Hendo")

Interview date: November 29, 2006

Interview location: Honolulu, Hawaii (Henderson resides in Temecula, California)

Dan Henderson is a phenomenal wrestler who has evolved into a phenomenal mixed martial artist. Henderson's senior year of high school, he wrestled in the junior national championships, where he won both the freestyle and Greco-Roman titles. "I think I had twenty-one matches in five days, so I was pretty sore. But I only had two matches that really went the distance. I pinned or tech'd everybody else." Henderson also wrestled in college at Arizona State University, but his biggest accomplishment was representing the United States in both the 1992 and 1996 Olympic Games in Greco-Roman wrestling. Said "Hendo" of the Olympics, "It was great. I wouldn't trade it for anything." Henderson transitioned into MMA in 1997 and made a huge name for himself in Japan in Pride FC. A relatively small light heavyweight, Henderson was able to win the Rings: King of Kings open weight tournament in Pride FC which included victories over five heavyweights. He has also won four different international MMA tournaments in three separate weight classes. Henderson then went on to win the Pride FC Welterweight Title in 2005 by defeating Murilo Bustamante (Jensen, 2006). However, he truly made a name for himself in the United States on February 24, 2007 when he knocked out the esteemed Wanderlei Silva to win the Pride FC Light Heavyweight Title, thereby making him the only man to simultaneously hold two titles in different weight classes. Henderson would lose the Pride FC Light Heavyweight Title to Quinton Jackson later that year in the sport's first unification title bout, although in the loss, Henderson pushed Jackson for five close rounds. He was thirty-six years old at the time of interview and holds a 22-6 professional MMA record.

Travis Lutter

Interview date: November 29, 2006

Interview location: Fort Worth, Texas

Travis Lutter defeated Patrick Cote to become the Middleweight winner of *The Ultimate Fighter IV—The Comeback* reality show. In winning the competition, Lutter was able to compete in the main event of UFC 67 where he lost to Anderson Silva. A former wrestler at Northern State University in South Dakota, Lutter is also a black belt in Machado Brazilian Jiu-jitsu, and was an Ultimate Submission World Champion. Lutter owns and operates two Brazilian jiu-jitsu schools in Fort Worth, which have benefited greatly since his success on the UFC reality show (Jones, 2007). Lutter provided us with an extremely forthright interview and referred us to some of his students for interviews. Lutter has competed in a wide variety of MMA organizations in the United States and internationally, and holds a professional MMA record of 9-4.

Frank "Twinkle Toes" Trigg

Interview date: February 10, 2007

Interview location: Honolulu, Hawaii (Trigg resides in Las Vegas, Nevada)

Frank Trigg is known as a renaissance man in MMA. He is articulate and frequently commentated for Pride FC. Trigg was born in New York and has seven brothers who taught him to be competitive. His first MMA match was in 1997 and since then he has held championship titles in the WFA and Icon Sport. He was also a 2000 Olympic trials wrestling finalist. Knowing that life as a professional athlete cannot last forever, Trigg plans to continue honing his career in commentating and advancing his clothing line. At the time of our interview, Trigg was thirty-four years old. He is a 1997 graduate of the University of Oklahoma where he earned his bachelor's degree in Public Affairs and Administration. At a recent MMA card, a fan was following him around, asked him to sign three pieces of memorabilia and then told Trigg he was so disappointed when he left World Wrestling Entertainment for Total Nonstop Action (professional wrestling organizations). The fan thought Trigg was professional wrestler Kurt Angle. Trigg went on laughing as he told us this story: "Yeah, he thought I was Kurt Angle. And then he asked me, 'Well, who the hell are you?' I told him I was Frank Trigg and he just walked off." Trigg's professional MMA record is 15-6.

Chris Bowles

Interview date: March 24, 2007

Interview location: Dallas, Texas

Chris Bowles grew up in Oklahoma. He wrestled in high school before going to the University of Oklahoma. Bowles considered wrestling at the powerhouse wrestling university, but opted not to since he started out as a pre-med major. He eventually graduated in 1994 with his degree in business administration and now works as a manager in the information technology (IT) field. After being out of athletics for many years, Bowles saw some people practicing wrestling and kick-boxing in Guy Mezger's gym. Missing the athletic competition, Bowles decided to give it a try and since then he has strung together a strong 7-1 professional MMA record at 155 pounds. He and his wife are the parents of two young children. In addition to working in IT, Bowles teaches MMA classes in Mezger's gym. Bowles was thirty-six years old at the time of interview.

Joshua Gilley

Interview date: March 24, 2007

Interview location: Fort Worth, Texas

Joshua Gilley was born and raised in Chicago, Illinois. Gilley wrestled in high school, and as described in Chapter Eight, he was part of an informal fight club that developed among friends through his high school wrestling network. Gilley now works integrating satellite systems. He trains out of Travis Lutter's Gym and had competed in one jiu-jitsu tournament when we interviewed him. Speaking about his interests in MMA, Gilley said, "… this is my hobby. This is what I do for fun…. This isn't like a focal point for me to grow from as a career. This is just something for me to build on emotionally, physically, and mentally." Gilley was thirty-three years old at the time of interview and has a thirteen year old daughter. Said Gilley of his daughter and her feelings on his MMA hobby, "Man, she thinks it's the coolest thing."

Paul Halme

Interview date: March 24, 2007

Interview location: Fort Worth, Texas

Paul Halme grew up in South Dakota. He dabbled in high school wrestling and played golf. While attending Northern State University in South Dakota, Halme met Travis Lutter. Said Halme jokingly, "Travis and I kind of joke around how we met in college, cause he was wrestling and I was playing golf.… He got me started lifting weights and stuff and I couldn't even do a pull up." Halme graduated with a bachelor's degree in sociology with an emphasis in criminal justice. Following college, Halme worked as a stock broker before opening up his own jiu-jitsu school in Fort Worth, which he now runs fulltime. At thirty-one years old, Halme has competed in major jiu-jitsu tournaments, and was in preparation for his first full MMA competition at the time of interview.

Takuhiro Kamikozono

Interview date: March 24, 2007

Interview location: Dallas, Texas (Kamikozono resides in Tokyo, Japan)

Takuhiro Kamikozono was born and raised in Tokyo and has been competing professionally in MMA since 2000. He moved to Denton, Texas in 1995 to attend college, attaining a bachelor's degree in business. Following college, Kamikozono worked in Dallas for a firm that assisted Japanese nationals in moving to the United States and those in the United States to move to Japan. While working there, he began training under Guy Mezger and competing professionally. Kamikozono has competed professionally in the United States, Denmark, Sweden, and Japan. He holds a professional MMA record of 7-5 and was thirty-one years old at the time of interview.

Guy Mezger

Interview date: March 24, 2007

Interview location: Dallas, Texas

Guy Mezger was born and raised in Texas and has been competing in various sports (combat and non-combat) all his life. Prior to starting a professional career in MMA, Mezger competed extensively in wrestling, judo, boxing, and kickboxing. He had a 42-1 record with the World Full Contact Karate League and was a 20-2 kickboxer. Mezger made his MMA debut at UFC 4 in 1994. Speaking candidly on his first UFC experience, Mezger stated:

> You know, and I was scared. I didn't know what the hell these guys were thinking. I mean there were guys going, "I can't wait to get in here," and they hadn't even had any fights. I was like, they've got to be insane! And I remember doing the interview, they were talking and saying they couldn't wait to get in there, and they asked me, and I said, "Man, am I the only one who's scared? Cause I haven't slept good since I agreed to do this."

Those comments notwithstanding, Mezger not only won his UFC 4 fight, he came back and won again at UFC 5 and eventually amassed a professional MMA record of 28-14-2, competing a great deal in both Japan and the United States. Mezger owns and operates the Lion's Den Dallas and at the time of interview was thirty-nine years old. Mezger was recently selected by billionaire and Dallas Mavericks (NBA) owner, Mark Cuban, to be in charge of talent development and matchmaking for Cuban's newly formed MMA organization that plans to be aired on Cuban's HDNet (Gross, 2007a).

Cleyburn Walker

Interview date: March 24, 2007

Interview location: Fort Worth, Texas

Cleyburn Walker was born and raised in Texas and joined the marines before considering a MMA career. He and his wife have two young daughters. Walker is just getting started in MMA, with only one professional competition. Although he lost that match, he went into it with no MMA training, an issue discussed at length in Chapter Seven. Walker was twenty-three years old when we interviewed him.

Chris Reilly

Interview date: April 1, 2007

Interview location: Honolulu, Hawaii (Reilly resides in Los Angeles, California)

Chris Reilly is a longtime martial artist who has competed professionally in muay Thai both in the United States and internationally. Although he has never competed in full MMA competitions, he works with some of the top mixed martial artists in the world, including interviewees for this project, Quinton Jackson and Jason Miller. Reilly grew up in southern California, but graduated from Boston College where he played football and rugby. Reilly is part owner of Legends Gym in Hollywood, California and was thirty-five years old at the time of interview.

Ku Lee

Interview date: June 16, 2007

Interview location: Honolulu, Hawaii

Ku Lee grew up in Palolo, Hawaii—a neighborhood in Honolulu. He moved around extensively as a youth within Hawaii but also spent significant parts of his adolescence in Washington DC. In comparison to Hawaii, Lee said of Washington DC, "… you know, more crazier…. A lot more guns, knives, that kind of stuff." Lee periodically teaches MMA classes in Hawaii and hopes to eventually headline local Hawaii MMA cards. At the time of interview, Lee was an undergraduate student at the University of Hawaii about to finish his bachelor's degree.

Steven Saito

Interview date: July 2, 2007

Interview location: Honolulu, Hawaii

Steven Saito was born and raised in Hawaii. He grew up surfing on Oahu's North Shore. Although he did not play high school sports, his parents had him and his younger brother involved in the martial arts since about the time he could walk. Saito graduated from Lincoln Christian College in Illinois with a bachelor's degree in teaching English as a second language and was twenty-seven years old at the time of interview. An avid reader and historian, Saito is extremely proud of MMA's rich history in Hawaii, as well as the influence that Bruce Lee has had on the sport. Thus far, Saito has only competed in amateur MMA competitions, but is planning to move into a professional career. He works at Fighter's Corner with interviewee Nolan Hong.

Anthony "The Crush" Torres

Interview date: July 11, 2007

Interview location: Honolulu, Hawaii

Anthony Torres was one of a few people we interviewed who was a participant on *The Ultimate Fighter* reality show (the second season). It was on the reality show that he got his nickname, "The Crush," from his coach, Rich Franklin. Born in Saipan, Torres is of Chamorro, Irish, and Spanish ethnicity. Before finally settling down in Hawaii as a teenager, Torres lived in Guam, Tennessee, and California. After playing high school football in Hawaii, Torres got into judo and jiu-jitsu and eventually moved into full MMA competition. Torres works as a federal correctional officer and was twenty-nine years old at the time of the interview. Torres has competed in SuperBrawl, Icon Sport, and the UFC and at the time of writing holds a 5-1 professional MMA record.

Darin Goo

Interview date: September 22, 2007

Interview location: Honolulu, Hawaii

Darin Goo was born and raised in Hawaii, growing up in a Honolulu suburb. He attended private school before studying at the University of California, San Diego where he earned his bachelor's degree in structural engineering. Afterwards Goo attended San Diego State University, acquiring his masters degree in civil engineering, and he now works as a civil engineer. Goo considers himself a MMA hobbyist, having done fourteen years of Brazilian jiu-jitsu, some wrestling and boxing. He has competed in a few amateur jiu-jitsu tournaments in Southern California, but said half jokingly, "I know I could never become a top level competitor just based on seeing the typical types of training they do, and the athleticism that they have, so that's why I'm a hobbyist." We're sure Goo is doing just fine in his life as a civil engineer. He was thirty-four years old at the time of interview.

Terrance (pseudonym)

Interview date: September 23, 2007

Interview location: Kaneohe, Hawaii

One afternoon, I was sitting in a Starbucks waiting for traffic to die down before heading home when someone asked if he could check his e-mail on my laptop. He noticed that I was reading the latest MMA news on Sherdog.com. The next thing we knew, we were talking about riding motorcycles, MMA, and scheduling an interview. Terrance (pseudonym) asked that his identity be kept confidential. He was born in central California but moved to Oregon at age ten. He's been wrestling since he was in first grade and placed very high in the Oregon high school state championships before forgoing his senior year of high school to attend junior college on an academic scholarship. Currently a year short of getting his bachelor's, Terrance joked, "I've been going to college a long time. I think I'm probably about the most educated undergraduate out there." He currently works construction and trains about twice a week at a MMA gym in Oregon but considers himself a MMA hobbyist, truly enjoying wrestling and jiu-jitsu. Terrance was twenty-six years old at the time of interview.

Chris "The Crippler" Leben

Interview date: September 27, 2007

Interview location: Honolulu, Hawaii

Chris Leben is the third graduate of the UFC's reality show *The Ultimate Fighter* (*TUF*) that we were able to interview. Leben was portrayed on the show's inaugural season as a controversial figure and has since become a household name in MMA. Currently living, training, and coaching in Honolulu, Hawaii at Icon Martial Arts and Fitness, Leben was born and raised in Portland, Oregon. He got his MMA career started after his older brother saw some guys training MMA in the back of a used car lot. Leben described what he saw when he went to check it out:

> I walked into Matt Lindland's USA Auto Wholesale. That believe it or not was the beginning of Team Quest ... Matt Lindland had a used car lot, and they were training in the back of it in this old broken down shed, a mechanics shed. They had boarded down the walls and had mats down, and I walked

back there and saw Randy Couture and Matt Lindland goin' at it.... I believe I was their twelfth student at Team Quest.

Leben is well known as a dangerous mixed martial artist with strong knock out power, holding an impressive professional record of 17-4. Leben was twenty-seven years old at the time of interview. Said Leben of his experience on the UFC's reality show, "... when *TUF I* came out, I was driving an $800 car.... It was awesome for my career. But it was like boot camp.... Something you only want to do once."

The UFC Octagon (picture taken at UFC 63—Matt Hughes vs. B.J. Penn, Anaheim, CA).

Brotherly Love: Mike Onzuka (back) demonstrates application of a rear naked choke during class on brother Chris (Honolulu, Hawaii).

Mixed martial arts on display.

Nolan Hong (left) congratulates Steven Saito after an amateur kickboxing victory in Honolulu, Hawaii.

Frank "Twinkle Toes" Trigg (right) shoots in on "Ruthless" Robbie Lawler (Honolulu, Hawaii).

From left: Jeremy Williams, Traci Hess, JJ Ambrose, Giovanni Vasquez, Jimmi Jones, and Alberto Rios, after Ambrose won the WFA Welterweight Title (Santa Monica, California).

Jesse Juarez holding his "Invincible" title (Lakewood, CA).

Quinton "Rampage" Jackson (top) gives Jason Miller a tough workout (Hollywood, CA).

Darrin Goo (top) competing in a jiu-jitsu tournament (Photo courtesy of Alicia Anthony).

Antonio McKee counsels a youth at his gym, the Bodyshop Fitness, in Lakewood, California.

David Mayeda (left) meets then retired and former UFC Heavyweight Champion, Randy "The Natural" Couture (Honolulu, Hawaii).

Michael Frison (left) training with Dustin Phan (Irvine, California).

Chris Reilly (left) and "Rampage" Jackson cornering Jeremy "Half Man, Half Amazing" Williams (seated) (Honolulu, Hawaii).

Antonio McKee (left) motivating Jesse Juarez (Lakewood, California).

Pride FC Champion and two time USA Olympian, Dan Henderson, after giving a seminar at Chris and Mike Onzuka's gym in Aiea, Hawaii.

Chris "The Crippler" Leben, after teaching his MMA 101 class at Icon Martial Arts and Fitness (Honolulu, Hawaii).

Deena, Travis Lutter, and their son, Jordan (Fort Worth, Texas).

Chris Reilly (left) and "Rampage" Jackson (Honolulu, Hawaii).

Jason Miller (top) in Nolan Hong's guard (Honolulu, Hawaii).

PART II
INTO THE LIVES OF MIXED MARTIAL ARTISTS

UFC Light Heavyweight Champion, Quinton "Rampage" Jackson and his son, Elijah, at their home in Irvine, California. (Photo courtesy of Cathy Tanaka).

4

NURTURING A FIGHTER

BY DAVID MAYEDA

Growing up with Violence ... or Not

I remember how nervous I was when I was going to interview Quinton "Rampage" Jackson. I was staying with "Rampage's" long time friend, Jason "MayheM" Miller and his girlfriend at their place in Hollywood, California. As we were driving from Hollywood down to "Rampage's" house in Irvine, Jason was telling me that "Rampage" was in kind of a bad mood that day and may not give the best interview. I had watched a few Pride FC videos of "Rampage" picking up his opponents in the air and slamming them into the mat en route to victory. But it wasn't the slams that were freaking me out; I knew "Rampage" would not actually go into a rampage. It was "Rampage's" scowls—his angry pre-fight glares. I could just picture myself asking him a politicized question that we asked everyone else, but then triggering a nerve with an already upset "Rampage" and seeing him scowl back into me with an irritated, defiant frown.

As I reflected back on my emotions, I realized that my perceptions of fighters we interviewed for this project varied greatly. And try as we may, researchers simply cannot help but be influenced by our own biases. Was it his size, his blackness, his image? Could I really have been falling into a subconscious racist dogma? Or was it that we come from two completely different worlds? Not only is "Rampage" a substantially larger human being than me, but he comes from a much different background. True, "Rampage" now lives in upper-middle class Irvine, California (my hometown), but Irvine definitely does not resemble the type of community where he grew up.

Jackson was born and raised in South Memphis, Tennessee. In describing his upbringing, Jackson (QJ) stated the following:

> DM (David Mayeda): Okay, talk to me about growing up in Tennessee. Is that where you grew up?

QJ: Memphis, yeah.

DM: What was your life like as a child, that kind of thing?

QJ: It was kind of rough. You know, middle child, black sheep of the family. Nobody liked ya, that kind of thing. It was kind of different. It is what it is. Everything happens for a reason. It made me the kind of person that I am today. You know, I live in California, away from my family. You know, I've never been homesick, you know what I'm sayin'. So, everything happens for a reason. It was a tough, tough childhood. You know I had to fight to survive. I had to basically take care of myself. I been on my own since I was about fourteen.

Jackson's statement, "I had to fight to survive," exemplifies the viewpoint I had of mixed martial artists before I began this project—that most of these men grew up enmeshed in violence, whether it be at home, in school, in their neighborhood, or a combination of these domains. Said Jackson in another interview with *The Orange County Register*, "Growing up in Memphis, it was a tough journey, man. Some of my friends that I grew up with … they didn't make it. I'm blessed to even make it" (Swiatkowski, 2007). As we spoke with more and more individuals for this project, we heard childhood stories that made us realize why MMA did not seem like an especially violent endeavor for these men. They were the types of stories that would make a burnt out youth social worker from the impoverished streets of Chicago casually think, "Yeah, violence breeds violence. I see this stuff all the time."

An articulate and outspoken Antonio McKee set the tone for many of the interviews we held. McKee hinted into his life as a child by saying, "I haven't met a person who's had a worse life than me yet. And when I say that I mean from the time I came out, it was just hell …" Whether or not other fighters interviewed for this project viewed parts of their childhoods as "hell" remains unknown. However, the descriptions of youthful violence we heard expressed by mixed martial artists simply cannot be dismissed.

Like Jackson and McKee, Savant Young grew up in a community where it often times seemed as if violence was a part of everyday life. Said Young:

I'm from South Central (Los Angeles) originally. I live in Pasadena now. So I definitely grew up fightin'. You know, livin' in L.A., South Central was pretty much one of those, you know, if you don't fight, you'll get backed into a corner and you know, you have to deal with that every day, so that's what kind of pushed me into training and doing different kinds of martial arts …

As Young indicates in the closing part of his statement, the high levels of violence in his community were a contributing factor that drove him into the martial arts world, and eventually into MMA. The need to protect oneself and taking formal measures to do so were reoccurring themes that many fighters raised, irrespective of race or class backgrounds. Chris Leben, for example, spent most of his childhood and adolescence in Southeast Portland in a rough community known as "Felony Flats." Similar to Young, Leben said he started wrestling in high school because other athletes were picking on him:

> My neighborhood was pretty crappy. Almost everybody there was high on meth. You know, everybody's ridin' around robbin' each other with kitchen knives for VCR's and stuff like that.... I'd skateboard every day, smoke weed, and hang out. Then one day I just decided to start wrestling because the jocks were pickin' on me in high school.

Although now heralded more for his striking capabilities, Leben's wrestling skills eventually benefited him when he began his MMA career. More importantly, it is important to note current MMA fighters' trajectories as they moved from childhood into their current professions and how community violence drove them into various combat sports at early ages.

However, it was not just that fighters spoke of engaging in combat sports as youth. Their environments also provided opportunities for them to witness different types of community violence. In articulating some of the violent images he was exposed to as a youth, Jesse Juarez stated, "I grew up around a lot of violence. I had two brothers that were in gangs. I saw their friends get shot, right in front of me. You know, a lot of violence when I was young." Other fighters spoke casually of witnessing violence in their families, among friends, in schools, and their neighborhoods.

And not surprisingly, many of those we spoke with talked about being in fights themselves in their younger days. Jason "MayheM" Miller talked openly about getting into fights throughout his adolescence with peers and his father. "Me and my dad would fist fight every once in a while.... yea out of anger. Or sometimes it would be playful. There were times where it was probably borderline abuse." Illustrating how he perceived his past fights with his father as not terribly consequential, Miller went on to explain, "It's funny now, ya know, to me. And we laugh about it now, me and my dad. We made our peace." Like Miller, many of the other MMA practitioners we spoke with viewed their personal histories of childhood fighting as fairly typical.

Emanuel Newton, for example, spoke frankly of how media designated for youth provided him with a pretext for starting fights and bullying others while in grade school.

> I was really into the Ninja Turtles when I was a kid. So what we did at school, and we just (said), "Eh, you wanna play Ninja Turtles?" And I'd punch a kid in the face, and then we would fight…. It's just, that's usually how my fights started. Playing, you know, rough playing, and then a kid gets mad, and then you're fighting him.

Just as being professional mixed martial artists was not seen as a big deal in their present lives, many interviewees did not perceive their personal experiences with childhood violence as out of the ordinary. Interviewees frequently defined fighting as an activity that just happened amongst young males—boys will be boys so to speak. Seen as an inevitable part of their lives, community violence and interpersonal violence were not seriously questioned by those we spoke with. This is not to say that interviewees approved of the violence that entrenched their lives, but its presence was accepted without skepticism.

Moreover, youthful violence among interviewees spanned across regional and socio-economic lines. JJ Ambrose was raised in Bullhead City, Arizona, a small city with a population of only about 50,000. Ambrose's description of his rural hometown went as follows, "… there wasn't much to do out there except get into fights with locals, and wrestle…. I never lost a fight, but you can't really say anything, you know, wrestling, you take the guy down, the fight's pretty much over." Travis Lutter also grew up in an extremely rural community of South Dakota. When he was in fourth grade, he and his cousin would force some of the fifth and sixth grade students in his school to build his play fortresses during recess, and they could easily bully other students because of their athletic superiority. Lutter said, "… little kids ain't gonna mess with ya, you know it was gonna be the older kids that were gonna mess with ya, and we just never really put up with it, and so you'd end up getting in fights."

Chris Reilly talked about growing up in Woodland Hills, California, which at the time in the early 1970s was more of a working-class community. In discussing his childhood pastimes with his friends, Reilly stated:

> … there was a whole group of neighborhood kids that lived within the surrounding blocks that were various ages, and we used to ride dirt bikes together, play tag football and that kind of stuff, so you know like I said, it

wasn't the hood. But it was a bunch of boys out in the neighborhood, and yeah, we certainly got in fights. It definitely happened.

As can be seen, whether they were raised in impoverished, working-class, urban, or rural communities, there were MMA practitioners we interviewed who were quick to talk about dimensions of violence in their childhoods. Of course, the levels of violence that these men were exposed to and/or partook in as youth varied. Still, their numerous stories help to understand how and why these men moved into the MMA world and do not see that move as especially problematic or dangerous.

Two participants we spoke with brought up the issue of race as a variable that contributed to getting into fights as youth. In particular, these interviewees brought up the issue of being multi-ethnic that played a role in having to deal with peer conflict. Jamie Yager was one of these interviewees. He discussed how his racial distinctiveness influenced how often he got into fights. After asking him if he got into fights during his childhood and in adolescence, Yager stated:

> I'm multi-cultured. My mom's white. My dad's black, and my dad's been in jail my whole life, so growing up with a white family and an all white and Asian community, it's been kind'a tough, cause just fitting in. So growing up, I did get in a lot of fights, and I did have people trying to pick on me, and so fighting was something that came out of me naturally.

Robert Otani, who grew up in Oxnard, California, made a similar statement, explaining that his father is Japanese American and mother is Caucasian, making him "the odd ball kid," something I could truly identify with since my parents come from the exact same ethnic backgrounds. Otani (RO) begins the discussion below describing his childhood in Oxnard:

> RO: It was good, it was rough as far as you kind of had to fend for your own over there. I mean it wasn't as bad as a lot of people say. Everyone wants to say that their town is the toughest, you know and all that. And I'm not gonna say anything like that. But it was definitely, I mean you definitely had to be a tougher type of kid to be able to do well.

> DM (David Mayeda): Did you get into fights when you were a kid?

> RO: Yeah. Yeah, I think just for the simple fact that I was kind of the odd ball kid. You know I wasn't white. I wasn't Asian, you know what I mean.

> DM: I know exactly what you mean.

RO: A lot of Mexicans too in the Oxnard area, so they always wanted to test you, and they always thought that I was Mexican, so I got always placed in the Mexican group, and they wanted me to be part of gangs, but I wasn't really about that.

Prior research on multi-ethnicity has been inconclusive in determining whether or not mixed heritage impacts social adjustment in adolescence (Cauce et al., 1992). However, for these two interviewees, not fitting in because they were identified as racially conspicuous by their peers was a said factor that significantly impacted how often they fought with their peers, or as in Otani's case, were recruited to be in ethnically-based gangs.

As the above data illustrate, violence was not an atypical aspect of youthful life for many mixed martial artists. More to the point, fighting was both a concept and a reality that has characterized many interviewees' lives for many years. In other cases, youthful fighting may not have been the norm, but it was not rare either. Thus for these competitors, it is not surprising at all that they do not view MMA as a dangerous profession, nor that they enjoy being involved in this profession. What may be surprising to many readers are the numerous other people we interviewed for this project who grew up in extremely nonviolent surroundings.

Allan Goes is a MMA veteran. He was born and raised in Brazil and began learning jiu-jitsu at a very young age before coming to the United States to compete professionally in MMA. When speaking with us, Goes initiated a conversation about his childhood. He stated that when meeting him for the first time, people often assume he was raised in an abusive household or community:

> ... many people have the conception, I born poor, I been hit by my uncle, my friends hitting me, my friends don't respect me, my aunt beat me with a bat, my family hit me with a stick. I cannot speak for that people because for myself, when I grew up, I always grew up with a lot of respect, with a lot of love. I don't have anyone hitting me. I don't have my father beating me. I don't have my mother beating me. I don't have my grandpa beating me with a stick. I grew up with a lot of respect, with a lot of love, lots of discipline by my grandpa. But never hitting. They never hit me.

As Goes states, the common perception that so many people hold of those involved in MMA is that their personal history is muddled with violence. Without holding any animosity about such assumptions, Goes felt it was important to point out that like him, many mixed martial artists had upbringings that were nonviolent and loving.

Derek Stadler is a very young mixed martial artist who grew up in Hilo, Hawaii, which is a relatively rural community on the big island of Hawaii. Stadler expressed that fighting was fairly common in Hilo. However, outside of professional competition, he has yet to ever be in a fight. Speaking of Hilo, Stadler said, "I would always go out and I would see a lot of fights and everything. But I was, I would never be in those fights. It just seems like everybody had that mentality over there." As will be detailed later in Chapter Six, Stadler credits his decisions not to get involved in fights to the values he learned through martial arts as a child. Like Stadler, Paul Halme was raised in a rural area in South Dakota. Halme said of his community, "Pretty boring. Real Mid Western, not violent. Rural, yeah, we were a small town. You know, the whole state's pretty rural."

More to the point, a good portion of interviewees added that their families and neighborhoods were so peaceful that they never felt a need or desire to get into fights as youths; violence was hardly even on their radar. Takuhiro Kamikozono and Yoji Matsuo were both raised in Japan, and both stated that violence (or any kind of crime or delinquency for that matter) was not something they had to consider in everyday life. Said Matsuo, "we never really had to worry about it because of where I grew up ... the average, normal kid in Japan of that age didn't really have to deal with any kind of violence, at least where I grew up." Matsuo went on to say that even after he and his family moved to Irvine, California at age thirteen, he never got into fights.

Likewise, many interviewees from the United States said that violence has essentially been a non-issue in their lives. Interviewee Dustin Phan also grew up in Irvine, California. A current undergraduate student majoring in math at the University of California, Irvine and a jiu-jitsu instructor, Phan stated, "I've never been in a fight. Even today, I haven't got into any street fights ..." Dan Henderson grew up in Victorville, California. Answering whether or not he got into fights while growing up, Henderson said, "No, almost never," and further explained that violence never emerged as a topic in family discussions. In reference to his parents, Henderson stated:

> They didn't really say, you know, don't go out and get in fights. I never had a problem with it anyway. I was always pretty low-key. I wasn't a shit-talker. You know, I kept to myself. Nobody bothered me either. I never had a problem with that. I never had the desire to go out and get into fights. I had, a lot of that I got out of wrestling, you know, that kind of competition. I think my brother probably got into a couple more fights than I did, but still, he didn't

get into that many. But they didn't really have an official talk and say, "Don't go out and get in any fights," you know.

Randy Couture offered a similar description of his childhood environment in Lynwood, Washington (a Seattle suburb), in which violence was more or less a non-issue. He stated that all through grade school, he might have been in two fights, which he hardly even remembers, and that violence was not a significant neighborhood or family issue:

> … well it was never an issue. I think we had some teenage kids break into our house once when I was in junior high, or it might have been when I was a freshman in high school. But that was the closest thing that happened that was violent that I knew of. Um, it wasn't a regular part of our lives. It wasn't something that we had to deal with. It wasn't a rough neighborhood or anything like that.

These accounts demonstrate a side of the MMA world that is rarely, if ever noticed or promoted. Representing a large proportion of MMA competitors and hobbyists, their nonviolent pasts should not be disregarded.

These interviewees' histories disrupt the overarching label that bothered Allan Goes. Contrary to this prevailing stereotype, many MMA competitors and enthusiasts were raised in relatively nonviolent environments and moved into the MMA industry by way of their natural athletic abilities as wrestlers or traditional martial artists. True, many mixed martial artists we interviewed did observe and/ or engage in violent youthful behaviors, but that characteristic certainly did not typify the interviews as a whole. Oh, and by the way, my interview with "Rampage," it transpired without any menacing scowls, grimaces, or glares. He was actually a quite gracious host.

Families, Fathers, and Father Figures

Toby Grear is another MMA practitioner we spoke with who has never been in a fight outside of the ring. He grew up attending private school in an Ohio suburb and graduated from a private Catholic university with a degree in business administration and a minor in psychology before moving to Los Angeles, where he is now pursuing a full-fledged MMA career. In conducting this project, we heard a lot of crazy stories, but Grear may have had the craziest of them all. Grear played many different sports as a youth, and his parents went to all his competitions. However, when he got into MMA, they could hardly bare to watch.

Before getting further into this story, we should quickly explain the role of a "cornerman." A cornerman stands in a fighter's corner of the ring to help coach him or her during the competition, in between rounds, suggesting strategic adjustments, to provide water, and patch up cuts when necessary. Note the gendered nature of this term—it's not termed "cornerwoman" or even "cornerperson." The term can also be used as a verb, as in, "So and so is going to corner me." In any case, can you imagine watching someone compete in a MMA competition in a small, dirty, smoky bar while his *mother* cornered him? Neither could we. Toby Grear lived it:

> When I got into the fighting thing, my mom was, she could barely watch. So there was one time, it was five years ago maybe. You know I was doing the small shows. It was a real small show, you know in the bars and stuff like that where they set it up. But my cornerman's car had broken down and it was in a small country town in Ohio.... my Mom showed up, all in her sweater, gold chain, know what I mean? All "country club'd" out, and I asked her, "Mom you have to corner for me." She was like, "No way, no way!" And it was like, it was totally, totally, really out of place, you know what I mean? She ended up cornering for me.... It was one of the craziest fights I've ever had, cause I'm in there and it's like rough and tough. You were still allowed to smoke in Ohio, so it's a smoky bar scene ... more of a dance club type thing. And ya got my Mom over here! And the fight starts, and all you hear [is her yelling], "Balance! Balance Toby!" Cause she didn't know what to say, that's all she knew! And I must have not looked balanced.... I ended up hitting the guy with a swinging backfist, and one of the weirdest things that happened to me was I hit him and you could tell I just broke his nose, and he looked around, threw his gloves off in the ring, you know, sixteen-ouncers, and he ran out of the ring to the bathroom. I'm just standing there, like, that was an odd victory. It could not have been a more odd night, you know what I mean?

Yes, we know what you mean. These days Grear's mom does not corner him, but she's now a big fan and will fly to Los Angeles from Ohio to watch his MMA competitions. There were a few other people we interviewed who discussed their mothers being influential in their childhood development in ways that impacted their future lives as mixed martial artists. Randy Couture, while not having a story as unusual as Grear's, explained that he grew up with his mom, who as a single parent, got him playing almost every sport she could. And Jamie Yager discussed his mother's advice regarding youthful fighting:

> My mom was always like, "Don't be an instigator," you know, "don't go pickin' fights, but by any means, if anyone puts their hands on you, you have

the right to defend yourself." So growing up, you know, if anyone gave me a reason to retaliate, then I would …

Thus, there were occasional accounts of mothers who influenced these men's eventual lives as mixed martial artists. And like Yager, there were a number of other individuals we interviewed who grew up without fathers during their formative years.

However, another interesting trend observed with some interviewees was how often they tried to hide their involvement in MMA from their mothers. After MMA veteran Guy Mezger won his first MMA competition in 1994 at UFC 4, he was in the stands being congratulated by friends. He had not told his brother that he was competing in this event since he knew his brother would tell his mom, but his brother found out about it and was present. Mezger recalled this experience, explaining how his brother surprised him in the stands:

> … he comes and gives me a big hug and goes, "Man you made me so proud out there, and tell me you'll never do this again," and I go, "Don't worry," cause at the time, I had no intentions of doing it (again). And he goes, "Good," and he hands me the phone and says, "Now call mom." I go, "What?" And he goes, "Yeah, they watched. She threw up three times before your fight!"

Mezger laughed about this story and went on to explain how his mother eventually supported his long-term profession as a mixed martial artist, trainer, and gym owner. Yet this is just one of a number of stories communicated to us regarding competitors not wanting their families, and especially their mothers, to find out about their involvement in MMA. And there's not much I can say to criticize these men. I did not tell my parents about my participation in an amateur MMA event until after I had gotten through it unscathed.

In cases where fathers were present, a far more common thread was that of fathers being prominent figures in interviewees' youthful lives, who encouraged their movement into the MMA world. And even when fathers were not influential, it was common for interviewees to talk about other male family members affecting their future lives as mixed martial artists. Chris Bowles provided a good example, exemplifying how his relationship with his father influenced his eventual passage into MMA. Bowles is a 1994 graduate of the University of Oklahoma with a bachelor's degree in business administration. He now resides in Dallas, Texas working as an information technology (IT) manager. Although

Bowles works over fifty hours a week at his IT job, he is a successful MMA competitor with a 7-1 record. Bowles said of his father:

> ... my dad, you know it's funny, my dad was a minister. But one of the tougher guys I ever knew, and has never fought probably once in his life that I can remember, but was a fighter in a sense. I mean he just was a tough guy that was, he would push us.... We had a mat in our house for that matter, down in the basement, which was for the wrestling and so forth. And he was just one of those guys, if we played a sport, he coached it, and he studied it as much as he possibly could. I mean we were in camps year round. We were training. He was teaching himself along the way, and trying to instill an ability not to quit. So we grew up that way.

Bowles's description of his relationship with his father was much more typical of what we heard from interviews in this project. Numerous interviewees spoke of fathers and/or other older male family members who introduced them into the combat sports. As Bowles explains, these older male family members were not necessarily violent themselves, but they placed a premium on physical toughness and athletic discipline.

While Bowles talked about his father influencing his high school wrestling endeavors, there were a number of other interviewees who told stories of their fathers' influence in the traditional martial arts. For example, when discussing his upbringing, Derek Stadler stated, "Well, I always liked judo and wrestling because my dad did it. He's a black belt. So he always had me in martial arts. And that's before MMA was really popular." Emanuel Newton made a similar statement regarding his father: "My dad was a big muay Thai guy. He died when I was pretty young. But he showed me some stuff, and I'd say I got his genes. And then I just went into wrestling ..." Finally, Robert Otani credited his father as a significant figure that like Bowles, constructed a part of their family's house so that it was conducive to teaching a combat sport, in this case judo. After I asked Otani, "What were your family's views on violence?" he responded:

> My dad actually, it's weird because he's just kind of warming up to what I'm doing now, but when I was growing up, they used to call our house "The House of Pain" and "The Dojo" because we used to have a mat room and everything. And everyone would come over and my dad would get everyone in the room that was acting up, or talking crap or whatever, and he'd get all the guys in there and make 'em go at it. So he kind of condoned it, or not condoned it, but promoted it in a sense, but in a controlled fashion I guess.

Interviewees' repeated descriptions of their fathers who inspired and mentored them athletically through combat sports illustrate how critical fathers frequently are in mixed martial artists' lives. As mentioned earlier in this chapter, other interviewees for this project, like Jason Miller, spoke of times when they and their fathers would actually get into physical fights on a regular basis, which contributed to their current normalization of sporting violence.

Still, it was not just fathers. Interviewees also spoke of other male family members who were influential in introducing them to MMA. Although Toby Grear's account of his mother cornering him may be more overtly memorable, Grear was actually introduced to MMA by his uncle. Grear recalls that at age thirteen, he and his uncle watched the early UFC tournaments together.

> My uncle had me watch it. We were at home. He got me into it. And I mean I was young, and we're talking years of me and him watching it.... So I mean that kind of got that ingrained in my brain. And so maybe it's always been in the back of my head to be a fighter.

After I asked Allan Goes how he got into MMA, he answered, "My grandpa was a judo player and boxer, and he always motivated us to do sport, always. Yeah, it was mainly my grandpa that gave me the support with this whole thing."

Interviewees also brought up brothers as significant in their days of childhood. In most cases, interviewees referred to older brothers "toughening them up," or essentially picking on them, something this book's photographer, Stephen Mayeda, can probably relate to quite well. For example, interviewee Terrance mentioned that his MMA hobby was normalized largely by his family dynamics: "I grew up with three older brothers. We fought and wrestled all the time. So for me, it's just like, I don't know, it's natural for me." Note how Terrance naturalizes his involvement in training MMA that stemmed from his older brothers' socialization practices. A graduate of the UFC's reality show, *The Ultimate Fighter II*, Anthony Torres also spoke of his older brother "toughening him up": "I got picked on a lot by him ... I got the beat down by him, you know. It was his way of toughening me up." In addition, his older brother reportedly made Torres fight with his own friends at parties:

> ... like family parties, and I'd be playing with my friends. For entertainment, him and his friends was for me to fight with my friends. And I didn't want to, but hey, just stuff he'd keep saying, (like) you'd better fight now, or when we go home I'm gonna give you a beat down. And it was like, shit, I didn't want

to go home to get a beat down, you know, so I had to do it. You know? I had to do stuff like that.

Once Torres began training in jiu-jitsu and other combat sports after high school, it was far easier to resist pressure from family or peers to get into fights. Nevertheless, Torres's socialization to see fighting as not terribly unusual began largely with his older brother's influences.

However, Chris and Mike Onzuka probably raised the most glaring example of how they influenced each other to eventually become prominent in jiu-jitsu and in Hawaii's overall MMA scene. Now in adulthood, the twin brothers jokingly explained how they used to compete with one another in virtually every activity—sports, school, work, and of course, fighting. Chris (CO) started out this topic, with Mike (MO) jumping in afterwards, both laughing at themselves throughout the conversation:

> CO: … we were competitive with each other. We couldn't get along with each other. We both have hard heads.
>
> MO: So when we woke up, it would be who woke up first. Who brushed their teeth faster? Who ate breakfast faster? We'd run to school, race to school. Who'd get their homework done quickly? We'd run home. Who'd get home first? Who'd get their homework done? We'd go out to play. If we were playing basketball or whatever, who'd beat each other in basketball or soccer or volleyball, or whatever we were playing at that time. Then we'd run home. Then it's like grades, everything—grades, working, you know, who makes more money. Everything. Who is more successful in school?
>
> CO: We used to fight, not like brothers would fight normally but we used to fight up until (age) nineteen…. Just walking in the hall, shoulder bump to shoulder bump, to a punch, and then we'd start fighting each other. You know we wouldn't stop until we knocked the door off its hinges or our mom came home or something like that.

These stories conveyed by so many different interviewees of fathers and other male figureheads demonstrate the profound stimulus men and male peers have on boys in their development as athletes, and in particular as athletes in the combat sport of MMA. What's more, these accounts exhibit the different ways that males normalize violence with one another. Whether it be through an informal but controlled atmosphere in which fathers set up in-house wrestling or martial arts gyms, uncles sitting down with nephews to watch combat sports, father-son fights, or fights among male siblings, the nurturing of mixed martial artists so often included male influence. And in some cases, the gendered aspects of MMA competition still impact interviewees' lives today. JJ Ambrose talked about the importance his father and other male family members play in his current MMA career, and the way women in his family tend to discourage his MMA career goals:

> Yeah, my family, it's kind of weird, you know, all the men are all about it. "Yeah, go fight, sweet!" You know. And then all the women, you know, they just kind'a stay out of it, try to get me a different job or something. But nothin' else is for me, and my dad knows that better than anybody. I love when he comes to the fights cause afterwards he's gonna go to work the next day and tell all his buddies.... You know, that really helps me when I'm in the ring sometimes too, I'll be in a bad situation, and I'll be like, "There's no way I can let my dad go to work tomorrow and have to say my son lost." So that pushes me hard.

Undoubtedly, there is a gendered dimension to MMA that will be displayed further in Chapter Eight. As we look to make sense of how mixed martial artists progressed into their current profession, specifically how their early experiences in childhood and adolescence pushed them into this violent sport, we can clearly see the influence fathers and father figures had and still have in shaping so many mixed martial artists' lives.

The Importance of Amateur Athletics

Along with familial influence, most interviewees we spoke with discussed having a long history competing as athletes throughout their youth, high school, and/or college lives. There were a few interviewees who took on MMA as a hobby or profession having never been in sports beforehand. Aspiring mixed martial artist, Cleyburn Walker, never played high school sports, but had his first professional MMA competition in Texas after being in the marines. Despite never playing sports extensively beforehand, Walker stated, "I'm doing everything within my power to make this my career." Yoji Matsuo is another individual we spoke with who never truly got into sports before entering the MMA industry.

DM (David Mayeda): What sports did you compete in or play in besides this?

YM (Yoji Matsuo): Nothing. I mean, I played soccer when I was a little kid, like in elementary school. I was in sixth grade, and I competed once in an elementary level soccer match.

DM: So in high school, you didn't do any sports?

YM: Nope, no sports whatsoever.

Matsuo, while engaging in amateur jiu-jitsu and pankration competitions, has no ambitions to compete professionally in MMA. Instead, the civil engineer and entrepreneur views MMA as a hobby and has moved into the business side of the industry as part-owner of an MMA retail store.

But as should not be surprising, most interviewees we spoke with played sports as youths and played them avidly. Unquestionably, the sport that came up the most frequently in these discussions was wrestling. Derek Stadler was a high school wrestler who switched schools during his senior year because he wanted to live with his mother. Unfortunately, in doing so, he was declared ineligible to compete in Hawaii's state wrestling tournament. After we asked him if not getting to finish his high school wrestling career was influential in his decision to try MMA, Stadler said, "Ah yeah, I think so.... I felt like I wasn't finished." Stadler's sentiments regarding an unfinished wrestling career exemplify what so many others felt regarding their own wrestling endeavors that were halted at various levels. Some other wrestlers we spoke with who stopped at the high school level included Chris Bowles, Robert Otani, and Jamie Yager.

Many MMA competitors we interviewed wrestled at the college level and were quite successful, even if they did not complete all four years of their collegiate athletic eligibility. Some of these athletes interviewed included Emanuel Newton, JJ Ambrose, Chris Leben, Travis Lutter, Jason Bress, Bao Quach, and Quinton Jackson. Said Quach for example, who earned his college degree in kinesiology, "I did wrestling in high school, some college, then I started doing jiu-jitsu. I was mainly a grappler. Then I started training with Colin (Oyama), and now I'm everything, you know, kickboxing, muay Thai." Before winning an N.A.I.A. collegiate wrestling championship in 2005, Jesse Juarez was introduced to MMA while wrestling in high school and community college. Juarez said of former UFC Light Heavyweight Champion, Tito Ortiz, "he would come into our wrestling room in high school and do a little wrestling.... And, he actually helped out at Golden West Community College where I wrestled ..."

JJ Ambrose stated that after wrestling in high school in Arizona, he moved to Southern California to attend junior college and wrestle, but he dropped out so that he could focus fully on a MMA career. This issue of leaving college early is an issue Guy Mezger had a great deal to say about and will be addressed more thoroughly in Chapter Nine. Finally, we were able to interview men who had established world class wrestling careers, including previous Olympic hopefuls Frank Trigg, Randy Couture, and Antonio McKee, as well as Dan Henderson who competed in Greco-Roman wrestling for the United States in both the 1992 and 1996 Olympic Games.

Nevertheless, the common thread among these former wrestlers was that regardless of how successful they were in wrestling, there was no professional career for them in their particular sport. Randy Couture began wrestling at age ten before competing at the international level in the U.S. Army and subsequently at Oklahoma State University, where he was a three time All American, not to mention an alternate on four Olympic teams. With those types of credentials, one would think athletics could yield a lucrative professional career. Yet after attaining a bachelor's degree in foreign language and literature, Couture told us he "started coaching basically to continue to pursue the Olympic endeavor and as a way to make ends meet and stay on the mat. So I got hired at Oregon State University, coached as an Assistant Coach …" Later in our interview, Couture (RC) expanded on the lack of financial opportunities for wrestlers, even if they were elite, world class athletes.

> DM (David Mayeda): You know, you bring up the financial aspect and before mixed martial arts got really popular, there wasn't an avenue for wrestlers, and you know, people who were world class athletes to make a profession out of it, unless you got a good job as a coach.

> RC: That's true, there were only so many coaching positions. And so it was very difficult for wrestlers especially. We're not one of the particular Olympic sports where you're getting appearance fees, and it's not as lucrative on an Olympic level like a gymnast or a track and field athlete. So finding a coaching position was very important for me to take care of my family and still compete and train at the level I needed to train. And fighting certainly changed that a lot. I left my coaching job to pursue fighting full time. I mean I was making a lot more money, stepping into the ring competing.

And while Couture was on the cusp of making the Olympics, Dan Henderson actually wrestled in two Olympic Games but still could not make a substantial living athletically. Thus in 1997, Henderson cut down to 175 pounds and gave MMA a shot in a tournament called "The Brazil Open Fight," in which he won both his matches on only two weeks of MMA training. The nurturing of these MMA competitors emerged largely out of the desire to keep competing and make a living out of the skill that they had honed for so many years. Unfortunately, amateur wrestling is not a revenue producing sport, but with MMA steadily gaining popularity, a new athletic pathway materialized that offered financial opportunity.

Still, wrestling was not the only influential sport interviewees brought up. Many MMA competitors mentioned that they grew up learning traditional martial arts. When we interviewed Tony Fryklund, he had already been competing in martial arts for twenty-two years, since age thirteen. Said Fryklund of his youthful days, "I was a little bit hyper active ... I was always you know, very athletic. I was always doing as many sports as I could." And like so many other MMA competitors we interviewed, Fryklund enjoyed the individual combat sports over team sports: "I liked the contact and it was individual. You know, it was completely up to you, if you win or lose, and I saw that right away." At a YMCA in his hometown of Boston, Fryklund was introduced to boxing and eventually to a variety of martial arts that later took him into the MMA world, debuting in 1997 at UFC 14. Fryklund went on to explain how critical it is to be proficient in a variety of martial arts and other combat sports if one is to compete in MMA today:

> ... right now, you really have to get a deep, deep understanding of each art that you're training, be it boxing, muay Thai, judo, jiu-jitsu, wrestling, and then tying those all together, you can only understand how to tie those together if you train them all as a separate martial art. Otherwise, just cause you're an MMA guy, and you throw some low kicks, it means you're probably good enough to get yourself killed ...

Fryklund's martial arts history stemmed from trying out a wide variety of different sports and eventually finding a love for the individual aspects of one-on-one competition. He also spoke at length of appreciating traditional martial arts values, discussed further in Chapter Six. Other interviewees got into the martial arts because of their fathers.

As described previously, fathers and father figures played a huge role in many interviewees' eventual decisions to get into MMA. Chris Reilly spoke of growing up in a rough, working-class community. Said Reilly, "When I was growing up, I didn't know we were poor; I didn't know until later. But we were poor. We didn't have much, and although again, it certainly was not the hood, it was a rough enough neighborhood ..." Reilly then described his father's wishes for him to be able to protect himself physically, as well as his personal fascination with the martial arts that he developed by watching Kung Fu Theatre as a child.

> And so my dad wanted me to know how to fight. So, you know, I went to the local karate school, and I remember I wanted to do it. I remember we used to watch Kung Fu Theatre together back in the day when there weren't so many options on television. It was Kung Fu Theatre, which was all the old Kung Fu movies and they would run it all day …

Although he also played high school football, college football, and rugby, Reilly became engrossed in the martial arts. After graduating from Boston College and trying a brief career in business, Reilly returned to training and competing in martial arts, having professional matches in Turkey, Cambodia and the United States. Though not a full MMA competitor himself, Reilly now trains a number of elite MMA athletes and runs a MMA gym where he is part-owner.

Finally, many interviewees discussed jiu-jitsu as a combat sport that steered them towards MMA careers. Allan Goes, who grew up learning Brazilian jiu-jitsu, began competing professionally as a means to take care of his family at the time when MMA was just getting started in the United States. During this time in the mid-1990s, MMA competitors did not have the hybrid styles they have today. Thus, Goes previously saw himself as a jiu-jitsu representative, trying to prove jiu-jitsu was the superior discipline within the combat sports: "… nobody would expect some Brazilian would have such great martial (art), that would shock the world. That's what was my goal when I first came over here. I fought for the jiu-jitsu. I was like a missionary." Today Goes has changed his outlook and sees his participation in MMA as a means of having fun, building friendships, and supporting his family as both a competitor and trainer.

Even former wrestlers used their wrestling experience to immerse themselves into jiu-jitsu before trying out full fledged MMA careers. When wrestling in college in South Dakota, Travis Lutter watched the second UFC tournament and was impressed with Royce Gracie defeating so many larger opponents. Lutter was also dabbling in muay Thai kickboxing at the time. However, jiu-jitsu became his passion: "… me and my coach ordered tapes, and there was a group of guys and we started doing jiu-jitsu off of tapes." Lutter then talked about merging his wrestling and jiu-jitsu skills which give him a strong MMA ground game: "The ability to take the fight and end it quickly because of my jiu-jitsu and my wrestling, I can kind of control where the fight's at. Things like that, it's a big advantage for me."

Another common sport interviewees played was football, probably not surprising given that football is a collision sport. There were numerous interviewees we spoke with who played high school football, and a few who played in college. Jamie Yager played as a free safety at the collegiate level for two years in Kansas, and Robert Otani played linebacker for the University of Southern California, winning two national championship titles. In short, the men we spoke with largely expressed that playing sports was a way of life for them, and something they still do not want to relinquish. Not wanting athletic careers to end is an extremely common feeling among athletes, especially men, and can have adverse physical health consequences should athletes "age out" of their abilities but continue competing (Messner, 1992). In addition, interviewees noted that MMA could serve as an occupational possibility that was previously not available for them. This topic that addresses financial aspirations will be addressed further in Chapter Nine. In Chapter Five, we inspect the inner thoughts that stir within mixed martial artists' minds, now that they are adults.

5

DISSECTING A FIGHTER'S MIND

By David Mayeda

While interviewing people for this project in Texas, I was able to interview MMA competitors and hobbyists at Travis Lutter's gym in Fort Worth and Guy Mezger's gym in Dallas. Known as "Guy Mezger's Lion's Den Dallas," Mezger operates his gym within a larger fitness club. While at the Lion's Den, I first interviewed Takuhiro Kamikozono before simultaneously interviewing Mezger and Chris Bowles due to time constraints. Mezger had just finished running Bowles, Kamikozono, and a number of other athletes through what looked like a grueling workout. After Bowles cleaned up, he joined me and Mezger in the gym office where we chatted extensively about MMA. As noted in Chapter Four, Bowles is a college graduate, with a bachelor's degree in business administration and works as an IT manager. He is also the father of two children—a young son and a baby girl. One would not normally think Bowles also enjoyed choking people out to win MMA competitions.

Towards the end of our interview, Mezger admitted that for the longest time he also had difficulty understanding why Bowles wanted to compete as a mixed martial artist. True, Bowles had a high school wrestling background and enjoyed athletic competition. But he also held a great job, was—along with his wife—raising two young children, and simply a calm, kind person. Said Mezger of Bowles:

> There's always something that's not quite clicking right in an individual that wants to fight for either sport or for money.... I'll admit it. I don't hit on all cylinders. Chris doesn't hit on all cylinders. In fact, I wouldn't let Chris fight for the longest time because I met his family, and I said, "Chris you're not screwed up enough to fight."

As the two chuckled at Mezger's comments, Mezger went on to state that many of those who are work-a-holics in a variety of professions don't "hit on all cylinders." Yet Mezger's comments still struck me and made me think more carefully about what goes through MMA competitors' minds, including how they view themselves within and outside of this rapidly evolving sport.

Soaking in the Pain Principle

In speaking with the forty individuals interviewed for this project, it became obvious that those engrossed in MMA held self-concepts that were linked heavily to the concept of pain. Obviously, athletes in all sports must manage physical pain and injury. However, MMA interviewees brought up pain as something they had to cope with in unique ways and on a regular basis, more similar to the way men conceptualize pain in other collision sports, such as rugby (Pringle & Markula, 2005). Naturally, pain was seen through the physical bumps, scrapes, and bruises MMA competitors endured. But it was also seen mentally in the ways fighters conceptualized pain, describing it sometimes as a factor they welcomed, and sometimes as a factor that needed to be ignored. This fixation on pain management was a major aspect of these fighters' personal identities, woven intimately into their self-concepts.

After interviewer David Ching asked Bao Quach how he coped with pain, Quach answered in a way that typified most other interviewees' answers:

> You know in a fight I really don't, you don't really feel the pain. And, I can handle pain pretty good, you know? You should be able to handle pain if you're a fighter. Because you're going to be constantly hit, hurt, whatever, so you know, you gotta be able to take it (laughs).

Repeatedly, fighters mentioned that during professional fights, pain is a non-issue. They generally reported not feeling it and that it is hardly even part of their consciousness, especially during competition. As Savant Young said, thinking about pain can contribute to losing competitive focus and in turn, an actual loss: "… during a fight, you never think about the pain cause when you do, that's usually when you lose the fight, so you kind'a try to numb yourself to the pain." Emanuel Newton expanded on this topic, even explaining that while in competition, he wanted to be on the receiving end of manageable strikes that fire him up psychologically. Describing pain management, Newton said:

> Well, in the ring is one, and out of the ring is another. When you're in the ring you're not thinking about it, you know. It's like unless you break a rib or you seriously break something, to the point where you can't move because it just stops the motion in your body, you know, usually you don't think about getting punched in the head. Like, personally, I hope I get (receive) a good punch in the head when I'm in the cage. That turns me on, it's like my switch, you know. But out of the ring, I mean, after you get out of that cage and back and the adrenaline stops rushing, that's when the pain kicks in. You know what I mean, but that's just what we do for the sport, and that's just what's gonna be expected.

Note Newton's ultimate acceptance of dealing with pain. It is an unquestioned expectation that comes along with being a MMA competitor, part of a mixed martial artist's normal, everyday identity. Other interviewees agreed with Newton that absorbing a solid punch (though not a knockout punch) could be a good thing in competition. Said JJ Ambrose, "… you know, you get punched in the face and that just kind of wakes you up and puts you in your fight mode." In fact, disregarding pain while in competition and training is common among athletes of both sexes in multiple sports (Charlesworth & Young, 2004; Pike, 2004). My (DM) exchange with Quinton Jackson (QJ) further illustrates how interviewees viewed pain in different contexts:

> DM: Define pain for me. How do you cope with pain in training and competition?

> QJ: It depends on how I got it. And is it the type of pain where I gotta keep training with it, or the pain after the fight where I got hurt, and I'm just chillin' out. You know what I'm sayin', you go through pain every day. It's just, that's a good question, I don't even know how to answer that.

> DM: How about this, a stereotypical fan, like myself who's never competed and hasn't been following the sport that long might watch a fight and be like, "This is the most brutal thing I've ever seen. Those guys gotta be hurting."

> QJ: Ah, hell no. In a fight, it don't even hurt. The only thing that hurts in a fight is probably body shots and leg kicks. When you get punched and stuff in a fight, it don't even hurt. And that's me, cause I can't feel somebody else's pain. But when I get punched in the face, it don't hurt unless somebody hits you right here on this orbital bone or something like that. I noticed that hurt before in practice. In a fight, your adrenaline's pumping so much, that you can't even really feel it.

As can be seen, MMA athletes viewed pain as part of their competitive world and in certain scenarios actually welcomed it. Though for the most part during competition, pain was constructed as much as possible as a non-issue. Yet outside of the ring or cage, feeling physical pain was not denied or ignored. To the contrary, it was an important topic. However, it was made bluntly clear that within competition, pain was either positive or nullified, and it needed to be constructed as such to be a successful mixed martial artist.

Outside of competition, interviewees still conceptualized pain as part of their lives, but in different ways. To begin with, physical pain was seen as a constant in mixed martial artists' lives. It was normalized and never ending. In David Ching's conversation with Bear St. Clair, Ching stated, "Define pain from a mixed martial artist's context." St. Clair responded, "Oh, pain from a mixed martial artist's context. If you're talking on a professional level, is that, that's how it is, get used to it. All day, every day ..." Thus, being a professional mixed martial artist meant being able to accept pain as part of one's standard routine in life, even when one was not training or competing.

Additionally, many interviewees regarded pain as a positive feeling outside of competition. It reminded them that they were in good health and that they were functioning somewhat normally. In other words, they had not become physically numb while outside of the competitive arena. Said Travis Lutter, "It's not a bad thing, you know, feeling pain is definitely part of this, but it reminds you that you're still alive. And that's a good thing." More to this end, pain was viewed positively as a motivator. Jesse Juarez explained pain from this point of view: "Pain makes me work harder. If I get hurt, I get mad at myself because I let my guard down. I didn't train hard enough.... So, I work harder. I train harder if I have pain." In short, physical pain was transformed into a contributor to these athletes' overall development and progress in MMA. Sabo (2004) refers to this perspective as "meritocratic pain," in which athletes believe that the pain acquired during training and competition will springboard them into greater athletic success. Being hurt (e.g., getting bumps and bruises) was part of the game. Pain was viewed by interviewees as making them stronger, and it distinguished them as mixed martial artists from non-athletes and athletes in non-collision sports. Even co-author Dave Ching stated that, while at first the pain in his leg from receiving leg kicks from his brother-in-law during sparring was extremely uncomfortable, it eventually became something that indicated a good workout and something that, in a "twisted way," he desired.

Being injured, however, was something different. A common understanding in athletics is that when an athlete is injured, he or she must stop training and competing all together, or modify training significantly so the injury can heal. Emanuel Newton touched on this distinction previously, noting that an injury would be something akin to sustaining a broken rib. Whereas when one is hurt (e.g., having a bruise), the athlete can and should push through the pain during practices and while in competition. After interviewer Stephen Mayeda asked Travis Lutter, "… what are the differences between being hurt and injured?", Lutter responded in a way that reflected this common athletic orientation:

> Being hurt and injured, that is a great question. When you're injured, that means you can't train no more. When you're hurt, that means it hurts. You know, but that means you're gonna train tomorrow. And that's the difference in between the two, and it's a very common question I ask my guys, "Are you hurt or injured?" You know, cause it's two different conversations that we're gonna have. If you're injured, you need to go get this fixed. I'll see ya when it's better … If you're hurt, suck it up, let's train. I'll see ya tomorrow …

Again, this doctrine is hardly unique to MMA. Coaches in numerous sports will ask their athletes if they are hurt or injured, and if they are only hurt, to continue practicing and/or competing. Moreover, as mentioned previously, this athletic doctrine is accepted by both male and female athletes. Nixon's (2004) work reveals how pervasive attitudes are among male and female athletes regarding what he deems the "culture of risk," in which athletes readily accept that they must accept physical risk and play through pain since doing so earns respect, shows character, and illustrates unselfishness (p. 87, 88).

Of course, although the socialization of athletes promotes such acceptance, that does not mean it truly promotes health. This sporting socialization is well known among even the most marginal sports fans. Within sporting circles, "Slogans glorify pain only to slickly slide it into non-existence. The phrase 'no pain, no gain' beckons athletes to 'push yourself to the limit,' 'sacrifice your body,' … Such slogans encourage athletes to disregard pain …" (Sabo, 2004, p. 62). Chapters Seven and Nine will investigate how dangerous this culture of risk is within MMA and offer suggestions for safety promotion. But for this chapter, it is critical to demonstrate how easily mixed martial artists consented to the culture of risk, welcoming physical pain into their everyday lives and constructing how they saw themselves as physically tough athletes. Robert Otani even went so far to say that receiving pain was fun. In describing a recent fight he had lost, Otani said, "I still look back at it, and I got stitches in my eye, but I had fun."

Interviewees did discuss pain in negative terms, but this was done when commenting on activities that were not necessarily physical and unrelated to their lives as mixed martial artists. Travis Lutter contributed a great deal to this topic. Contrasting the differences between physical pain and emotional pain, Lutter said:

> ... it's like we're all gonna end up in some kind of pain as we get older. We're all gonna end up in a rocking chair at some point in time. It's just a matter of how you get there. And I choose to get there under my own terms, and that's important to me. Yeah, I mean training hurts, getting hit in the head hurts, but at the same time, you get to do it cause [you] can. You know, I'm sittin' at a desk in an office—that's pain. There's pain. And sittin' and fighting traffic as you go to work, that's pain, you know. Hearing your kid scream cause he doesn't have food, that's pain. This is just physical pain.

Other interviewees made similar comments, stating that it would be painful to work a desk job and cope with a more mundane lifestyle. Allan Goes likened pain to being completely incapacitated or having an acute disease, thereby de-emphasizing the physical pain he may acquire while in training or competition.

Still, MMA interviewees did not deny feeling physical pain outside of competition, even if it was welcomed and/or accepted. Savant Young, like most other interviewees, admitted having to cope with physical pain after competitions. Said Young, "After the fight, that's a whole other story. You know, after the fight, there's the ice, and there's the Motrin. There's the whatever you could have for the pain, but it's all temporary ..." And many interviewees readily discussed how over the counter medication was used to help with pain management. Travis Lutter had his medication down to a science. Speaking about his Ibuprofen intake, Lutter said, "... the doctors have explained to me that the most you're supposed to take in is like three or four times a day, 800 milligrams, you know, if they give you a prescription ... four Ibuprofens, 800 milligrams, that's what I do ..." Countless interviewees also mentioned taking glutamine supplements regularly, which is said to optimize muscle growth and recovery and can be purchased over the counter at any nutritional supplements store. Consequently, in addition to pain being a normalized part of these MMA practitioners' lives, so too were the medical and supplemental products that are readily available to help handle physical soreness.

It is important to remind readers outside of the athletic sphere that people react to sporting injuries and bumps and bruises in completely different ways, depending largely on their own frames of reference. Curry and Strauss's (1994) research illustrates how college wrestlers perceive being hurt and getting injured as par for the course, and that viewing pictures of their sometimes graphic injuries is an uneventful activity. When other college athletes and medical students saw the pictures, they had similar unemotional reactions. However, when college students who were not athletes and attendees at a sociology of sport conference viewed the pictures, reactions were starkly different, with the college students unable to believe how athletes normalized injury and conference attendees defining the athletes as human capital exploited through the big business of college sports.

Furthermore, the normalization of sports injuries made by male athletes has become a heavily studied topic. Men in a variety of sports accept pain and take different approaches to dealing with it (e.g., hiding it, tolerating it, playing through it; Young, White, & McTeer, 1994). However, having worked out with as many female as male athletes during and after college, I would argue that soaking in the pain principle is no longer a sex-specific phenomenon, and as mentioned previously, the research (Nixon, 2004) seems to verify this. True, the acceptance and welcoming of pain in sport may stem from a patriarchal model, but it certainly is not specific only to men, and I would be surprised if female mixed martial artists conceptualized pain in ways notably different from the men interviewed for this study. What may be more crucial is helping athletes to see the long term deleterious effects of ignoring and playing through pain, and that incessantly having surgeries to prolong an athletic career can lead to severe health problems in the not so distant future. In short, athletes (especially those in sports that have high injury rates) need counsel in establishing identities and skills outside of the athletic realm so that they are not forever stuck in a physically and emotionally harmful livelihood and are comfortable moving into a life that promotes general fitness over athletic excellence as they age out of competition.

Riding an Emotional Rollercoaster

Although coping with physical pain was not perceived as a major problem by interviewees, coping with anxiety was, in particular among those MMA practitioners who competed professionally. First, however, it is important to note that coping with sports-related stress is a sports issue, not merely a MMA issue. Coaches and parents so frequently rattle off how sports build character, self-esteem, promote physical health, and so on. A former high school and college athlete myself, I can't tell you how many times I felt like dirt after sporting competitions, including those that I won. One would think after winning the Big West Conference Championship as a college senior in the 400 hurdles I would be celebrating, not sitting alone in my room depressed and crying because I didn't run fast enough to qualify for the national championships.

Sports should be fun, and hopefully they normally are, but when one internalizes mottos such as, "You can never be satisfied," then the standards for excellence leave little room for personal fulfillment. The fact is, the societal pressure inflicted upon athletes at all levels can be so emotionally taxing that innumerable athletes break down mentally all the time. Of course, these institutional models that apply unrelenting psychological pressure stretch far beyond athletics. Sports sociologist Michael Messner (1994) writes, "I am coming to see academe and sports as the same pyramid. The same ego game" (p. 27). Likewise, I have heard my share of friends who are graduate students and university faculty express feeling depressed and saddened by their career choice, pressured by academic clichés, such as "publish or perish," and "your tenure clock is ticking."

Returning to MMA, emotional anxiety was not discussed as a serious problem by all professional mixed martial artists with whom we spoke, but a great deal admitted that many mixed martial artists carry psychological stress that stems from their personal lives and/or an erratic MMA lifestyle. A few interviewees indicated that MMA is a sport that attracts individuals who already have pre-existing anxiety problems. Jason Miller held this perspective. We asked interviewees if mixed martial artists had to deal with psychological issues and problems. Miller responded in the following manner:

> … the sport definitely attracts people that already have mental problems. Cause it's not really natural, well, I think it's natural, but it's kind'a, supposed to be bread out of you by the time you get older. Uh, you don't punch people in the face. You know, you don't fight people…. it's a freakin' lonely sport, man…. when you get out there, guess what. Your friend's not there, nobody's there. All that's there is you and him … I think it plays into it, like the psychological stress that you go through.

Miller made two key points. First, he thought MMA competitors tended to have psychological issues they were dealing with before getting into the sport, and secondly, that the individualized nature of the sport furthered anxiety problems and personal stress, as MMA athletes can often times feel lonely and isolated. Bear St. Clair agreed with Miller's first point, that MMA competitors entered the MMA industry already holding psychological problems. After David Ching asked St. Clair, "Do you notice that fighters in particular, have to deal with psychological problems, like depression, anxiety, and rage?", St. Clair stated:

> Listen, if you're a fighter, that means that right there … it's a qualification as a fighter to be crazy in some manner. One way or the other, there's something

wrong with you. And let me tell you why.... Everybody seeks and wants comfort, and fighters run into the fray, into the pain, into the discomfort, okay? Most people want it safe. Fighters obviously don't.

St. Clair's and Miller's sentiments on this issue were not the norm amongst interviewees. Rather, most interviewees felt that although MMA competitors do deal with psychological problems, the sport does not necessarily attract those who already have emotional concerns or make them more unstable. As Darin Goo said of MMA, "I wouldn't say that it makes people troublemakers or more likely to get into trouble with the law." Goo went on to say that as MMA has become more of a legitimate sport, more people are training at higher levels, leaving them less time and energy to find or cause trouble.

Returning to the issue of loneliness, it was far more common for interviewees to agree with Miller's second point, that the one-on-one nature of MMA could cause severe anxiety levels for competitors. Interviewees talked casually about seeing would be competitors back out of matches at the last minute, not so much terrified of the competition itself, but of the public view and scrutiny that could accompany a loss and having to deal with that possible loss alone, unable to share the shame with teammates. JJ Ambrose (JA) and Savant Young (SY) spoke about such occurrences:

DM (David Mayeda): Do people have psychological problems sometimes with depression or anxiety?

JA: Definitely. You have opponents walk out of the arena all the time, you know. They just get the cold feet and are like, "I'm out'a here. I can't do this."

DM: Really?

JA: Yeah. That happens a lot.

SY: They get all the way to the venue and decide they don't want to fight no more. So I think there's definitely some anxiety issues, a lot of fighters go through.

Young expanded, stating that MMA competitors who go through with competitions tend to get used to this type of stress, which is part of the process of becoming a professional. Nevertheless, the angst competitors frequently dealt with was not dismissed as insignificant. Even at the amateur level, this type of anxiety was said to occur. Yoji Matsuo made the following comments based on observations he has made at amateur jiu-jitsu and submission grappling tournaments: "There are fighters that have anxiety problems ... and on the days of the tournaments some guys might kind of wilt mentally from anxiety." These are certainly anxieties that athletes in general experience. Furthermore, there are a variety of individual sports (e.g., tennis, track and field, swimming) in which competitors normally cannot rely on teammates, and athletes in these sports often times train mentally as much as they do physically (Vernacchia et al., 2000).

But for MMA athletes, anxiety was said to intensify because in MMA, your opponent is actually trying to harm you. Unlike virtually all other sports (except for example, boxing and kickboxing), intent to harm is fully legal in MMA, or more candidly, it is expected. Building off the previous section that addresses perspectives on pain, Robert Otani expressed his ambiguous feelings on pain, inflicting it on others, and whether or not holding such feelings was moral. Otani articulated his uncertain feelings while discussing what he enjoyed about MMA competition:

> I really do like the pain aspect of it, as far as inflicting pain on other people, and I really do like that, and I know it sounds weird or cheesy or whatever. You gotta like that. If you don't like inflicting pain or you don't like doing damage to another person, I mean you're not trying to hurt that person. I mean it sounds like you're not really trying to, but that's the name of the game. And if you're not gonna do it, that person's gonna do it to you.

As Otani jumps back and forth attempting to justify the violent sport he enjoys so much, he closes with the reality that if one does not physically hurt his or her opponent, the opponent will strike first—it's "the name of the game." Knowing that one's opponent was striving to win via breaking a personal pain threshold was said to take a toll on many MMA competitors' emotions. And the individualized nature of getting hurt in front of others exacerbated anxiety levels. Dan Henderson and Travis Lutter explained this viewpoint in two separate interviews, highlighting MMA's distinctiveness from other sports:

> If you're not there mentally in any sport, you're not gonna be the top guy, especially in fighting, it comes out even more. I think because [there's] more anxiety out there. It's a little bit more stressful knowing that the guy is gonna hit you, and you gotta be okay with that. You gotta almost welcome it.—Dan Henderson

> ... it takes kind of a special individual, or different individual. I don't know about special. But it takes a different individual to step into the octagon, and

shut the door behind you. And you're alone, I mean that's a very alone place to be. Cause like in boxing even, I've got two things to worry about, his right and his left. In this sport, I gotta worry about his right, his left, his knee, his elbow, his foot, and then oh, guess what, he's gonna take me down and then he's gonna try and hit me with those things down there, and then he's gonna try and crank my neck, you know break my arm. I mean, there's just literally how many different ways to lose in this sport versus, you know, boxing or kickboxing? So it's not a very natural act. You know, you talk about the other sports, and I'll hear [commentators] talk about, "Well you know, it was a very tough fight, scrapin' and clawin' right 'till the end," and we're talking about tennis. And it's like, man, I hate to tell it to you, but nobody hit you in the head. Let's see you be composed, when that guy hits you in the head. And how composed you would be if that guy jumped the net and whacked you in the head, and then went across and got his tennis racket? And I like tennis, I like tennis a lot!—Travis Lutter

Henderson's statement illustrates the linkages between pain and sporting violence that comprise a great deal of these competitors' identities, along with the inability of some fighters to accept being on the receiving end of pain within the public sphere. On a side note, his comment about having to welcome getting hit made me think a lot about my decision to jump into a watered-down MMA match at age thirty-four, not having wrestled to any degree in well over a decade, even if the competition was a small amateur one. At one point before training, Steven Saito said to me, "We have to spar. You have to know what it's like to get hit. It's, it's shocking bro." We never did spar. Lutter builds off of Henderson's comments, pinpointing how lonely the sport can be, as well as how the multiple forms of losing via knockout or submission can add to competitors' anxiety. Again, athletic performance anxiety occurs in all sports. However, as told by interviewees, the intensified anxiety issue for MMA competitors was related to the likelihood of being deliberately hurt by an opponent via so many different methods.

Along with the stresses of being hurt, MMA practitioners stated that anxiety and general stress was common because of the extremely fast rate at which a competitor could rise and fall in popularity, and tied to this was an erratic rise or drop in monetary compensation. A seasoned MMA veteran, Frank "Twinkle Toes" Trigg spoke extensively on this topic. Trigg felt that depression was quite common among MMA competitors and athletes in general. Trigg (FT) explained his perspectives:

FT: If you look at this sport, you can go from making a ton of money one month to making next to nothing the next month. One month you're fighting in a main-event level fight in Pride (FC) in front of 47,000 people, and the next month you're just trying to find a fight. So people go through all kinds of depression.... We have egos. Athletes have egos. Fighters have egos. I have an ego.

DM (David Mayeda): So it's not just the contact and collision sports?

FT: No, it's all sports.

Nolan Hong made a similar comment to Trigg, stating that some fighters "can't handle failure, or you know, they can go into depression. Especially a high level of competition where [monetary] success is based on winning or losing." But unlike most other interviewees, Trigg was adamant that MMA athletes were no different from athletes in other sports, in that they usually held fragile egos that were tied to their fame, wealth, and pursuits for athletic excellence. Colin Oyama agreed with Trigg that depression and other psychological problems are common among athletes, irrespective of the sport. Said Oyama:

> I think a lot of those types of qualities come through in athletes in general. I think you can have a tennis player that's, you know you watch John McEnroe, some people call it aggressiveness, you can call it whatever you want. For me, I look at him, and that guy, it's called drive.... I think the pressure to win, in any sport, can make an athlete act that way.

Oyama then cited a few elite athletes from other non-contact sports who had engaged in deviant and/or criminal behaviors in their attempts to win (Ben Johnson in track and field, Tonya Harding in figure skating). Returning to MMA, there certainly is an erratic element that plays with competitors' egos. Travis Lutter spoke about mixed martial artists' emotions, and how such a great deal of their lives' "hopes and dreams" can get ensconced in one match. In describing a fellow mixed martial artist that Lutter beat on the reality show, *The Ultimate Fighter IV*, Lutter said:

> You know, it's literally, he didn't land a punch on his feet. He threw some punches from the bottom, but he didn't win a second of the fight. And to lose (for) fifteen minutes, that's part of what he's going through at that moment. The other thing is it's the hopes and dreams. The hopes and the dreams that were lost that day for him—money, fame, and a title shot.

Thus, with a sole loss, mixed martial artists may not only have their egos tarnished, but also lose the financial benefits that would otherwise have assisted themselves and their families. It is dangerous for the individual mixed martial artist when he or she has so many different life aspects invested in one fight.

Frank Trigg returned to the topic of MMA being a lonely sport that many other interviewees raised. Trigg, however, added an additional twist, stating that MMA was not just a lonely sport while athletes are in competition. In addition, the sport can isolate athletes who need to train and cannot always rely on training partners. Said Trigg, "MMA can be a lonely man's sport. You have to go into the gym on a Sunday sometimes and just train by yourself, nobody else around." Like many other individual sports, MMA can detach athletes, including those who are so motivated that other athletes do not want to work as hard or try to keep up.

Despite the psychological rigors that interviewees brought up, a good portion of the men we interviewed conversely felt that mixed martial artists do not run into psychological problems any more than people in other societal sectors. These interviewees admitted MMA athletes can and do have personal problems, but that those problems are not out of the ordinary. Although he commented extensively on the anxiety MMA competitors often feel before and during competition, Travis Lutter felt that mixed martial artists do not deal with psychological problems any more than other conventional professionals. After being asked if mixed martial artists deal with issues of depression, rage, or anxiety, Lutter said:

> Not really more than any other walk of life. I don't think fighters, I mean we're definitely disturbed for doing what we to do, but I think that people are fucked up in all walks of life to put it bluntly. It really doesn't, I think there's guys that do deal with it very poorly, and I think it's like that across the board …

Lutter then questioned how many accountants, lawyers and other professionals deal with depression, rage, and anxiety and felt that their rates would not be significantly different from those who are MMA professionals. In fact to some degree, scholarly work confirms Lutter's comparisons, as a significant proportion of professionals working in high-status occupations (e.g., attorneys, university faculty) endure severe levels of work related depression (Jago, 2002; Benjamin, Darling, & Sales, 1990; Ross & Mirowsky, 1989; Pearlin & Johnson, 1977), and that generally speaking, job status is a major factor for men that can lead to depression when recognition for work and other attributes are not made by superiors (Zimmerman et al., 2004; Real, 1997).

Even MMA hobbyists (e.g., Joshua Gilley), rookies (e.g., Cleyburn Walker) and trainers (e.g., Michael Frison, Dustin Phan, Paul Halme) who we interviewed felt that MMA does not seem to attract those with major psychological problems, nor that the sport incited such concerns. Robert Otani put it bluntly, contending that mixed martial artists are as diverse as people in any other walk of life, but that the extreme emotions of MMA can cause competitors to cope with the emotional ups and downs in a variety of ways, some healthy, some unhealthy:

> … it is an emotional high and an emotional roller coaster. You get so many different feelings and emotions before a fight, and after a fight your adrenaline is crashing, so you dump, and then, it's crazy. I mean, I've only been in the ring twice, experienced it twice, but I've seen other fighters after the ring, and they're one person before and another person afterwards.… You know, there's fighters that are almost like little children, you know. They have to be coddled and nurtured and weaned … fighters have issues just like anyone else, but the game that we're in is so emotional.

Recall from Chapter Four, I was nervous before interviewing Quinton "Rampage" Jackson. When I asked him whether or not mixed martial artists dealt with psychological problems, he responded quickly and calmly, "I'm pretty sure. We're human." I have to admit, Jackson's answer made me feel a little bad about asking the question, as if the question itself was predisposed with prejudice.

Mixed Martial Arts and Sporting Toughness

Another topic we explored in order to gauge mixed martial artists' perceptions on their sport was how physically and mentally rigorous the sport was relative to other sports. Interviewees provided responses that were across the board. A few interviewees flat out stated that it would be hard to identify a sport that was more physically demanding than MMA. Said Savant Young, "None. There's not a tougher sport out there than MMA. I'll say that, mark my word on that one." David Ching's (DC) conversation with Dustin Phan (DP) also exemplified this viewpoint:

> DC: Okay. What's your opinion, do you think there's a tougher sport mentally and physically than MMA?
>
> DP: No, honestly. I don't think so, both physically and mentally, no.
>
> DC: Can you expand on your answer?

DP: Yeah. I think you know, it is physically you know, you're expected to perform under pressured situations while your body's taking damage. I think psychologically, it can really break you down, and obviously physically … you're receiving pressure at the same time. It's not like if you're playing soccer, one team's going on the offense while the other's going on defense, and then it switches.

Young and Phan were not alone in holding this perspective. Additional interviewees believed that other sports did not measure up to MMA when it came to how taxing the sport could be on one's body and mind, including interviewees who had played other sports and those who had never played other sports.

It was critical to listen to those athletes who had played a range of sports and could make comparisons based on their varying experiences in analyzing this topic. A few MMA practitioners explained that what made MMA so difficult physically and mentally was having to become proficient in such a wide variety of disciplines within the combat sports. In other words, having to learn wrestling, boxing, kickboxing, judo, jiu-jitsu and all the intricacies of these different disciplines made MMA an especially difficult sport to master. After asking Robert Otani about MMA's difficulty relative to other sports, he focused on the sport's mental rigors, as he stated:

> From what I'm told, no. I mean I've only played baseball, wrestling, judo, football. And yeah, this is the most demanding and most strenuous as far as mental-wise, cause … you gotta know everything.… You can't just be a big, strong guy and expect to win. You gotta be well rounded. As far as physical, I don't know, I mean I've been pushed to the limit in football too …

Quinton Jackson felt the same way as Otani and provided an interesting analogy to illustrate his perspective that being a well rounded mixed martial artist was a primary factor that made MMA especially mentally strenuous.

> … a good fighter, you have to be well rounded. You have to know three or four different martial arts, and be okay at 'em. You don't have to be great at each one, but you have to be okay at 'em.… It's kind'a like a, a chess match, or it's kind of like multi-tasking, your brain gotta be sharp, you gotta be quick.… you gotta be ready to switch it up at the drop of a dime. You gotta be able to be punchin' and kickin' somebody, and the next thing you know, you gotta be able to take him down, or keep him from taking you down. So it's very mental.

As we heard interviewees provide different answers on this topic and the rationale behind their answers, we began to realize that most interviewees did not automatically view MMA as the ultimate example of athletic toughness.

In fact, a slight majority of interviewees with whom we spoke either cited other sports they felt might be more rigorous or felt comparing sports in such a manner was not possible. A few former wrestlers felt that wrestling was either just as physically demanding as MMA or slightly more difficult. Randy Couture stated, "… there's huge similarities between wrestling and mixed martial arts. Wrestling becomes much more limited in tactic and technique … but they're very, very similar intensity-wise, and the physicality of them both is very, very similar." Jesse Juarez and Emanuel Newton, on the other hand, felt that their days of college wrestling were more laborious than their current training and competition in MMA. Juarez, who won a national championship as a college wrestler, said of his wrestling days:

> I quit mentally twice in wrestling, but I never quit in MMA…. The training, the training is constant, constant, hard, hard training. I mean, especially when you have coach on you, saying you're terrible, you suck. It's gonna push you, and then it's gonna push you over the edge.

Newton agreed but claimed wrestling was more difficult, in that the conditioning for wrestling was geared towards competing in multiple matches in one day, which happens far less frequently today in MMA. Said Newton on two separate occasions in his interview, "I think wrestling is almost harder conditioning than fighting…. you're gonna go to a wrestling tournament and … wrestle, you know, three, four, five times in a day. You know, it's tougher. But in MMA you have one match …"

Jason Miller added that the ways in which people viewed different sports' physical rigor also depended on those individuals' physical attributes, stating, "I think different athletes are built for different things …" Noting that his genetic composition was not geared towards running at an elite level, Miller went on to say:

> I don't know, I think the triathlon's gotta be pretty damn hard. Serious man, I tell you bro, look, twenty-five minutes, that's the title fight. Twenty-five minutes, fuck it, even if I'm getting my ass kicked the whole time, I don't think it can compare to like running forever. Being in a marathon looks fucking terrible. Man, that's just like, why? Why are you doing that to yourself?

Like Miller, many other interviewees completely relinquished their sport-specific egos and stated that although MMA is up there in terms of physical and mental toughness, it is impossible to compare different sports in such a manner. Said Bao Quach, "It's hard to compare the sports too, you know? … it's like apples and oranges. You can't compare basketball to fighting." Colin Oyama brought up other extreme sports as being highly mentally and/or physically difficult and at least on par in some ways with MMA: "NASCAR drivers, you know, physically not too demanding, mentally very demanding…. you know physically demanding, these extreme ski guys going downhill, I mean, those are physically demanding, crazy ass sports."

Some interviewees even brought up sports historically considered "soft" and "feminine" as more physically demanding in some ways than MMA. After Stephen Mayeda asked Travis Lutter, "Is there a tougher sport mentally and physically than MMA?," Lutter responded in the following manner:

> I'm sure, you know, I mean MMA is a tough sport. I mean, no disrespect. Could I play golf? No. Could I play football? No. You know golf, what a frickin' sport, you got 18 holes and it takes forever. I get to be done as quickly as I can get the opponent out of there. And the *most* time is twenty-five minutes. You know, I'm done. Those guys play for hours. You know, tennis match—three hours … four hours sometimes. You know, that's a grueling sport.

It was interesting and at times surprising to hear mixed martial artists discuss how they conceptualized their sport of choice as no more difficult than other sports that may not even involve physical contact. Finally, Dan Henderson believed that irrespective of the activity, the mental anxiety one holds is directly related to his or her preparedness and experience. With regard to his perception of the mental toughness required for MMA, Henderson said, "I don't think it's that tough, but for somebody that hasn't done it for that long, (they) might think it's pretty tough." In contrast, Henderson made comparisons with bull riding and a non-sporting profession:

> … (bull riding) would probably be a lot more dangerous … and more nerve wracking for me than to go out there to fight. But it's just a matter of being prepared for what you do, you know. I'd probably feel the same way going out and teaching one of your classes. There's no way I'd want to do that either. I wouldn't be able to do it real well. And you gotta be prepared to go out there and teach; I gotta be prepared to go out there and fight.

Aside from boosting our own egos, Henderson demonstrated the humble perspectives that many interviewees shared, able to define their own sport's rigor while accounting for an assortment of variables that play into physical and mental toughness.

Thinking about the Future in an Erratic Industry

Whether or not MMA is tougher physically and mentally than other sports, like other sports, MMA is one in which athletes' careers can end very abruptly. As Frank Trigg stated, the MMA industry is highly erratic. A main event competitor can lose a match or two and suddenly find himself out of work. Trigg also mentioned that even within the biggest MMA organizations, many fighters make very little money: "In mixed martial arts, guys work their asses off, and they might get paid three-and-three ($3,000 to compete, and $3,000 more if they win their fight)." In smaller, regional shows, MMA competitors are paid even less. With regard to his first competition, Cleyburn Walker told us, "I was paid $300 for my fight, which I lost. The guy that beat me got $900." Given these financial realities, it is important to examine the combat sports' financial structure and how competitors fit into that structure.

Within the boxing business, fighters fall into different tiers. Wacquant's (1998) rich examination of the boxing industry exposes how boxers in these different tiers are utilized by promoters and matchmakers to make money. At the top are main event fighters, who hold major titles, are top contenders to titles, or prospects who are expected to become title contenders. In many cases, these main event fighters are protected by promoters, who match them up with lower-level fighters. Thus, the main event fighters will likely win fights and in turn pad their won-loss records. Below the main event fighters are the "journeymen." Journeymen are considered average fighters. They win some and lose some. They are highly respected for their capabilities and experience. However, promoters, fighters, and knowledgeable fans know that they are essentially used as a test to see if the top prospects are indeed worthy of moving towards a title shot and to hype the prospects' reputations. Journeymen are expected to put up a good, exciting fight, but they are not expected to win. At the bottom of the rung are those fighters who rarely, if ever, win, sometimes called "bums." They may be used to maintain a journeyman's reputable record or to build the record of a young prospect.

In short, the different classes of fighters serve a purpose, which is tied to putting on an exciting show with a ton of hype, that will attract fans, who will pay big money to watch, and ultimately make the promoters a hefty profit. From this Marxist analysis of the boxing industry, one can make direct comparisons to the

MMA world. There are top level competitors, mid-rangers, and those whose won-loss records have very few wins. Additionally, competitors in the combat sports vary in terms of experience. But the bottom line is, mixed martial artists are pawns in a larger capital industry.

Truth be told, there has recently been a number of enormous upsets in the UFC (e.g., Randy Couture over Tim Sylvia, 3/3/2007; Matt Serra over Georges St. Pierre, 4/7/2007; Gabriel Gonzaga over Mirko "CroCop" Filipovic, 4/21/2007; Keith Jardine over Chuck Liddell, 9/22/07), illustrating that the promoters and matchmakers are not always matching aged-out journeymen with top-tier fighters. With regard to these upsets, UFC president Dana White has stated that in MMA, "You can't [book fights] like you do in boxing. You can't build a guy up to 39-0 with 39 knockouts" (Martin, 2007). Still, the fact remains that the MMA business does not compensate most competitors with huge financial rewards.

As Guy Mezger told us, aspiring mixed martial artists frequently hold faulty perceptions that the financial prospects in MMA are bountiful: "… to be honest man, most of the guys, a lot of the guys, they think there's a huge amount of money in this sport, and there is, for a very small amount of people." According to reports posted by MMAWeekly.com, Mezger's comments are dead on. For example, established MMA light heavyweight star Tito Ortiz recently made $210,000 for fighting to a draw with up-and-comer Rashad Evans. Evans on the other hand, only made $16,000. And even champions in the lower weight classes do not make huge sums of money. On the same card as the Ortiz-Evans draw, UFC Lightweight Champion Shawn Sherk only earned $28,000 for defeating Hermes Franca, who earned $14,000 in the loss. Other lower-tier fighters were only paid $3,000 after losing on this same card (Pishna, 2007a).

Mezger went on to explain the moral difficulties he has in training hopeful mixed martial artists, so many of whom see big money to be made in MMA and therefore, choose to pursue a career in MMA rather than advance their education:

> The average boxer cannot support his family on the money he makes. He can barely support himself, so the problem that I have with what's going on is that these kids believe, and it's tough to tell kids that their dream isn't gonna come true, that they are gonna make this millions and millions of dollars, and that's just generally not the truth. And so I would hate for them to forego education.

Mezger also stated that fewer and fewer MMA athletes are entering the business with college degrees. As mentioned in Chapter Four, many current MMA competitors are former college wrestlers who want to utilize their athletic foundation in MMA. However, in the past, college wrestlers would more often complete their college degrees before moving into the MMA world. With MMA becoming so popular now, less high school wrestlers are going to college, and instead are entering MMA schools, provoking the question: If MMA does not work out, what do these young men have to fall back on?

Travis Lutter raised similar concerns, explaining that if a fighter only makes $2,000 for a competition, there is a good chance he will only break even. For example, there are other major financial costs for MMA fighters that Lutter raised, such as medical licensing and training expenses (e.g., payment for schools/gyms, dietary supplements, practice equipment). Another interviewee, Ku Lee, observed that MMA is becoming a sport reserved for the middle and upper classes. As the sport has grown in popularity, gyms are increasing their monthly prices for those who want to train. Said Lee, "I think it's becoming more of a rich sport now.... places are opening up, you have to pay two hundred bucks (per month) to do it. So I think it's changing." Not to mention, if a MMA competitor sustains an injury either in training or competition, attaining further income through future fights is nullified until the athlete fully heals. Frank Trigg added, "There's no pension plans for fighters." In light of these financial concerns, we thought it would be crucial to ask up-and-coming MMA athletes what their future plans were in or out of the MMA industry.

Most young MMA competitors stated that following their athletic careers, they wanted to open up their own MMA gyms. After asking what their long-term plans were, Savant Young (SY) and JJ Ambrose (JA) responded:

> SY: For me, I probably will get into the management aspect of it. Maybe open a gym, um, probably become a promoter since those are the ones that make all the money ...

> JA: My long term goals are to make it into the UFC, but eventually I want to open up a school.

Jamie Yager made a similar statement, saying he wants to eventually give back to the community by opening a gym for at-risk youth and utilize MMA as a venue for teaching young students pro-social values:

> Long term.... I want to open up a gym where I can teach kids that, "Look you know, this is a self-discipline right here. You learn this and you do this in the right environment. You don't do this at school. If you have you know, if you have problems ... you can get this worked out here. You know, get your emotions worked out in the gym." You know because I've grown up. I've had a lot

of problems, a lot of adversity, so my way out was always something physical. Whether it was lifting weights. Whether it was taking a run. Now my outlet is the MMA game, and learning.

Like Young, Abrose, and Yager, numerous other young MMA competitors we spoke with had similar aspirations of opening and owning gyms. Many of these aspirants held such goals despite not holding college degrees. And in fact, many of their role models who own and operate successful gyms do so without having completed their college education.

The obvious danger in holding such a goal is that not every MMA competitor can eventually move from competitor to gym owner and operator. Obviously the market would be saturated with gyms, and furthermore, given that young mixed martial artists rarely make substantial sums of money, acquiring the capital to purchase and maintain a gym is actually extremely unlikely. Furthermore, as with all sports (even non-contact sports), sustaining a permanent injury is always a possibility that can unexpectedly stymie an athletic career in the blink of an eye. Young MMA athletes must be made keenly aware of these unfortunate possibilities and take the proper steps to plan for their future lives should their careers as athletes end prematurely.

From left to right: Takuhiro Kamikozono, Guy Mezger, and Chris Bowles (Dallas, Texas).

Anthony "The Crush" Torres (left) being interviewed by David Ching in Honolulu, Hawaii.

Boys and girls waiting for their amateur competitions (Honolulu, Hawaii).

Jason Bress, overseeing his class at L.A. Boxing in Aliso Viejo, California.

Jason "MayheM" Miller celebrating with his new Icon Sport Middleweight Title (Honolulu, Hawaii).

From left to right: B.J. Penn, "Rampage" Jackson, Randy Couture, Dan Henderson, and Jens Pulver (Honolulu, Hawaii).

Robert Otani (left) with his coach Tony "The Freak" Fryklund (Las Vegas, Nevada).

The Ultimate Fighter IV winner, Travis Lutter (Fort Worth, Texas).

"Rampage" Jackson (left) keeping "MayheM" Miller loose before his MMA competition (Honolulu, Hawaii).

Jason "MayheM" Miller (left) and Dan Henderson. (Honolulu, Hawaii).

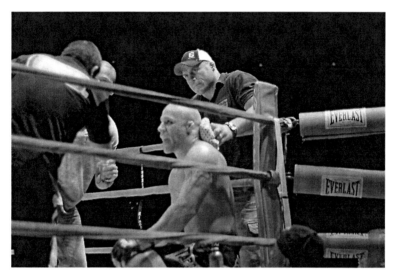

Frank "Twinkle Toes" Trigg (seated) being cornered by Randy Couture (Honolulu, Hawaii).

Allan Goes and son (Aliso Viejo, California).

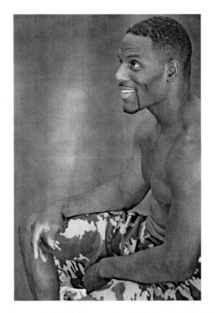

Antonio McKee, taking a break (Lakewood, CA).

Savant Young (left) and Emanuel Newton working out (Lakewood, CA).

Steven Saito (left) and Nolan Hong after a tough workout (Honolulu, Hawaii).

From left: Jeremy Williams (seated), Chris Reilly, Dan Henderson, and Jason Miller pummeling with Ryan Parsons (Honolulu, Hawaii).

Dan Henderson and David Ching (Aiea, Hawaii).

From left to right: Jason Miller, Stephen Mayeda, and Randy Couture (Honolulu, Hawaii).

PART III
MIXED MARTIAL ARTS, VIOLENCE, AND AMERICAN SOCIETY

Ambulance taking away an adolescent boy after he was kicked in the head at an amateur competition in Honolulu, Hawaii (June 3, 2007).

6

MARTIAL ARTS, TRADITION, AND NON-VIOLENCE IN SOCIETY

BY DAVID CHING

There is a question, an endless debate, over whether fighting makes you more aggressive and prone to violence, or less. In my case, it was definitely more. For the first time, I kind of, secretly, *wanted* to hurt someone (Sheridan, 2007, p. 287).

A friend once told us that the problem with mixed martial arts is there is too much "martial" and not enough "art."—Chris Onzuka

Mixed Martial Arts and Violence on the Street

As the growth of MMA has accelerated in the last couple of years before the eyes of American mainstream culture, its long time viewers have certainly seen some changes in the sport. For example, the rules have evolved significantly in the UFC, which thus far, has been the oldest and most prominent vehicle in America for MMA's advancement. Specifically, the notable rule changes are the additional rules (addressed more extensively in Chapter Seven). The early years allowed head butts, groin shots, bare knuckles, no time limits, head stomps, soccer kicks, and the list goes on.

One thing however that has not changed over the years, is the physical venue where the fights take place—the UFC's highly recognizable octagon shaped ring surrounded by chain link fencing. Arguably, there are other types of material that could be used to surround this octagon shaped ring, material that would not be conducive to grabbing for support or leverage (prohibited under current UFC rules), but certainly less evocative in imagery. This chain link ring conjures impressions of back alley street fighting—certainly imagery from which the early years of the UFC did not shy away. On the conscious curiosity level, the UFC accomplished a great deal in satisfying the question of how different fighting styles matched up under these caged conditions. The raw emotions conjured by the physical visuals of the arena, however, tickled the imagination of the typical male viewer, bringing to mind the question, "What style of fighting would really work on the street?" That was the core question ostensibly on every male viewer's mind when watching these early MMA competitions. As MMA fighter/coach Bear St. Clair stated:

> I honestly think that it's a primordial thing, and if you get down to the basic instinctual thing of what we are, we are animals. Combat and territory and superiority and genetic selection and survival is ingrained in every single last one of us.

Whether or not St. Clair's assumptions about our "innate" tendencies toward violence are true or not, with MMA's growing audiences and the prevalence of organizations like the IFL, UFC, Bodog Fight, WEC (a UFC subsidiary), and Dallas Mavericks' owner Mark Cuban's HDNet Fights, there has been and will continue to be increased MMA exposure through network television and prime-time programming (Downey, 2006). This now begs the question, "Will increased exposure of MMA increase violence on the streets?" This question is a particular point of interest for Dr. Mayeda, since much of his academic and professional work deals with at-risk youths and violence prevention in communities. For this reason we specifically sought opinions from those involved in different aspects of the fight game, including trainers, fighters, competition judges, and hobbyists. In short, are we truly ingrained with a predisposition for violence as St. Clair suggests, or will institutions like MMA organizations create and add to societal violence?

In discussions with trainers, fighters, and purely spectators, I often find that it is the "pure spectator" who will enthusiastically attempt to give fight analyses (let's call this person "*Joe Spectator*"). Although he has never competed or seriously trained, *Joe Spectator* will commonly give analyses ranging from discussions of style match-ups, effective striking techniques, grappling and submission nuances, and even training tips (much like a Monday morning armchair quarterback). It smacks of that old saying, "A little bit of knowledge can be a dangerous thing." This ability to see and learn those fighting techniques through observation opens up the possibility that spectators who are visually processing the fight may feel empowered with the knowledge gained from viewing trained fighters practice their craft. I know to a small extent, I am guilty of that deluded thinking as well.

With very little variation, the trained fighters' consensus was that MMA's growing popularity would either decrease street violence, or at worst, that street violence would remain the same. Those interviewees who stated that there could be an initial increase in violence in the street all followed up by stating that it would probably return to normal. Added Quinton "Rampage" Jackson, "Yeah, they might want to try some stuff, but if they ain't trained in it and stuff, they probably won't be able to pull it off in a fight anyway. That stuff takes time to train and stuff like that."

And while one reasonable concern would be that as an individual's training advances, MMA gyms are arguably arming a potentially misguided individual with life and bodily threatening skills, it was a common observation of those interviewed that this skill development influences positive change in such individuals. Chris Onzuka shared his perspective on training in martial arts and effects it normally has on individuals, based on his personal experiences:

> They're gonna learn how to fight, and then what I've seen is when you first get into a martial art, when you start getting good, you start feeling that power, and if you're young and you're irresponsible, you go out there, and I'm a perfect example of being irresponsible too, going out there, getting into fights, showing how tough it is, and you know, it's fun beating up guys, whatever. And then after the maturity level comes in, where you say, this is wrong and there's a lot of ramifications to this kind of thing, legal, physical, financial, then people, they tone that stuff down.

So if the case is that for those techniques being discussed by *Joe Spectator* need to be taught and practiced repeatedly to actually have any chance of success, then he will need to find a place to be trained. Subsequently, as the training process advances, it would seem natural, or at least hopeful, that positive revelations on different levels would be achieved. Randy Couture commented:

> I think if done properly it won't increase violence in the streets. I think if people are getting their training and seeing what really happens when someone gets punched in the face, what it's really like to be in those situations, if they learn the discipline and garner the confidence that comes from the style of training, they're not gonna put themselves in those situations. I don't think that it's gonna create a problem. I think it's gonna be the opposite. You'll have more people educated about fighting, they learn more technique and get into that aspect of it, they don't want to go out and put themselves in a situation

like that where nobody wins. You know, even if you win the fight, you still lose.

Thus, as *Joe Spectator* goes through the training process, learning and experiencing how it feels to use MMA and have it used on him, this process hopefully leads to an acquisition of internal wisdom regarding these skills. And while the initial motivation for involvement in MMA may have been to gain "weapons" or "fighting tools" that could be used in street altercations, a more enlightened perspective may begin to emerge. Chris Reilly contributed:

> And there's no doubt that some of these guys come to the sport with some misconceived notions about it, and who do want to just be able to beat somebody up, and you know, early on, they're getting taught how to kick and punch. And it can have, what I would call, some negative effects cause I certainly don't think that that's a good thing. What tends to happen over time, is if you stay with it, you learn how hard, how much hard work goes into developing these skills. And you get a chance to bang around and to get banged around on such a regular basis that you get to know it, and you get comfortable with it at some levels. And you get to understand that real violence, true violence, you know, street violence and stuff outside of the martial arts, where you have a mutual agreement of two guys who go in and shake hands ... You know, anything outside of that is real violence, and it's something that's really, really ugly and really scary, and has potentially really life changing consequences. And so I think in the end, the end result of that is that there's much less violence. I mean anybody you know who's studying (MMA) for a long time, regardless of how good they get, a professional fighter or a hobbyist who's just stuck with it for a long time—those guys are gonna be the last guys who are gonna get involved in some kind of an altercation outside of the gym.

So it is quite possible that MMA's growing popularity will reduce levels of street violence as *Joe Spectator* if he decides to begin training at a responsible gym and truly integrates within a conscientious MMA community. A number of fighters mentioned that initially, in the short run, there may be a spike in the level of street violence. However, as fighters become trained, educated, and given a controlled arena to release any aggressive urges, the long run effect may find the communities' base levels of violence either return to normal or even drop below the original baseline level. Pride FC world champion Dan Henderson's opinion reflected this viewpoint, as he stated:

> I think that if guys go to a bar and watch any fighting event, it used to be boxing but now that MMA is more popular, they're gonna get kind of worked up

and want to get into a fight. And I've seen it, and I've heard that happens after the fights here (in Hawaii) quite a bit. But I think, as far as the growth of the sport, a lot of guys from the street get into the sport, and if they go in and train and compete MMA in the gym, they don't have the need to go out and fight in the streets. I think the biggest change would be it would lessen the fights on the streets if anything ...

And with the growth of the sport, some would say that in their subjective views, they are seeing the effects. Southern California is considered one of the hotbed areas of MMA popularity, not merely in viewership and relative community acceptance, but also in the number of places to train and hence, the number of trained fighters. Huntington Beach hails notable gyms and fighters specifically identified with Huntington Beach, such as Tito Ortiz and Tank Abbott. As Bear St. Clair, a fifth generation Costa Mesan, night club bouncer, trainer and owner of Bear Essential Combat observed of Huntington Beach:

> The way it is now, Huntington Beach is calmer than ever, because you don't want to mess around with anyone there, because it seems like everybody is training now, it's ridiculous. I'm serious. Like, it's cool man. Everybody is like, "Okay, alright, whatever." Because you don't know. I mean, he might like, you know, jab you in the face, he might round house you, he might choke you out.

Bear St. Clair's statement is based on the observation that, much like a wild west scenario, violence is kept in check due to the potential for a violent response; if you draw your gun, so will others, so why do it? And if you do, are you ready and willing to accept any consequences or ramifications that come with that action? These circumstances could certainly be one anticipated result of the proliferation of advanced fighting skills. Interviewee Tony Fryklund also theorized street violence would ultimately decrease due to a "might makes right" aura that would ensconce communities where MMA was popular. Said Fryklund:

> ... the little cliché, might makes right, I don't go poking the tiger, so hopefully people see, oh well there's a lot of fighters out there, there's a lot of people. And the more of those people that are into that sport, into combat sports, into boxing, all those things, should know that, men, women, kids, young, old, it doesn't matter. Everyone's doing some sort of combat sport or is at least adapting.

But should this be the reason for a reduction in violence? In an advanced culture, should the curbing of violence be due to fear, or rather, enlightenment?

Respect and Humility in Mixed Martial Arts and "Traditional" Martial Arts

The traditional martial arts, styles such as Tae Kwan Do, Aikido, styles of Kung Fu and Karate, have all reached widespread community acceptance. In many of our communities awash with minivans and soccer moms, you will also see all types of traditional martial arts schools catering to our suburban youths and adults. A common stereotype of such martial arts schools is that they are rigidly structured with strong foundations in respect, humility, and tradition. The irony is that while sending a youth to a school of fighting, they will learn the interpersonal skills and discipline that will keep them from fighting. It seems common enough to hear anecdotal evidence presented of how wild or undisciplined youths found discipline and respect through these schools of traditional martial arts.

While these traditional schools certainly have many positive impacts on individuals, such as those stated above, along with the expected physical health benefits, it seems that with the introduction and development of MMA, these types of schools now face harsh criticisms in terms of their applied effectiveness. Has the modern day MMA practitioner gotten it right? Are mixed martial artists the superior hand-to-hand combat athletes/practitioners? Well sure, MMA has created a blend of the styles that has certainly proven to be superior in this type of competitive arena. Especially as MMA continues to develop and evolve, these traditional arts may be destined to go the way of the dinosaurs in today's arena of combat. MMA has established itself as the ultimate combat sport. As trainer and former UFC fighter, Guy Mezger, commented on MMA versus the traditional martial arts:

> … we have found tremendous weaknesses in traditional martial arts as a real, to be able to back it up so to speak. I mean mixed martial arts works. It's a more effective style. It's a modern system. Traditional martial arts are like fighting wars with flintlocks. Great gun in 1776, but not today. Today an Uzi is a great gun. MMA is like an Uzi compared to traditional martial arts' flintlock.

So while the new breed of martial arts, MMA specifically, has grown and replaced the more rigid traditional styles, another question may be brought to mind. Is the ability to best your opponent in combat the only pursuit that matters when choosing a martial arts style? Because the traditional arts have not been able to measure up in the arena of a MMA ring or octagon, have they lost their relevancy?

It would certainly depend on the individual's goals in question. It is relatively clear that the sport of MMA has become just that, a sport. In the early years of the UFC, it seemed as if the technically superior fighter would eventually win, ala Royce Gracie. Then, as the UFC developed and evolved, it seemed like the explosive athletic wrestler type would consistently have the strongest results, ala Don Frye, Marc Coleman, Tito Ortiz. Now arguably, the consensus is that MMA has developed enough so that you need to be the explosive, athletic, technical fighter with mental acumen and strong conditioning, ala Randy Couture, Chuck Liddell, Georges St. Pier, and a host of other champions from various organizations.

So is MMA to be viewed more as a combat sport and remain as such? Or will it head in the direction of traditional martial arts, where generally a strong sense of tradition, respect, humility, and discipline are blended with the development of physical skills? Should MMA gyms take up that responsibility to deliberately instill values such as humility, discipline, and respect, like the traditional arts attempt to do? It can be argued that if a gym is teaching potentially destructive and harmful "tools," isn't it that institution's responsibility to do its best to make sure its recipients will wield those tools responsibly? Chris (CO) and Mike Onzuka (MO), producers of the local Hawaii show, *Fighters Club TV*, and who opened the first licensed Gracie Jiu-Jitsu gym in Hawaii under Relson Gracie provided their conflicting opinions on where they saw the MMA industry moving:

> CO: I think mixed martial arts is going in the way of almost all martial arts.... I think mixed martial arts is a young type of martial art, but right now it's so based upon fighting and technique, that eventually as it grows older, people will find out that there is discipline in it. I believe that it'll grow more toward more of a traditional martial art. Not nearly as much as traditional arts, as like bowing, I mean maybe bowing. But I think the discipline and stuff will eventually come as structured teaching happens, structured schools happen. More schools are involved in it, and they find out these kids are getting into fights at school, and they have to bring these kids back and say, "Okay now you guys, you have to have some kind of discipline." And so I think a lot of the martial arts way is gonna come into the mixed martial arts. I think it's just a matter of time.

MO: I think I kind of disagree with that. I think it's gonna be more like box-ing. The guys go to the gym. They don't know how to box, no real disci-pline. A lot of gyms are gonna be like that, you know. All they're gonna be concerned about is winning MMA fights. It will have nothing to do with spirituality. It'll be all about toughness … you know you can kind of see it now. There's so much schools out there. Everybody and their brother is hav-ing a school now, and they're in their garages and stuff like that. And these guys don't usually come with no background. They don't have any tradi-tional martial arts background, and I don't even know if you'd consider jiu-jitsu a traditional martial arts background, cause we don't bow, we don't meditate. Basically, the reason we emphasize the stuff we do, you know stuff to keep kids out of trouble, is because of our upbringing. We're trying to emphasize our values on our guys, and realize that there's a bigger picture outside of our school. It's not just them. It's affecting us. We're reflecting on jiu-jitsu as a whole, which ties into mixed martial arts and all these other schools. We try and emphasize that to our guys. But I really don't think that the majority of instructors are gonna do that. And I don't really see it hap-pening, you know with all these guys coming up.

Chris Onzuka's statement expressed that as the sport develops and schools start to develop a formal structure to their fighting curricula, a natural progression would include incorporating formalities and structure, which should in turn bring in the traditional roots and discipline that are typically stressed in estab-lished martial arts. On the other side of the discussion, Mike Onzuka countered that he doesn't see the majority of MMA instructors taking the responsibility upon themselves to instill these traditional values in their students, as winning in sport becomes the paramount objective. Randy Couture agreed to some degree with Mike Onzuka, but ultimately took a middle ground, noting that with the growing popularity of MMA, some gyms will open that will be responsible in promoting nonviolence from a traditional martial arts perspective and others that will not:

> Like anything else, there's good schools and there's bad schools. There's good people and bad people that are running and are in charge of these situa-tions.… the majority of the guys that I know that are competing and that are competing at a high level do have that discipline, do have that humility and all those things that are indigenous to martial arts. So I think that's how in a lot of ways it's different from boxing or a lot of the other combative sports.

Some gyms may have the curriculum of tradition, humility and respect that Couture alluded to for the younger age students, but not necessarily for the older students, who train for sport or fitness. Instead, the issue of respect can be used as a tool to reveal adults' character and thereby act as a weeding out instrument, allowing the trainer to focus freely on teaching one to fight, as winner of *The Ultimate Fighter IV*, Travis Lutter, affirmed:

> The reason that the kids are there is for them to learn things and to cement the ideas that their parents are bringing to them—you gotta do good in school. That's a big part of the kids' class. Respect your teacher, respect your instructor, respect, things like that. And that's just cementing what their parents are already telling them. But as an adult, I shouldn't have to tell you that. If I do, you're probably not gonna survive very long in the class anyway. So that's my attitude towards martial arts. I'm teaching people how to fight. And that's all I'm interested in doing. I'm not trying to make 'em better people. You know if you're a good guy or a bad guy, if you're a bad guy, you're just not gonna last here. You're just gonna have to become a good guy, or you won't last. I'm not into changing people. So, you know, like I've said, I've never done a traditional martial arts class. And when people come to me looking for that, I tell them I don't offer that. This is what I teach. I'm gonna teach you how to fight.

Whether they are "good" or "bad," violent or nonviolent, adults have already experienced significant character development. They may not need or want to have their gym attempt to mold or direct their personal character issues. Lutter's informal "weeding out" system, however, eventually exiles the wrong types of students from the gym. Chris Leben has also noticed that when people take MMA classes for the wrong reasons, they normally cannot release their egos, and their misguided attitudes eventually influence them to quit. Said Leben:

> You know you'll get tough guys that come to the gym that wanna learn moves and try to use 'em in the street, and the problem is they can't leave their ego at the door when they come in to train, and so their ego kills 'em in the gym just like it does in the street. So as you work hard and you check your ego cause you're getting beat up in the gym all the time, you're not gonna want to go out and do that in the street.

Consequently for adults, more informal systems can be built into gyms that help impede those with dodgy motives from utilizing MMA gyms for the wrong purposes. Additionally, gyms are supposed to have adult students sign standardized forms in which students acknowledge their understanding that legally, they are not allowed to use their combat skills in initiating fights (one can be charged with "assault with a deadly weapon" if he or she assaults someone and is a combat sports expert, even if no added weapon is used). It seems on the other hand that for children, parents have identified martial arts schools as places not merely to learn self-defense skills and achieve physical fitness goals, but to also have positive influences systemically address their children's social development.

Still, as the sporting aspect of MMA develops, there is a strong and sometimes misguided motivation for enrollment on the list of parental goals, which Jason Bress observed in ethnically and socio-economically diverse Southern California:

> Yeah, like I'm, I'm in different areas all the time so I get to see here … the parents have a lot of money. You know, they have their problems. It's passed down to the kids, where you know, they're spoiled brats. No one, they have no discipline. They're always in trouble at school, either the teachers have to take care of them, cops take care of them, put 'em on all these plans, put 'em on drugs. You know, they come here, it's sad to see how it is. And then, they have money so they can train in all these places, like around here, there's so many places they can learn jiu-jitsu. They have money, you know, they can afford to watch the UFC's (pay-per-views), and get all the equipment. You know, it's just different. But they don't have no respect, cause they haven't been bopped around and cause their parents aren't taking care of them, in my opinion. And it's all about the respect thing, and it's just not around here. Now, if you go to Fullerton and that area, Orange, Fullerton, Brea, where it's lower-income, there's a lot of Hispanics, there's a lot of Asians. There's more respect. I think they're more family-oriented, so there's more respect.

Bress essentially describes how socio-economic diversity can complicate the implementation of martial arts tradition, especially in wealthier communities where more youth take for granted their abundant familial and community resources. Conversely, in working-class communities of color, Bress feels it is far easier to put into practice those values historically associated with traditional martial arts because for youth in these communities, the respect is already there. The rewards MMA instructors feel when instilling this sense of discipline through the traditional martial arts model extends beyond that of mere fighter skill and fitness development. As Paul Halme observed:

> Yeah, a lot of things with the kids is trying to teach them leadership, how to be leaders, you know.… with the kids we try to teach 'em to be a good kid, to be a leader. Because to be a leader, you're out in front, like one thing we do with our kids' class is whoever's like the highest ranked kid, he actually leads the class with myself or my assistant instructor, so it kind'a gives him or her some

responsibility, and everybody's watching them, so then they know they've gotta be doing everything right. It's neat to see it change a kid's self-esteem.

Formalized tradition and respect embedded within MMA curricula may only be found within those schools/gyms catering to or involving youths, with the exception of an adult school already structured under the more traditional martial arts (see also Chapter Eight for a discussion on kids and combat sports). It is unlikely that many adult MMA schools springing up during this incredible growth of popularity will deviate from the sport fighting aspect. Therefore, it is less likely that these schools will resemble those with traditional martial arts structures.

Of course it also depends on the lead instructor. So while those like Chris Reilly do provide a bit of tradition for those who wish to find a MMA school with that type of structure, it does not need to be an imposition on other students. Said Reilly:

> You know, everybody bows at the beginning and the end. I have a Buddha there so that if some of my instructors, they want to do a formal respects paying period before and after the class, that's available to them. If they don't choose to do that, I don't enforce it. You know, for some people, it's a sport. For some people, it's about discipline and respect. For some people, it's about getting in (the gym) and whoopin' someone's ass.

There are different ways to approach the issue of respect and tradition. It is certainly worth examining where these issues fit into this sport or art, because as Bear St. Clair stated, "MMA is brand new, and it's a bastard child. And it needs culture. Okay, and that's what needs to be developed. That's what's lacking." Frank Trigg added to this:

> Yes, there is a responsibility where we need to go back to the traditional martial arts. We need to teach kids that there are winners and losers, and the winners are going to get more in life. So if you get a kid into kickboxing and he's beating other kids, I mean in kickboxing in the sport, not on the street, you're teaching him that he's a winner. And even for the kid that loses, he's a winner too in a different regard. But it's in sport.

Considering the observations and thoughts provided by some of the interviewees quoted here, there is not an especially strong consensus as to how to structure traditional martial arts values in MMA schools, but there seems to be a general consensus that issues of respect and humility should certainly be involved. Whether those values are integrated into the curriculum as mentioned in the hopes of

Chris Onzuka, or for the issue of respect to be a tool that can be used to ultimately weed out those students lacking humble qualities, as alluded to by Travis Lutter, MMA schools do have a responsibility to instill the traditional martial arts values that encourage nonviolence outside of the gym.

Educational Responsibility in the Mixed Martial Arts Community

The avenues in which an individual can access information have developed and branched in so many ways, expanded largely by the growth of technology, especially the internet. This growth in exposure has allowed individuals to experience, learn and disseminate information regarding topics such as MMA at a rate so accelerated that the sport is breathlessly trying to keep pace in digesting and understanding its possible implications on society. Considering MMA's recent growth and its exposure to society through television and the internet, adults and children alike are being exposed to and in a sense educated in the science of fighting, whether they train in MMA or not. Thus, with this increase in exposure to the science of fighting, the media and MMA organizations are potentially raising the frequency and intensity of violent altercations. In essence, MMA's growth could very well have a dangerous effect, as JJ Ambrose states, "I mean, fights have been happening in the streets since the beginning of time, you know, now there's just gonna be more skill involved. So it'll just be better lookin' street fights." More importantly, Toby Grear adds a crucial point—that MMA is unique from other sports as the "sport of fighting," and fighting is what people use when violently settling disputes:

> … that's another thing that sets us apart from other sports. Our sport is something people do all day, every day. I mean, somewhat, whether it's an argument or an altercation, whatever it is. That's what it is about our sport. You don't see people settling things with pro wrestling or whatever it is.

In other words, fighting is a major concern in American society, and more often than is acceptable, individuals settle their disputes by fighting. True, groups of people may occasionally straighten out a conflict by playing a game of pickup basketball, street football, or some other competitive outlet. However, it is far more common that when heated, spontaneous conflicts are addressed physically, they are addressed in one-on-one or group fights. Given this newfound knowledge of hand-to-hand combat that is being spread through MMA media, there are other societal issues of education that may need to be addressed, on many levels.

One of potentially many topics that could be addressed would be a different slant on the analysis of street fighting from the paradigms that the typical MMA community may be viewing. A tragedy in the sport fighting community caused me to rethink the whole concept of MMA and its place in "street fights." In August of 2003, the popular American muay Thai champion Alex Gong was gunned down and killed in a confrontation with a driver in a hit and run incident, where a driver had hit Gong's parked car outside of his gym. Gong reportedly witnessed the incident from his gym during training, ran outside to confront the offending driver, was subsequently shot at point blank range, and killed almost immediately. While some may criticize that his training and skill as a fighter was an underlying factor that led to this incident's escalation and thus this tragic crime, those of us without training as fighters may argue that they are not necessarily causal variables in this situation.

All of us have probably experienced some sort of anger while driving in urban conditions. However, for many reasons, lack of confidence in physical confrontations possibly being one, may not have allowed our anger to escalate to the point of initiating an argument. Regardless, the revelation I had from Gong's tragedy was that in our increasingly violent culture, all the hours of mental and physical conditioning that can go into preparing us to incapacitate another human being in a hand-to-hand combat situation, can be ultimately neutralized once the conditions of the sterile fight environment have been violated, *i.e.* with weapons. As Michael Frison pointed out during his interview:

> ... I don't think people realize that street fighting and MMA are very different, you know. There are similar aspects to it, yeah, but I mean the last thing I'm gonna do is pick someone up and suplex them on a street cause the last thing I wanna do is be down on the ground with some broken glass and curbs and the guy's buddy kickin' me in the head, and you know, everything else. So you know, I think it's um, the average MMA guy is gonna do better than you know, a karate guy or just some guy at the bar. But I think that it's still, it's (MMA) not street fighting.

The concept of confidence in defending themselves on the street gained through their MMA training was a common theme expressed by many fighters. They had the confidence that their training had prepared them for situations of street violence. And yes, in general, when dealing in situations with mere "punks" that are out there to start trouble and prove who is the toughest, they may be better prepared. I suppose the problem is when the punk is not looking to prove what a tough guy he is, but rather takes the more predatory mindset of not looking to prove anything, rather than simply to defeat or punish his opponent in whatever manner necessary. This is a potentially significant difference in attitude from that of the MMA practitioner. It is the "whatever manner necessary," that separates the attitude, as it may often involve weapons, such as knives or firearms. Nolan Hong, co-owner of Fighter's Corner, a MMA based retail supply store commented:

> I never want to get into a street fight just because we've learned that anything can happen, and especially when you're trained within a structure of rules and know that these rules are there to protect you from what could happen. And then you see in the street that there are no rules. It's something that you don't, you know, leaves you with something you don't want to be a part of.

Hong's statements also echo the sentiments of Paul Halme who stated, "… a lot of times it never ends up well for either person…. You know, street fights are never fair."

I believe it is important to note that the original utility of martial arts, arguably at their core, was not for the purpose of sport competition. The development of the martial arts was originally for purpose of preservation—of the self, family, and community. This is not to say that there are not arts that have been developed and used solely for competition purposes, as competition types of arts in China and other geographical regions can be traced as far back as 700 BC. However, there are important distinguishing characteristics between combat and competition arts. Competition arts in society today, with some marginally popular exceptions, tend to focus on the weaponless hand-to-hand aspect of combat. In this case, I would then consider hand-to-hand as an important subset within the concept of martial arts. Technique, conditioning, and reactive reflexes are supremely important combat skills gained through competition combat sports. Modern day competition sports would include the different types of wrestling, judo, karate, Brazilian jiu-jitsu (BJJ), and what we now call our modern day sport of MMA. In modern society, when the topic of martial arts is addressed, whether it be in social conversations or popular media, it is generally focused on the hand-to-hand aspect of martial arts. This myopic view of martial arts appeals to the romanticized concept of defeating an opponent sans weaponry, and has misplaced an important reality of survival combat—that in survival situations, the least appealing position to be in, is unarmed.

Gracie-style BJJ is an enormously popular brand named martial art. They provide hand-to-hand combat training to the U.S. armed forces. In a dinner party discussion I was involved in with an army captain, whose list of military credentials include special operations intelligence, and two tours in Iraq, Afghanistan, and Bosnia, the topic of hand-to-hand training in Gracie BJJ came up. I posed the question, "What technique would you favor in a hand-to-hand life and death situation?" Who better to pose this question, than one who has literally faced numerous true life threatening situations? I expected to hear the response of a certain type of choke, or a technique focusing on breaking an opponent's limb. His casual response, "I'd try to grab a rock or something to smash his head in." In my opinion, his response highlights the paradigm shift when interpreting combat conflict situations, from one who would fight competitively for sport versus another who would fight to survive. The competitive fighter typically fights to best an opponent, to highlight a superior level of physical, technical, and possibly psychological skills or toughness, as opposed to the goal of surviving a life threatening confrontation. It is far less likely that true life or body threatening survival scenarios will come into play while in a purely hand-to-hand sporting combat competition. It is actually far more probable that the stripped bare combat scenario that we see in competitive MMA is the least likely scenario that one would encounter in a true life threatening situation. We believe that this should be an important distinction between MMA violence and the potential levels of violence one could encounter on the street, reminded to us via champion Alex Gong.

Currently, our society, whether it wants it or not, is a rich fertile ground for MMA. But due to MMA's rapid growth, it is showing signs of developing without a clear structure that would give it healthy direction. There are so many areas where it is having an effect, economically, legally, academically, and the list can go on. From where should some of the educational guidelines for these areas come? Who, if anyone, should bear some of the responsibility for directing this sport's growth, which has begun to bring much to many? To name a few, promoters, trainers, parents, and fighters are some of the primary participants who could bear different levels of responsibility. There are those who have taken certain levels of responsibility to educate the public of the dangers of using MMA in an unstructured environment. One that we took particular notice of was a commercial segment put forth during an IFL television show, where the popular former kickboxing and MMA champion and IFL commentator, Bas Rutten, offers a community service announcement encouraging viewers not to fight and understand that MMA is purely a sport that should not be taken to the street. Interviewee Terrance also saw this community service announcement and commented on it, saying:

> I saw Bas Rutten on TV and he just took a minute to say, you know these are professionally trained people. If you want to do this, go to a gym, get some training. And fighting's no way to solve problems outside of the gym. To see more guys do that, it would be great …

However, based on MMA's current and potential growth rate, that example is just a proverbial drop in the bucket. While most interviewees expressed some off the cuff noncommittal opinions on where the burden of education and responsibility in the MMA community should fall, it seemed that there was no general consensus as to which party held the largest responsibility to disassociate MMA from street violence and encourage peaceful resolutions.

There were those who saw the role of education and direction provided at the root level of schools and within the training and development of fighters. And some saw a role of the traditional structure of martial arts that was examined earlier in this chapter as vital. Tony Fryklund, current MMA fighter and trainer, links the idea of teaching kids how to fight to teaching them to practice it responsibly:

> I think kids have a responsibility to protect themselves. And if our sport brings the martial arts back into it, and hopefully it becomes an epidemic that fighting becomes an epidemic in a good way. Hopefully it gets to the point where the instructors take responsibility, cause our schools get full again, and if they are new schools, we're teaching the old school values of that, to say don't practice karate, don't practice MMA, don't practice judo or jiu-jitsu in your bedroom. Don't practice in your living room. Practice in a designated space, just like you tell little kids, and just like their parents do a checklist, so at least as they're growing up with it, they're understanding, yeah, I will hurt someone just to show a little boy an armbar or a rear naked choke and let them go to school. I'm hearing that. That people are letting little kids go to school knowing a rear naked choke. "Oh he rear naked choked his sister yesterday." Dude, what? You gotta tell 'em no. The little girl's turning freaking blue. Ha ha ha? What's wrong with people? You know that's just responsibility on so many different levels.

Jesse Juarez added:

> It should be just like boxing, and other sports like that. You can practice it in the gym, where you train, but they should know better, I mean, not to practice it in a fight, not to practice mixed martial arts on another person in a fight because it's totally wrong if that other person doesn't know anything. Yeah,

there is a responsibility that comes with the sport. They should publicize, teach the proper approach.

Another interviewee who suggested the role of the trainer teaching pro-social values was Bear St. Clair. His opinion was also strongly rooted in the role of traditional martial arts, arguing MMA schools have the duty to instill in their fighters the proper values and to illustrate how MMA's image is affected by fighters' actions. He feels his role is:

> ... infusing the values, and traditions, and the respect, and the honor, which you saw tonight in my classes, which I demand and give from my students, which is the traditional martial arts values and respect. You saw my students clean up the place, take care of it, okay, I don't let anybody take, uh, lean down, hunch over, look all lost, do anything like that.... And right now MMA has absolutely no soul and no culture whatsoever.... I would change the lack of honor. I would change the lack of respect. I would change the lack of, you know, tradition, meaning I would start to instill some things that should be held and revered as tradition, and continued. I would take out the debauchery.... I would take out the screaming and the yelling, and the, the rock and roll (attitude). I would instill some respect, you know? I mean, I think it (MMA) really has a really, really, really a long way to go before it is truly ... a respectable venue, and a respectable thing.

Continuing with the discussion of the role of trainers is Colin Oyama, co-owner and trainer of No Limits gym in Irvine California. Oyama, who has trained such notable fighters as Quinton Jackson, "MayheM" Miller, Tito Ortiz and is now working with a stable of up and coming fighters, offers his opinion on professionalism and the sport's current image:

> And so I think the biggest thing, it should be trainers' responsibilities, or teachers, or instructors, or whatever you want to call them, that run these gyms, to say like, "Hey man, you need to act a certain way." You know? At least with our fighters and stuff, I'm not saying they're perfect but there's a code of conduct we have here.... So I think it starts from that level. You know, to where ... you need act like a professional. Your fighters should act accordingly. If we had some type of guidelines, or some type of regulations on how to act, you know? And how to conduct yourselves. I think, I think that would help to clean up the sport. At least the image of it, right away, you know?

Aside from trainers, it can be argued that they who have the most to gain from MMA's growing popularity have a responsibility to perpetuate and nurture the sport responsibly and with integrity. Promoters and the different fight organizations that are springing up are all trying to either gain a piece of this MMA phenomenon, or extend their financial assets as much as possible. So while there are many schools and instructors who work hard to teach responsibility and an understanding of the weighty responsibility that comes with wielding new found fighting skills, promoters may have the biggest responsibility. Mike Onzuka stated:

> I think promoters have to take the lead. They have the biggest financial gain. And we'll do what we can, but to tell you the truth ... there's only so much we can do, you know as far as taking time out of our own schedules to do this stuff. These guys that make their living off of these promotions, they should take the lead in putting these things out there to educate everybody because that's feeding themselves money.

While the promoters have at their disposal the ability to reach masses of people due to their business goals and connections, issues such as promoting education about and within the sport too often take the backseat to their goals of business development. Because critical demographic groups affected by MMA's increased exposure are youths and adolescents, responsibilities are often placed back upon the shoulders of parents. A common component that is certainly not limited to the MMA issue is that parental responsibility is key in getting positive messages to children in our communities. As Antonio McKee stated:

> Well, I think that comes from the structure in the home. If you lay your foundation right, the house will be built strong. If you educate your kids and spend time with them, and you work with them, and you show them the different variations of life and the world and what they can do, then I think you can guide them down the right path. Unfortunately, some of us, we're lost. So how can we parent somebody lost? You know what I mean?

Travis Lutter agreed:

> Yeah, you would think common sense would prevail, but it usually doesn't. You know, the WWE (professional wrestling), you know, do they have a responsibility for these kids in the backyards jumpin' off their house and onto each other, and you know, that's probably a job for parents, you know, to regulate their kids from not being stupid.

While there are different resources available to society to make us aware of the responsibilities that this sport's growth imposes upon us, the general consensus of all interviewed is that education and awareness of these responsibilities is a good thing. Jason Miller, who has held volunteer speaking engagements with youth in Hawaii, argued that MMA competitors also hold a responsibility to preach non-violence outside of the gym, but explained his pessimistic view on how responsibility is not being taken satisfactorily throughout the MMA community:

> Now, I can only speak for myself, and I would cause I feel a bit of responsibility to say, "Hey kids, don't be chokin' your brother unconscious," you know. Like me, that's how I am. But honestly man, I don't think people give a damn. I mean, yo, they wanna get paid.... I try to give a damn about everybody, you know I try to give back. I don't think most of the guys give a damn. They just are concerned with, hey, buy the tickets and come to the show. Ya know, that's, that's the truth. I mean, that's just the truth of it. That's the long and short of it.

Chris Leben expressed a similar viewpoint to Miller, noting that if one is a prominent mixed martial artist and MMA coach, he or she holds a distinct responsibility to role model appropriately. Said Leben:

> You know, if you're an ultimate fighter, if you fight in the UFC, and you're a coach like I am, then I think you're gonna have younger guys that look up to you, and I think they're gonna look at you as a role model whether you like it or not.

Thus, according to these MMA competitors, the athletes themselves also hold a societal responsibility that goes beyond building their own careers and collecting paychecks.

MMA has so many critical points of interest. The aspect of pairing different fighting techniques and stylistic match ups has incredible entertainment value, as displayed by the sport's burgeoning popularity. The societal impacts also have a seemingly endless flow of sociological, economic, and psychological discussion points. When discussing the MMA community's responsibility to educate the public that it is completely inappropriate to use MMA for street fighting or even associate the two concepts, some want to place the burden on the promoters, some on trainers/schools, some on fighters, and some on parents. Once harm via physical violence is an issue, it is arguable that all those mentioned above share the burden, including the general public. While it is tempting and often a common practice in today's society to always look to blame society's ills on others, Guy Mezger makes a valid point by saying, "I think it's everybody's responsibility to make sure that … this world's a better place, that people are educated in what we're doing, but then the other side of it is, it shouldn't relieve the public from using their brains."

7

SAFETY ISSUES IN MIXED MARTIAL ARTS

BY DAVID MAYEDA & DAVID CHING

America's Obsession with Violence—David Mayeda

American culture is absolutely obsessed with violence. Dramatic television shows and video games depict excessive levels of violence (Huesmann & Taylor, 2006), and although their stories and images are fictional, they are frequently far more brutal than what anyone would see in MMA. According to a study conducted by the American Psychiatric Association (1998), by the time most children reach age eighteen, "they will have seen 16,000 simulated murders and 200,000 acts of violence" just on television (quoted in Muscari, 2002, p. 585). These numbers do *not* include what youth will also witness in video games, movies, online, or hear listening to music. Moreover, research on media violence has argued that "exposure to media violence causes increases in children's, adolescents', and young adults' physically and verbally aggressive behavior" (Anderson et al., 2003, p. 104; see also Paik & Comstock, 1994; Wood, Wong, & Chachere, 1991). As Chapter Six discussed, violence among adults and youth is a major problem in our country, and the MMA community shares a responsibility in decreasing and preventing violence.

Given these concerns, this chapter will explore an additional violence-related topic relevant to MMA—safety. This chapter will examine how MMA rules have evolved, how MMA compares with other sports in terms of safety, and close out with a discussion on substance use concerns within the sport. First, however, we will scrutinize the ways audiences from different countries—namely the United States and Japan—receive MMA differently, as perceived by those interviewed for this project. If in fact fighter safety is a serious concern for MMA organizations, then it is also important to examine how much fans seem to care about safety issues, if at all. Japan is among the safest countries in the world, but it also has extremely high rates of media violence. Say Shelov & Bar-on (1995), "The only country in the world with nearly as much entertainment violence as the United States is Japan. Yet Japanese society is far less violent than American society" (p. 949).

Actually, there are different types of violence in Japan that are of high concern, such as suicide (Brooke, 2004) and domestic violence (Fulcher, 2002). As one report notes, "Although the Japanese population leads the world in longevity, it has a high rate of suicide that is globally ranked ninth" (Nakao & Takeuchi, 2006, p. 492). Nevertheless, Japan's violent crime rates (homicide, robbery, rape, and assault) are extremely low in comparison to those in the United States. In Japan, only 48 out of every 100,000 people were reported as victims of a violent crime in 2001 (Roberts & Lafree, 2004, p. 201). In 2001 in the United States, the correlating rate was 504 victims per every 100,000 persons (Federal Bureau of Investigation, 2002, p. 14)—a rate approximately ten times higher than Japan's.

Roberts & Lafree (2004) claim that Japan's low rates of violent crime have more to do with their healthy economy than cultural forms of social control. However, our interviews with mixed martial artists who have competed or witnessed competition in both Japan and the United States suggest that culture is significant. And while perpetration of violent crime is something very different from audience responses to MMA fight cards, interviewees remarked that there is a noticeable cultural difference in how American and Japanese audiences respond to violence, at least when watching MMA.

Actually, this was not a topic we had thought of investigating until Travis Lutter initiated a discussion on differences he noticed between American MMA fans and those from different countries. In addition to competing in the United States, Lutter has competed in different parts of Europe. "I've fought in Europe three or four times, four times, something like that. I've fought in Denmark, Sweden, and twice in England." This prompted Stephen Mayeda to ask Lutter, "And how does it compare fighting in America than fighting overseas?" Lutter answered:

> Well, I've never fought in Japan. I've been to two or three Pride (FC) shows with Guy Mezger when he fought. I cornered him, and that's a totally different ambiance, to sit there and have those guys, the way that they kind of, they appreciate the technical kind of things that Americans don't. Americans want to see blood, guts, and heads rollin', stuff like that. Whereas the Japanese, they want to see good technique.

Lutter's observation that Japanese fans were much more apt to appreciate technique (e.g., technically-based grappling and submissions), even if it did not involve vicious striking blows, ended up being a recurring theme other interviewees mentioned when comparing Japanese and American fans. Mayeda followed, "So what about in Europe, is it blood and guts or technique?" to which Lutter replied, "A little bit of both. More blood and guts, but they're not as bad as Americans. They definitely want to see some blood and guts, but Americans are the worst though." Interviewees said Japanese fans did appreciate striking in competitions, but they were not disappointed if matches were won and lost via submission holds and they did not crave vicious striking blows to nearly the same degree as American fans.

Like Lutter, Takuhiro Kamikozono has lived in the Dallas area. He has competed in MMA matches in Texas, Minnesota, and Colorado. But unlike Lutter, Kamikozono has also competed in his home country of Japan. Therefore, I asked Kamikozono if he noticed differences in the crowds from different countries. He responded in similar fashion to Lutter, saying:

> Yeah, um, fighting in Japan and America, it's very different. Japanese people are just watching the fight quietly, and they just want to see what's going on. The American people are just you know, showing up and making big noise, like they just want to see blood or something, huge action. And Japanese people are just totally different. They just want to see how good (mixed martial artists) are. Like they want to see some technique ... I can see a difference.

One might assume that Kamikozono, being a Japanese national, could hold a bias in addressing this topic, but again, he was not the only interviewee to make this point.

We should point out that MMA has been accepted as part of the mainstream sports culture in Japan for a longer timeframe than in the United States. Again, Pride FC was started in 1997 and was selling out huge stadiums years before the UFC hit America's mainstream. Thus, there may be a learning curve we are witnessing. Dan Henderson competed in Pride FC for many years until the UFC bought it out in 2007. Commenting on the differences between American and Japanese fans, Henderson first said:

> The fans in the U.S. are starting to get a little bit more educated about the sport. They still like to see the blood and all the punching and more of the standup war going on. You know, they don't understand a lot of the grappling and some of the smaller things going on.

American fans (more so than Japanese fans) are still learning the complicated aspects of wrestling, jiu-jitsu, and judo that are integrated deeply in MMA, but that have never been especially popular in our own sporting culture. However, Henderson went on to say that in addition to MMA being an accepted part of the mainstream sports culture in Japan for quite some time now, Japan has a long cultural history of propagating respect through traditional martial arts, and this respect can be seen in how fans respond to MMA competitions and competitors differently from Americans:

> I think in Japan, they understand the sport. It's been a part of their culture for a long time, and they're much more respectful in Japan than they are in the U.S. You hardly ever hear any booing in Japan. You know, they respect the fighters win or lose. They know that they're prepared … and you know, that's a big thing, rather than if there's a little bit of a lull in the action in the U.S., and the fans start booing. You know, I think that that's pretty disrespectful to the athletes out there.

In fact, Henderson's comments correlate nicely with what scholars have said about martial arts and Japanese culture. Take for instance the original intent of judo and the ways winning and losing are valued in that combat sport. Kelly (2007) states that there is "… a place for winning and losing in judo—not as its own objective but rather as training for life and for character building" (p. 480). In line with much of what was addressed in this book's previous chapter, the traditional and historical values within the martial arts seem to diminish Japanese fans' thirst for excessive violence, at lest in MMA. Thus far, the same cannot be said for American fans.

Truth be told, we should give American fans some credit. In the early- to mid-1990s, UFC fans were said to be far more aggressive and "bloodthirsty" than they are now. Randy Couture made a point of mentioning this, saying both MMA competitors and American fans have matured over the years: "Back in the days, there were fights in the hotels. There were a lot more fights in the stands than there were in the cage, frankly at the events. And I think that type of behavior hasn't been tolerated." Nevertheless, interviewees generally said American fans still have room to grow in terms of appreciating the intricacies that go into all dimensions of MMA. Seriously, can one imagine Japanese fans getting into fights at any sporting event, including MMA cards?

This contrast between American and Japanese fans is a bit confusing because the rules established in Japan's Pride FC were considered by most MMA practitioners we interviewed to be the most violent and dangerous of all MMA organizations. In Pride FC (before it was acquired by Zuffa, LLC), kicking an opponent's head while he was down was perfectly legal. This included allowing what are known as "soccer kicks" (standing to the side of a downed opponent and kicking his head like one would kick a soccer ball) and "head stomps" (standing over a downed opponent who is lying on his back, lifting one's leg in the air and attempting to stomp on his head with the flat of one's foot). Kneeing a downed opponent's head was also legal in Pride FC. None of these "techniques" are legal in current American-based MMA organizations. In the following section, David Ching quickly addresses an evolution of MMA rules in the United States and then offers perspectives from interviewees on the rules that they see as most favorable in terms of providing for safety and sporting fairness. Let's hope that the rules established by MMA organizations in the coming years do not cater towards Americans' excessive thirst for violence and that more American fans realize that MMA as a sport should never encourage injury.

The Evolution of Mixed Marital Arts Rules and Fighter Preferences—David Ching

Senator John McCain's labeling of North America's first high profile MMA competition, the UFC, as "human cockfighting" is duly noted by the MMA community. While many viewers and fighters take umbrage to this statement, he actually aided the sport in reaching its current popularity. Although current MMA competitors and organizers bristle at the "human cockfighting" association, they must realize that today's rules are a far cry from the original set of rules in the beginning years of the UFC. It is important to note that although the UFC is the dominant MMA organization in North America (and since its acquisition of Japan's Pride FC, the international market as well), there are other major organizations that have slight rule variations along with differences in physical venue, such as a boxing ring type of set up versus the UFC's chain link fenced octagon.

The first UFC competitions starting in 1993 had very few rules. Because the competition was originally constructed to determine the most effective martial art or fighting style in an open fighting event, rules were minimized and competitors had very little to worry about in terms of rule infractions. The most notable features of the early years that helped define MMA as barbaric were the allowable head butts, hair pulling, and groin shots. At some points, there were neither weight classes nor time limits, and there were no standardized gear requirements, including no requirement of gloves. What was prohibited? Not much—basically eye gouging, fish hooking (pulling on the inside of someone's check with one's fingers), biting, and of course outside weapons. Aside from being required to follow the referee's instructions, not much else was required or prohibited.

After having the opportunity to interview both past and present fighters and hobbyists, it is arguable that Senator McCain's description was relatively accurate, not in the sense that MMA was or is equivalent to human cockfighting, but that rules needed desperately to be added and enforced. With the exception of two interviewees, all others vehemently agreed with the current restrictions of the previously allowed head butts, groin shots and hair pulling. One of the interviewees who would prefer fewer rules was Chris Leben, who described himself as more of a "purist." Said Leben:

> Well, I'm kind of a purist as far as the sport goes, so I say bring back head butts. I say, it's fighting, so short of biting or sticking your finger in somebody's eye, if they can do it in a street fight, they should be able to do it in the cage. I mean, that's what we preach, we say we're not martial arts, we're MMA where it is as real as it gets. Well, the more you limit it, the more you take it away, the more like boxing it becomes.

Much like what Leben describes, early rules may have been suited for the initial purpose of the UFC—to supposedly showcase the most effective martial art in an "as real as possible" fight scenario. In this case, the less rules, it would seem, the better. However, due to the legal and political issues hindering any potential growth, as well as public preferences for increased safety, rules have evolved and been added over the years. Hence, McCain's statement was the first highly publicized wake up call for the sport's organizers that they must alter MMA's structure if they hoped to reach any sort of mainstream popularity. Now that mainstream status has been achieved, most interviewees we spoke with believed the current MMA rule sets are relatively safe. Quinton "Rampage" Jackson offered the following viewpoint: "In the beginnin', it was kind'a barbaric. It was a little bit, but they changed the rules up. They got it goin'. And it's very safe. It's good. I'm happy with the rules." Randy Couture added:

> I think the evolution of the rules was more than anything was for appearance. I don't think they were that interested in the beginning, uh, it just looked a lot rougher by most people's estimations. And there were some things that I was very happy to see taken out. Head butts and things like that, I mean how technical is it to ram somebody with your head? But things like that, we're better off with them taken out. And there's certain other things that I didn't think needed to be taken out, but for appearance sake, you know, were taken out, and that's important too.

Some of the current UFC rules now enforced include the following:

- Matches consist of three rounds (five minutes each) with one minute rest in between, except for championship matches, which have five rounds.

- Five separate weight classes have been established.

- No kicks or knees are allowed to a downed opponent's head.

- No striking to the spine or back of the head is allowed.

- The referee has the power to stop the fight if a fighter is not intelligently defending himself.

A complete list of the UFC's thirty-one fouls can be found on their website (http://www.ufc.com/index.cfm?fa=LearnUFC.Rules).

The brutality in the early UFCs has had some lingering effects on the sport of MMA in North America relative to Japan, which are arguably positive differences. Dan Henderson, who has years of experience in the Japanese arena, but who is now fighting in the UFC, observed:

> You know, they stop fights a little earlier in the U.S. than they do in Japan for the most part. But I consider Japan to be pretty safe, and I think most people consider, they think they're a little overprotective in the States, that's why they're stopping [fights] a little earlier, probably due to how the sport was portrayed when it first came out.

Some of the notable differences in rules are generally attributed to whether an organization follows the UFC or Pride FC model (although Pride FC now appears defunct, some MMA organizations still utilize some of its old rule set). It seems that the most debated differences in rules between the two organizations are that Pride FC allowed kicking and kneeing an opponent's head while he was on the ground, while the UFC does not. Conversely, the UFC allows elbows to a downed opponent's head or face, while Pride FC did not. In our interviews, many were critical of the usage of elbows under the UFC format. The primary criticism of elbows was that it seemed to end fights early, sometimes giving the win to the combatant that may have not been winning the fight, but was able to cut his opponent with a lucky elbow strike. Some comments from interviewees:

I'm pretty comfortable with the rules the way they are right now.... I think the one criticism that we get now most commonly is the elbows. It probably wouldn't bother me if the elbows were taken out on the ground to the head. You know, when you can take a guy and ram him into the bottom of the fence and limit his mobility to in some ways defend himself, the elbow strikes sometimes open cuts, and fights sometimes get ended by open cuts, and you don't always see the best fighter come out of it in that situation. And I've been on both sides of that. I've won fights that way, and I've lost fights that way.—Randy Couture

No elbows to the head. The elbows don't really knock people out too often. They can knock you out, but they mostly designed to cut people up. And you can get scarred for life. I don't like that too much.—Quinton "Rampage" Jackson

I like Pride (FC) rules the best. I would rather be able to knee to the head while on the ground than to elbow somebody at any time. The elbow just doesn't do that much damage to the guy other than cut a guy ...—Dan Henderson

Cuz elbows on the ground, boom, ya cut the guy open, man they stop the fight prematurely. Like, okay, we just wasted all that time, like the fight was stopped before it even started. Yea so ... I think the rule changes are necessary. Like you couldn't have guys head butting each other or kicking each other in the balls. That's just like ridiculous ... if you allow us to kick each other in the balls, there's gonna be guys who just get in position to kick ya in the balls. That's the whole fight, ya know, that's the whole fight, kicking in the balls. Wow, that doesn't make for a very exciting fight. It makes for a damn kick in the balls, ball kicking competition.—Jason "MayheM" Miller

I don't love the elbows, even though I like 'em when I'm on top. But I think you get a little bit cleaner technique without elbows. But you know, it's frickin', the main reason I don't like elbows in the UFC is because they end fights early with cuts, ya know.—Travis Lutter

Whether or not any particular fighter prefers to have a rule in place, such as one that allows or disallows elbows, it does raise the point that there are clear differences in rules that have a significant effect on MMA fights. These differences can have subtle effects on what positions fighters allow themselves to get into, and they certainly have been shown to affect the outcome of a fight, for better or for worse. As Paul Halme confirmed, "... just by making a small rule change, you can change the whole style of a fight."

Because different MMA organizations have slightly different rules, there are some concerns. Some fighters interviewed offered their thoughts on the need for a standardized rule set, to which all organizations should adhere. Dan Henderson explained:

> I would think for it to grow as an international sport you need kind of a set standard of rules, you know, that all the organizations use. It would be easier to unify belts that way. That's probably a big issue right now with they got Pride (FC) guys fighting U.S. guys, and the rules, it changes the game quite a bit.... So I would say a mixture of the rules would be good for everyone in the sport, and then we could start unifying some belts and growing the sport more.

Chris Reilly added:

> I mean, one thing that I would change is I would try to unify the rules. I think it's a big problem that it's the states that decide what the rules should be because this is an international sport. And so even within the U.S., we have different rules in different states, let alone the different rules that they put up internationally.

Because the different MMA organizations operate independently from one another, standardizing rules between them will be difficult. However, it is clear that mixed martial artists are in favor of the different organizations moving in the direction of rule unification. This notwithstanding, rule differences between different organizations are rather subtle. And the rule increases do provide for a much safer competitive environment than the early days of MMA. In fact, today's MMA organizations may have rule sets that make this sport safer than people realize, perhaps even safer than other mainstream American sports.

Safety Issues in Mixed Marital Arts and Comparisons with other Contact/Collision Sports—David Ching

The visual experience of a MMA competition for a first time viewer can often times seem a little disorienting and extremely brutal. With very rare exception, the general population has not had many opportunities to view the type of hand-to-hand conflict typical of MMA. Sporting collisions are usually seen in arenas like controlled boxing settings, where contact between fighters includes bursts of repetitive split second contact, or in other sports like American football, which is already so integrated and accepted in our culture that we have "pee wee" type leagues for children as young as elementary school. We are also exposed to the popular and choreographed setting of simulated violence found in professional wrestling and the fancified choreography of television and cinema violence.

In one's first exposure to a MMA match, an individual may see things ranging from a participant being knocked unconscious by a shin to the head, falling from a stunning right hook to the jaw or temple, being choked unconscious or forced to tap out, or any of the other multiple ways a combatant could win or lose a match. It is thus understandable that when the fledgling viewer of MMA first witnesses the sport, the explosive visuals of the conflict in the cage or ring can cause a mildly traumatic experience. This knee jerk, gut reaction first time viewers have often leads to an assumption that MMA is an incredibly unsafe and an excessively damaging sport.

What was very notable in our interviews with fighters and trainers about the issues of fighter safety and MMA, was that the participants overwhelmingly voiced that MMA was significantly safer than sports accepted by the American mainstream, such as boxing, football, hockey, and wrestling, these being the sports that have the highest level of physical contact among America's popular sports. Former UFC Heavyweight Champion Randy Couture reflected on what he has experienced and witnessed regarding the relative safety of MMA:

> I've certainly seen more injuries in Olympic wrestling than I've seen in mixed martial arts. In all my years of fighting, two broken bones. And in all my years of wrestling, I've seen a seen a whole bunch of pretty serious dislocations and joint injuries and things like that.

Randy Couture, being one of the senior successful competitors in the sport, is a multi-belt champion, achieving titles in both the heavyweight and light heavyweight divisions, and is arguably an ideal testament to the MMA safety record. As Frank Trigg commented:

> Look at Randy Couture. He's forty-three, or forty-two years old, and he's still competing at an elite level, and that is because the sport is safe. In what other sport could someone forty-two years old do that? Okay, well Barry Bonds, but what, he's a designated hitter in baseball, a sport where there is minimal contact. People talk about mixed martial arts being such a violent sport, but actually, it's one of the safer sports.

When discussing safety comparisons with other contact sports, a common comparison fighters made was between boxing and MMA. Boxing certainly has faced its trials by fire in our society on its way to becoming an "acceptable" combat sport (see also Chapter Nine). This is a natural comparison, not only due to boxing's current widespread societal acceptance, but also because boxing is one of many integral MMA components. However, although boxing can potentially be a large part of a MMA bout, as Quinton "Rampage" Jackson stated, the repetitive head punching in boxing is minimized in MMA:

> It (MMA) looks worse, but it's a hundred times safer than boxing or kickboxing. First of all, you don't get too much head trauma. On average, seven boxers die a year, on average. In our sport, we haven't had any deaths. In boxing, you watch a boxer, you see him get dropped, they fall down, they get an eight-count. And then they continue to fight. In my sport, if you get dropped clean like that, the fight is over. So that's head trauma right there. And then, boxers are skilled punchers, you know what I'm sayin'.… And I can't imagine what he took in sparring before they get there. That's where I get most of my punches, in sparring. And then, if I get punched too much, I still can take the guy down where he can't punch me.

At the time Jackson made this statement, there had been one death in MMA, but as will be explained shortly, that death came during an unsanctioned event in which a combatant should not have been competing. Colin Oyama, former trainer of "Rampage," added the following comments, highlighting that in MMA, the ability to end fights via submission holds helps to offset the danger of kicks and punches. Winning a MMA fight does not require harming someone through strikes to the head, or anywhere for that matter. Oyama explained:

> Ninety-nine percent of boxing punches are generated towards the head. Um, you're trying to knock him out, you know. Nobody's here to see you punch the guy in the stomach. I mean, you kind of wear him down with a body shot maybe, but the goal of boxing is to hit him in the chin, and put him out. The goal of MMA is to finish the fight, one way or another. Are we trying to hit him in the chin? You bet. We going try knock him out. But the guy gets taken down, and, his arm is there, or his neck is there, or whatever. Can you submit him? Absolutely. Are there other ways to hammer the opponent in MMA? Yeah, you can kick him in the leg. You can knee him in the stomach. Do those things hurt? Yes they do. But the last time I checked, nobody got brain damaged from getting kicked in the leg, or kneed in the stomach. He might have a busted rib, he might lost his wind, or he might have got hurt, but it did not affect him long term, so I think in MMA there's a lot of ways to go about breaking the opponent down without blasting him in the head.

MMA has many different fighting components that augment the striking aspects found in boxing and kickboxing. The non-striking, grappling aspects of MMA actually lessen the degree to which fighters are subjected to repeated concussive blows. Darin Goo chimed in, saying of MMA:

> People think it's less safe because you can do more things, or maybe they see more blood because the gloves are smaller and elbows are allowed, so you see more facial cuts. I would rather have a facial cut than a serious concussion. The long term affects of a facial cut are minimal, but lasting brain damage can affect you the rest of your life.

And while MMA clearly has its share of head trauma, not dissimilar from boxing, in terms of the kicks, knees, and elbows, it still has a strong track record relative to boxing because head blows are minimized. As Dan Henderson mentioned:

> I know there's deaths every year in boxing. We've had one death in our sport, and I think that was due to a pre-existing condition. The guy shouldn't have been fighting; it wasn't sanctioned. It was in Russia. And so, that was when the sport first came out, within the first two years of the sport being in the U.S....

Frank Trigg's statement also comments that increased safety has come with the addition of a commission to oversee and sanction events:

> In our sport, we've had one death in the Ukraine, in what was a completely unsanctioned fight. And the guy who died should not even have been fighting. He lied. He had two recent concussions prior to that fight, and he shouldn't have even been fighting. That was just stupid on his part. And, again, it was an unsanctioned event, that happened what, about ten years ago in the Ukraine. Today, with the commission, it's one of the safest sports.

When we interviewed Trigg, only one known death had been attributed to a participant's involvement in an unsanctioned 1998 MMA bout (Sherdog.com, 2007a). Jesse Juarez reminded us that boxing over time has shown to be very damaging and has a significant negative effect on too many of its participants, as he stated:

> ... it's because they've got hit so many times in the head, even though they are protecting themselves, it's just that constant hit, constant impact, constant impact. With MMA, I mean you don't go for eight rounds, ten rounds, twelve

rounds, getting constantly punched in the head. If the ref sees you're in danger and you can't protect yourself, they stop the fight. And with boxing, I mean you can get knocked out and get back up, and go right back at it, and get hit in the head, get hit in the head.

Boxing rules such as the "standing eight count," which allows the referee to temporarily stop the bout and give an eight-count respite to a fighter who he has deemed significantly "rocked," will actually allow a combatant to recover whatever wits he or she can in that eight-count, and then be allowed to resume fighting, and thus absorb more punishment. The "three knock-down" rule is a rule which states that if a fighter is knocked down three times in a round, then the fight is deemed to be over via a technical knock out. The standing eight count and three knock-down rule may seem merciful, but they actually increase the amount of concussive head trauma a boxer will face, and in comparison to the immediate and complete stoppage of MMA bouts, inflate boxing's dangers. As Dan Henderson confirmed:

> Boxing you get hit in the head, you know, twelve rounds straight, and you get your bell rung in boxing and the ref has to step in and give you an eight count. Then they let you go out there and let you get beat up again two or three times before they stop the fight. We get our bell rung, and the fight's over, so I think, I'd say we're wearing a lot smaller gloves, but either way, when you get your bell rung, the smaller gloves might be safer for your head. You know, you don't take all the multi-trauma to your head like a boxing glove.

Another issue that MMA fighters discussed when explaining why they argue that MMA is safer than boxing is the use of different gloves. As Bear St. Clair voiced his opinion, noting how the larger, softer boxing gloves actually increase head trauma:

> The gloves are a big problem. You've heard this before I'm sure, right? The padding, the soft padding that you think is helping you. It's not. It's killing you, okay? Because the cushion of the glove eliminates the natural barrier, you know, all your natural defenses, which is a hard skull, and you know, two hard objects hit, they knock off each other, they bounce. You put a soft glove on the round skull, it doesn't bounce off, it doesn't deflect, it just absorbs the entire blow, and furthermore, like I said, since that glove's not moving, that skull ... the blow, you know how energy goes, it's gonna travel through. And that blow is gonna concussively go through your brain, and out the other end. And that's not good for you.

And while boxing has been established in our culture as the mainstream American combat sport for decades, it is clear that it does not have an exemplary safety record. Many critics and observers cite past boxing champions who display compromised cognitive and motor skill functioning (pugilistic dementia, or being chronically "punch drunk"), thereby diluting meaningful comparisons between MMA and boxing. For this reason, many MMA fighters raised safety comparisons between their sport and other widely accepted contact sports, American football being a popular juxtapose.

Of the fighters interviewed, some had a significant amount of experience in organized football. One of the interviewees being Robert Otani, a former University of Southern California linebacker who was part of their national championship teams in 2003 and 2004. Otani offered his opinion, in comparing MMA's safety with football:

> Well, as far as safety in football, in my opinion, football's way more dangerous, even though you got all the protective gear. And just when you watch football it doesn't look as brutal, but the thing about it is you got 300 pound guys out there that are running 4.7, 4.8 (second) forty's (yard sprints), and moving at you, and you got a guy my size who weighs 215, and I gotta bang heads with that guy every play. And you get a running start, and even though you got that protective gear, I mean that's like a car crash every down. And in MMA, you got weight classes. You got those things set up so it's not unfair. I'm not saying football's unfair at all, and that's part of playing football, being an athlete, being able to beat those big guys and running with those fast receivers and running backs and all that. The thing about it is it's just a human collision course out there.

Other fighters who possessed a significant amount of football experience shared a similar analysis. An opinion that the padding, while certainly necessary in reducing injury, had the less obvious effect of allowing for greater levels of contact, and thus greater levels of impact damage. Chris Reilly continued, "Well, as I said, I have a fair amount of experience with football. Almost made it to the top level, and there's no question in my mind that that's much, much more devastating." He additionally explained:

> So what you've got, is you've got two big, strong guys, and you pad them up so that they feel even less vulnerable. You know, they've got a hard helmet and a face mask and pads. In their minds, they think that they're indestructible and you've got them set up to go head-to-head, full-blast directly into each other. The amount of impacts on your brain, and your neck, and your spine

in that sport are unbelievable. And then on top of that, all those pads make you top heavy, and so they also put a lot of pressure on your knees and your ankles, and there's a huge potential for both of those (body parts) to be severely damaged by any kind of a side impact when you've got all that stuff on you, which also inhibits your peripheral vision. You know, in fighting, you're virtually naked. You've got a small set of gloves on and some under-wear. And so it's you and another man, and so basically, we're all relatively even, in a pound-for-pound fight. You know, you're basically just in there with just you and another guy. And so if you're properly trained and properly conditioned, you stand a relatively good chance of getting out of there really unharmed.

Other interviewees raised observations regarding American football which coin-cided with Reilly's observations that increased "protection" does not automati-cally translate to enhanced athletic safety. Chris Onzuka commented, "People got hurt when they wore leather helmets and just covered their elbows. Okay, so let's put some plastic pads on, right? Let's *increase* the padding on 'em so they can hit harder." In short, as we make athletes feel more invincible in collision sports, in some ways the sports may actually become more dangerous.

Trainer Colin Oyama, who also played football at the collegiate level weighed in, posing the question that while MMA is a relatively young sport, football has shown to have serious long term detrimental effects on its participants, and won-ders how MMA will compare in the long run:

> Football, you know, I played at college level, you got some big guys. You can only imagine the NFL. Um, you see these guys getting drilled, you know quarterbacks are about 220, whatever. I mean, you got 300 lb guys running 4.9, 4.8. You know, you have that hitting you. Falling on you. What's the average life expectancy of a football player, versus an MMA fighter? I guess, MMA is kinda young right now to find that out, but I'm curious to see, like, a lot of these NFL guys, when they retire, how long do they live? And what's their quality of life?

Bao Quach, who is trained by Oyama added, "I majored in kinesiology and I studied a lot of all that on my bachelors and stuff, in kinesiology. And I know football, I've had a class where they are talking about football players. I know ... their career spans sometimes doesn't go past a year or two years." Interviewees also brought up hockey as a sport that sees numerous concussions. Darin Goo stated, for example, "Guys flying on the ice, twenty-five miles per hour, two ath-letic two hundred pound guys smashing into each other. Maybe their bodies can take it, but you know, maybe their brains can't." In fact, the National Hockey

League and NFL have had to address their guidelines regarding players returning to play after sustaining a concussion. "There are about 160 concussions in the N.F.L. and 70 in the N.H.L. each year" (McKinley, 2000, p. D1). It is often times difficult to know when you are about to be ear holed (hit in the side of your helmet with the crown of an opponent's helmet) in football, or blindsided and smashed into a wall in hockey.

The scenario of two combatants alone in a cage or ring where there are multiple avenues to defeat your opponent may seem like an intimidating prospect. However, the one-on-one nature of MMA is one of the primary components that interviewees felt made it safer than other team sports that had more unpredictability, namely football and basketball. As Toby Grear (TG) stated in his conversation with David Mayeda (DM):

TG: It's safer than boxing, but I joke around that I don't play basketball.

DM: How come?

TG: Cause you know, you can get injured, like real big injuries, like a knee, you know a lot of knee injuries, a hand injury. Just funky injuries. I like in MMA that I have more control.... I get hurt more in (MMA), there's no doubt about it, but the difference is you get hurt, not injured. In here, I get hurt all the time—a bruise, something will get bent out of shape, but the thing about like basketball or football is you really rely on things you can't see, things you have no control over. Guys rolling over on the back of your knees, if you go up for a lay-up, somebody takes your legs out. Um like when I played soccer, I played soccer in high school, somebody slide tackled me, and I ended up tearing the tendon straight across in my ankle.

Jamie Yager, who played Division I college football, agreed with Grear that the unpredictability of team contact sports made them much more dangerous than MMA. Said Yager, "... whereas football compares to MMA, I believe that the MMA game is a lot safer because in football you're depending upon ten other guys ... and (if) somebody takes a down off, and you're knee's blown ..." Virtually all interviewees said that their injuries sustained in MMA were very minor (e.g., getting bruised, mild sprains). For instance, Michael Frison made the following comment:

... you always get like the sprains and the strains and the black eyes and the bloody noses, and forehead cuts and whatever, but nothing that's ever stopped me. Most of my worst injuries have been out on the street, walking off a curb and twisting an ankle.

Dan Henderson mentioned that he tore his ACL, but that occurred just after he had won a MMA competition, jumping off of the ring ropes in celebration. Of course major injuries do occur in MMA, but they are far less common than people would normally think.

Culturally within MMA there is an additional aspect that minimizes injury. There is no shame in "tapping out" (submitting when caught in a submission hold). Mike Onzuka pointed out this cultural element within MMA saying, "I think it's way safer. And the number one thing, it's honorable for fighters to tap out and to give up." Likewise, after Stephen Mayeda asked Travis Lutter, "Is there shame in giving up during a fight?", Lutter said, "No, there's not.... It means that guy was better that day." What many first time viewers of MMA may not realize is that grappling and jiu-jitsu are huge components in the MMA arsenal, and they are relatively safe. Jason Miller, whose major strength is jiu-jitsu says of his general experience in MMA competitions:

> ... in mixed martial arts, man I've had fights with like nothin'. Unscathed after the fight, ya know. I didn't punch him, he didn't punch me. I'm like, damn, "Why'd I even wrap my hands?" ya know. I got on the guy's back and choked him.

And it is not as if submissions in grappling or jiu-jitsu injure competitors. Again, choke holds and arm or knee bars are not applied long enough to injure someone because it is not shameful to tap out. Mixed martial artists have the collective understanding that it is better to tap out and maintain one's health rather than try to fight through a deep submission and sustain a serious injury. As seen in many of the comments shared by interviewees, it is clear that from a fighter's perspective in terms of safety, MMA thus far has a relatively good track record. And while visually MMA may seem to have a greater propensity to result in serious injury, it may actually be safer due to the reasons expressed above.

Thus far in this section we attempted to address safety issues through an inter-sport comparison, primarily contrasting MMA with the two high contact/collision mainstream sports of boxing and football. Some veteran fighters revealed important intra-sport safety issues addressing the role of match-ups and fight promotions. Chris Reilly contributed:

> So you know, I really do think that in the overall, the sport is safe. Problems happen when you get guys in there with guys who are way more experienced and way better trained. That can be dangerous and so that's something that we've got to watch out for and caution against. This is an issue that comes down to the promoter.... I think that if you have two evenly matched, same-size athletes in there with a good set of skills, you're gonna end up with bumps and bruises, sometimes a little bit worse, but nothing that doesn't heal.

Essentially, Reilly is frowning upon the longtime boxing model that deliberately pits top tier fighters against lower-tier fighters in order to build up the better fighters' records and public hype. Tony Fryklund contributed to this topic, explaining that promotions can take advantage of young fighters' over zealous desire to be part of a professional MMA card before they are adequately prepared. Said Fryklund, "... there's pro athletes and there's sorry athletes that think they're pros. And that's what's scary about this sport." Numerous interviewees stated that this mismatching model is a recipe for disaster in MMA. Darin Goo, for example, stated the following with regard to MMA matches he has seen in Southern California: "... they've purposely picked big mismatches so that some guy gets destroyed just so the [crowd] gets all excited." Travis Lutter also expressed particularly strong viewpoints on this safety issue:

> I mean there's adults out there ... putting together fights where all you gotta have is a month's experience, I mean a month of training and you can come fight. I mean it's stupid. Why do you want to take a guy that knows basically nothing, and you know, he knows just enough to go in there and get his ass kicked against somebody that's been in there a year or whatever.... a no holds barred fight, you can go in there and get your cheekbone busted, you know, and you need to have surgery. You bust something. You could get knocked out, get a concussion, you get a trip in the ambulance. It's like, and some of the smaller shows don't provide insurance for ya, or worse yet, they're not gonna be paying your bills. I think that's really ignorant and stupid.

Lutter was not the only interviewee who felt some smaller MMA organizations were putting rookie competitors in especially perilous situations. Tony Fryklund went on to mention that he has seen some smaller organizations barely get by state regulations in order to make fight cards "professional," so that they can build fighters' reputations. Said Fryklund, "Cause they're finding ways to make some of these shows just sanctioned enough to get it past amateur to a pro fight for a local favorite." However, the true evidence of this mismatching happening came when we interviewed Cleyburn Walker (CW), a young MMA aspirant who competed in his first professional MMA competition with literally no MMA experience, as seen in the conversation below with David Mayeda (DM):

> DM: Alright, so why don't we get started talking about your first fight. How'd that all happen? You went in with no MMA training?
>
> CW: No, no MMA training whatsoever. I had just got out of the marine corps, and one of the things we did was wrestled, submitted each other a lot as way of establishing somewhat of a pecking order outside of our rank structure was to fight each other without actually fighting, so I thought I could fight on the ground, and from past experiences, I thought I could fight standing up well enough to defend myself, and I knew I was in shape. So I thought, what the hell let's just jump in head first and see how it goes.
>
> DM: This was at a sanctioned mixed martial arts event?
>
> CW: Yes it was a professional mixed martial arts competition where we were paid …

Walker was paid $300 for this competition, and he said it was a good experience. Thankfully, he was not severely hurt or injured. Walker's positive experience notwithstanding, this type of irresponsible matchmaking should never happen.

Unfortunately, this practice of allowing unprepared fighters to compete in MMA matches goes on much more than we thought. When David Mayeda interviewed Terrance, we heard a story that was even more surprising and disconcerting than that of Walker's. Mayeda (DM) was talking with Terrance about gender roles when he brought up a very disturbing story about a small fight card he had recently attended in Oregon. The litany of safety concerns Terrance (T) raised in telling this story is truly mind boggling:

> T: We had a cage fight in our town recently where two girls got in a fight in the stands, and then they told the girls to come down and (said) "Sign this and get in here if you want to fight," you know. And they did.
>
> DM: You gotta be kidding me!
>
> T: It was just madness.
>
> DM: They went down and signed a waiver?
>
> T: Yeah.
>
> DM: They may not have had any experience?

T: None whatsoever. And that's how it is. They're putting tons of kids in these rings. And these promoters are making bank. And these kids, you know, they'll show up at the gym a few times, "You're ready," you know, "sign here." I got a little off track there.

DM: No, I think that's a big safety issue.

T: That's a huge safety issue! And what I don't understand is I've been wrestling my whole life, you know. And I'm wise enough to know I'm not getting into a cage with these guys because, look, I have friends who fight at Team Quest. I have friends who fight for Bodog, and I know that if you get in there with a really good fighter, they're gonna hurt you, or me. Like I said, I've been doing this my whole life, and there's a good chance I could go out there and get injured. And these other kids don't realize it cause they've never wrestled at that level. They've never fought at that level, and they just don't understand. They think anybody can get in there and be like Chuck Liddell, or whatever. I go in the gym and see these kids. They've been in there for a month and they're fighting in the next cage fights. And they don't test 'em for anything.

Recall that Terrance has been wrestling since he was in first grade and was a highly accomplished high school wrestler; still, he realizes the potential danger of competing in a full MMA match. Promoters, however, will take advantage of young inexperienced MMA aspirants to the degree that people (in this case women included) may be recruited out of the stands for impromptu matches. These are exactly the types of irresponsible practices that keep MMA from gaining sporting legitimacy and public acceptance. Endangering people's health in order to satisfy rabid fans is inexcusable. As some interviewees suggested, fighters need to have a minimum amount of MMA training under responsible coaches and a minimum number of amateur MMA competitions before being allowed to partake in professional MMA matches.

In addition to this, there are other ways MMA organizations and promoters can better protect participating fighters. As the sport gains legitimacy in the eyes of the public, promoters and organizations will continue to increase profits, and in turn will likely spend a greater amount of resources. Mike (MO) and Chris Onzuka (CO), who have been rooted in MMA since its early days, serving as event judges, cornering MMA competitors, and producing their show that promotes MMA, shared their observations of safety evolutions thus far:

> MO: The UFC's, the Pride's. Icon Sport is really good about bringing legitimate doctors there. I think the problem is at the smaller events. I think those, they're limited towards, as far as bad contracts with the fighters, the doctors being present. Stuff like that. Typical things at the larger events—fighters get pre-fight checks, and it's not a huge thing, you gotta tell if the guy has heart trouble, but at least it's something, some legitimate doctor checking these guys out is a lot better than these guys not being there. And more importantly is after the fight these guys checking the fighter out, so I think that's the biggest difference as far as fighters' safety and the bigger events and the smaller events.

> CO: I think with financial backing comes increased safety, but there's a general level of safety that's like current employee laws, I think is pretty, fairly adequate. There could be some changes with it, but as far as getting a licensed physician on hand, experienced referee on hand, pre-fight checkups, post-fight checkups, stuff like that, a good set of rules. There's some basic things that *every* event should have. Some events will have like four doctors on hand, you know and that stuff.

Like the Onzuka brothers, Frank Trigg, Savant Young, and Tony Fryklund all felt that having competent referees was absolutely crucial in insuring fighter safety. Trigg and Young both mentioned that referees who trained in MMA were the most competent because they understood the sport's nuances and therefore, knew exactly when to jump in and stop competitions (e.g., they could see submission holds coming and knew when fighters were truly protecting themselves or not). Said Trigg of such referees:

> They can see when someone is sinking in a rear naked choke, that it may not be fully sunk in yet, but that it's getting close, or an arm-bar, and they are right on top of that because they understand the intricacies of MMA competition.

And finally, Colin Oyama argued that state regulations need to be tougher when certifying MMA instructors, making comparisons with other professions that require rigorous certification testing:

> Taking the bar gives me certain privileges as an attorney, taking the boards gives you certain privileges as a medical doctor. Uh, passing your CPA, or whatever, all these things give you rights to do certain things in a certain field. Then you got a "professional fight trainer," who pays $64 to the state. Basically that's about it.... How the hell are you a pro trainer?

Both gym owners and state regulations must take the steps to insure that instructors are qualified and advocate for the proper values that make students better fighters and citizens.

With the UFC's recent acquisition of Japan's Pride FC, we have already seen the marketing synergy created by the combining of those two organizations. The unification light heavyweight bout between the current UFC champion Quinton "Rampage" Jackson versus Pride FC's champion Dan Henderson had the highest ever viewership recorded for a MMA event. The ever increasing exposure in the U.S. market will simply result in greater revenues and profits by the owners of this merged organization. Similarly, newer MMA organizations are coming that have major financial backing, such as that being developed by Mark Cuban. This will almost certainly result in greater demands for safety and higher standards of professionalism and equity in fighter match-ups, which will hopefully raise the bar for all of the smaller organizations that need to follow suit. Anthony Torres applauded the UFC's safety measures but also made a numbing observation during his interview regarding the lack of safety measures in some smaller shows:

> I think the UFC, the way the UFC does it. You gotta get … a CT scan every two years, before every fight you get HIV testing, hep testing, bloodwork, eye exams, full physical, and then, once that's all done, then you have your pre-fight physical. We get the doctors on sight, and then afterwards they check you out again. You do all that.... compared to all these other events, these smaller events, they don't make you do pre-fight physical right then and there, and some guys get away with fighting injured, when they shouldn't be fighting …

Just as injured fighters shouldn't be fighting, these exploitive MMA organizations should not be operating. Compromising any fighter's safety to make a buck is inexcusable, period. Contemplating the likelihood of a critical injury occurring in MMA, interviewee Terrance said, "I wonder what's gonna happen when somebody does get seriously hurt. It is bound to happen, and luckily it hasn't happened yet. What's it gonna do for the sport? It's already such a controversial sport …" Unfortunately, Terrance was unknowingly predicting a horrible tragedy. On November 30, 2007, MMA suffered its second death as a result of a competition, and its first in a sanctioned U.S. event. As reported on Sherdog.com (2007a), MMA competitor, Sam Vasquez, died approximately six weeks after a MMA match held on October 20, 2007 in Texas, in which he received a combination of strikes, including a right punch to the chin. The thirty-five year old Vasquez was survived by his wife and seven year old son. Reportedly while hospitalized in November, an acute clot formed in Vasquez's brain, and he suffered a major stroke before passing away at the end of the month. MMA promoters, fans, competitors, and the entire MMA community must ask themselves if "exciting" strikes to the head are worth such tragedies and how these misfortunes can be prevented in the future. Next, we turn to another safety issue in MMA and many other sports—illicit substance use.

Substance Use in Mixed Marital Arts—David Mayeda

Numerous MMA fans should be familiar with the acclaimed 2002 HBO documentary, *The Smashing Machine: The Life and Times of Extreme Fighter Mark Kerr.* In this documentary, former world class wrestler turned elite mixed martial artist, Mark Kerr, opens up and allows viewers into his life, including his past addiction to pain killers. The footage is graphic, as Kerr illustrates how acutely damaging drug addiction can be physically and emotionally. Kerr has since admitted that he also used performance-enhancing drugs (Malone, 2007). Of course drug use extends far beyond the MMA world. In recent years, substance use has become a hot topic in the world of sports, especially performance-enhancing drugs.

Controversy regarding performance-enhancing drugs has arisen in a variety of sports including the National Football League (Hosenball, 2005; Weisman, 2005), cycling (Wyatt, Austen, & Macur, 2007; Wyatt & Austen, 2007; Rhoden, 2006), track and field (Associated Press, 2007; Milton, 2007; Patrick, 2006; Patrick, 2004a), and of course in the sport which has garnered the most public attention, Major League Baseball (Araton, 2007; Saraceno, 2007; Llosa, Wertheim, & Epstein, 2007). Athletes have been known to use various types of illicit drugs for different reasons. Like non-athletes, athletes may use recreational drugs in order to relax or attain a high. Athletes may also become dependent upon pain killers, and in the most publicized cases, some athletes take performance enhancing drugs to improve their athletic chances (Worsnop, 1991).

In 2007, MMA was also under heavy scrutiny due to a fairly large number of athletes who were caught for using performance-enhancing and recreational drugs. In July 2007, the California State Athletic Commission (CSAC) released a report overviewing competitors caught for using steroids and other "drugs-of-abuse" violations, specific to MMA, boxing, and kickboxing for the period of March 31-July 6 (Gross, 2007b). The report listed twenty drug violations for mixed martial artists, five for boxers, and two for kickboxers. Of these twenty-seven violations, nine were for steroids, seventeen were for drugs-of-abuse (e.g., marijuana, cocaine), and one was for an adulterated test; an additional violation was given to a competitor who refused to take a post-fight test (Martin, 2007).

Things got worse for the MMA community's reputation just a few days later. At UFC 73 held on July 7, 2007, Sean Sherk successfully defended his Light-weight Championship against Hermes Franca. Twelve days later on July 19, it was announced that both of these high profile mixed martial artists allegedly tested positive for using performance-enhancing drugs. Franca admitted his guilt in a statement posted on MMAWeekly.com, saying he used steroids to hasten the healing of an ankle injury and that he could not prolong the fight with Sherk since competing in MMA is his sole source of income. Part of Franca's statement reads, "As a lightweight fighter, our purses are comparatively small. The public sees the payouts. As lightweights, we do not pull down the money anything near the bigger guys" (MMAWeekly.com, 2007a). Sherk allegedly tested positive for elevated levels of nandrolone (Gross, 2007c) but is in the process of appealing the results.

The controversy swirled around the MMA industry as a whole, not just the UFC. Other high profile mixed martial artists competing in different MMA organizations reportedly tested positive for steroid use around this time, including Phil Baroni (Cain, 2007b) and MMA legend Royce Gracie (Rossen, 2007a). But no doubt due to the UFC's prominence in the sport, UFC President Dana White commented on the drug issue to *ESPN The Magazine*:

> People think if you get caught in the UFC, nothing happens, but that's wrong. Your life is ruined. You disappear for a year and you don't make any money. And now we're going to make it even worse if you cheat. And I'm not just talking about steroids—drugs period. If you get caught with anything, you're f---ed. (Hockensmith, 2007).

In this same interview White stated in his normal uninhibited style that aside from the standard punishment, it would be inappropriate to further stigmatize those who are caught: "You want to drag these guys and their families into the center of town and stone them?"

We asked interviewees to express their thoughts on drug concerns in MMA. Given our methodological approach that includes revealing interviewees' identities, we did not ask those we interviewed if they were currently using any drugs or had in the past. One interviewee we spoke with did admit that he was currently on suspension for testing positive for marijuana. Nobody admitted to having used steroids or pain killers.

Part of the problem in MMA may stem from the residual effects of organizations never having substance use testing systems in the past. It was commonly expressed by interviewees that Pride FC never tested until they had a fight card in Nevada and that smaller shows in the United States still rarely test. Mark Kerr said in a recent interview with *Ultimate Grappling* magazine that prior to Zuffa, LLC's purchase of the UFC there was no drug testing. "… you can go all the way back to the UFC in '96 and '97 when I fought there. The UFC had no testing policies in place. So it wasn't just Pride (FC)" (Malone, 2007, p. 58).

Some interviewees said that they simply didn't know how extensive drug use was in the MMA industry, but sensed that it could be a concern. Jamie Yager, for example, said, "I haven't seen that being a problem in the community, but it is something that worries me, that people are looking for the cutting edge." Most other interviewees agreed with the latter part of Yager's statement—that the pursuit for the cutting edge via performance-enhancing drugs was a big problem. Savant Young held this perspective. Said Young:

> It is kind'a becoming more of a problem because you gotta understand this is fighting, so it's not like basketball where you gotta be skilled at making a jumpshot. You know, this is something where you gotta be bigger, stronger, faster, all in one…. I mean, so to each his own. If they gonna do it, they do it. They know all the repercussions of doing it. They know if they get caught doing it, they get suspended. Your license is gone.

As Young states, basketball is one of the few sports that has not seen steroid issues as of late, but due to mixed martial artists' need to have the physical qualities Young lists, steroids are a concern in MMA. Paul Halme added an interesting insight, stating that the problem was greater in smaller regional shows because there was no public or legal pressure for them to test at all. Referring to steroids Halme said, "Actually I think they're probably more prevalent, unfortunately, in the lower level things that aren't testing, so you can get away with it."

Most interviewees saw the prevalence of steroids in MMA as inevitable. Interviewees seemed to think that not only have steroids been a problem in the past due to a lack of testing, but also that as MMA becomes more mainstreamed with more opportunities for greater compensation, steroid use will simply follow the same path as other professional sports. Initially, Michael Frison felt that testing was starting to bring down steroid use: "I think it's becoming less of a problem than it was a couple of years ago because just before it hit mainstream, that was when people were using more steroids cause they weren't testing for it at that point." But upon further speculation, Frison stated that use of performance-enhancing drugs will take place more often as the financial rewards increase:

> I think, in any endeavor you do, the more it gets popular, and the more is at stake, the more people are gonna try to use drugs and find ways to get around drug testing, and all that's gonna be, it's part of the game.

Having witnessed what is happening with other professional sports, other interviewees essentially agreed with Frison, expressing a kind of fatalistic perspective on steroid use in MMA. Interviewees claimed that Human Growth Hormone (HGH) was fairly prevalent. HGH helps to prevent muscle tissue from breaking down after someone stops using steroids and also helps to prevent tendons and ligaments from tearing, but also can lead to diabetes, thickened skin, heart disease, impotence, and a shortened life (Worsnop, 1991). Another drug that appears to be prevalent among those recently caught in MMA is nandrolone, which increases growth of certain body tissues and the oxygen carrying ability of blood. According to the website Drugs.com (2007):

> Nandrolone may cause liver tumors or bloody cysts in the liver and spleen. If they occur, they will usually go away once you stop taking Nandrolone. However, you may not know that you have one of these tumors or cysts until severe, possibly life-threatening bleeding occurs in the abdomen.

We interviewed Dan Henderson (DH) in November 2006, before the UFC acquired Pride FC and before the highly publicized steroid controversy emerged. Proclaiming that steroid use is a widespread sporting problem and one that is easy to get away with, Henderson also speculated that at the time, people in the UFC could also be using steroids.

> DH: I think it's a problem in a lot of sports, not just MMA, but there's not really a whole lot of regulations on it. You know, the athletic commissions kind of test, but from what I understand, it's pretty easy to, I mean if you know when you're gonna be tested to not test positive.

> DM (David Mayeda): As the sport gets more popular in the U.S. and there's more money to be made, do you think steroids might become more of an issue?

DH: Well, probably. I think it's an issue now, I mean there's a lot of guys that fight in the UFC consistently that I would think are on steroids, but they seem to not test positive. Pride (FC) doesn't test in Japan, so that could be an issue as well. It would be nice if they did.

Guy Mezger was another MMA veteran who felt use of performance-enhancing drugs was a general sporting problem and that use of such artificial enhancers in MMA was more a reflection of this broader corrupt sporting culture. Again, exhibiting a fatalistic attitude that performance-enhancing drugs were an inevitable reality in sports, Mezger said:

> Let's put it this way. People talk about the Olympics—if you're a performance athlete in the Olympics. There are two kinds, there's the guys that take steroids, and they're the ones who get the medals. And the ones that don't take steroids, and they're the ones that get a handshake for being there. And that's it. They're just better at getting past the drug test, and that's just the way it is…. Now there are guys in the fight business that don't do it. Don't get me wrong. There are plenty of guys out there who don't do any drugs … but there are plenty of guys with much tougher schedules and stuff that do take it. So the problem that I see facing this is that it goes down from the prime athletes who do the drugs, to the kids doing the drugs. And that's my main complaint with the whole thing.

Mezger closes out with another concern, that in addition to the perceived inevitability of performance-enhancing drugs clouding the business, such realities further tarnish mixed martial artists' ability to role model positively for youth. And Mezger's concerns about athletes masking their drug use are completely valid. Professional athletes have been known to beat the system by halting their intake of drugs early enough so that it cannot be detected, attaining urine samples from others, and having their own chemists design performance-enhancers that are not noticeable in tests. Further complicating the picture, some performance-enhancing drugs are not tested for and/or are simply hard to detect, such as HGH and erythropoietin (more commonly known as "EPO"). EPO is used more by athletes who compete for long time periods, such as distance runners and cyclists, but the drug can lead to blood clotting and in turn strokes or heart attacks (Worsnop, 1991) Finally, MMA organizations (especially smaller ones) likely do not test because it can be expensive, costing between $500 and $1,000 per test (Jost, 2004).

As for the possible prevalence of performance-enhancing drugs in MMA, again, most interviewees could not ballpark a rate, but simply said it was a big problem. One person we interviewed, however, whose identity shall remain confidential, said that although pain killers are no longer as common, over 80 percent of all serious mixed martial artists have at least experimented with some kind of performance-enhancing drugs.

Marijuana was the other drug interviewees brought up as being prevalent in MMA, and the CSAC report substantiates those statements. But addictions to harder drugs were raised as well. Jason Bress described the vicious cycle some MMA competitors get caught up in, engaging in activities and an overall "rockstar" lifestyle that includes terribly detrimental hyper-masculine behaviors. This conversation began with me (DM) asking Bress (JB) about steroid use, but the conversation shifted to a number of related concerns:

> JB: With the regulations now, I see that dwindling down, but you know, there's still guys still doing ecstasy, and speed, and coke, and those are the main ones that I saw.
>
> DM: And is that more because of the lifestyle, the popularity …
>
> JB: Well, just being poor, you're just around drugs all your life, just growing up. And hopefully they haven't done it. And pot is another one. I see, it's funny, I see a lot of jiu-jitsu guys likin' pot…. I think it's better than drinking (alcohol), in my opinion. Um, but drugs are involved. I think the whole stripper thing is involved. It all just comes hand-in-hand, strippers, drugs, fighting.
>
> DM: Why is that?
>
> JB: I don't know. I think we're all drama. I see a lot of these, I'm not mentioning any big names, but a lot of these guys have been given $500,000 contracts, $400,000 contracts, whatever. They get married. They cheat on their wives. Their wives find out. They get a divorce, and they lose all their money. Then they have to fight again, and they have to keep doing that. They've done that three or four times. They don't learn, you know. It's like we're little kids, and we don't know how to grow up sometimes, you know. That's sad. That's really sad because they get their bodies beat up even more, their brains even smashed around…. And we keep trying to make it.

One of this book's objectives it to paint a more realistic portrait of mixed martial artists' lives by disrupting the deleterious stereotypes that plague them. At the same time, for a substantial portion of men in this industry (and other sporting industries), there is so little counseling and mentorship that would help mixed martial artists adjust and have the foresight to plan for their future lives so that they can remain healthy financially, physically, and emotionally throughout adulthood. Furthermore, Bress's observation that marijuana is more common among those who especially love jiu-jitsu was substantiated by other interviewees. Sheridan (2007) writes of the correlation between jiu-jitsu communities and marijuana use, "The weed smoking is another part of it. There is a whole contingent of jiu-jitsu players all over the world who self-medicate with THC" (p. 95).

Living in the moment, living like a rockstar is a lifestyle to which many young people are drawn. Since promoters and MMA organizations as a whole benefit from these athletes' performances and the training that goes into their performances, it is only fair that the organizations do a better job of providing education and mentorship on the issues presented above. Tynes (2006) suggests that in Major League Baseball, every player be tested randomly five times per year. Certainly in that sport there is adequate financial backing to carry out such procedures. If in fact the UFC was able to purchase Pride FC for $70 million, the organization must have enough resources to implement a more robust drug testing system. And again, it is not just the UFC. It is absolutely imperative that the other major MMA organizations and smaller organizations test as well, and not be exonerated from dismissing drug testing systems simply because a local community does not care.

Finally, drug testing systems should not be completely punitive. People make mistakes. Athletes are under tremendous amounts of public, personal, and financial pressure to succeed. By no means does this excuse them from using illicit substances (either performance-enhancing or recreational). However, the policies implemented in track and field are so egregiously punitive that they do not help athletes recover. Instead track and field's drug policies totally ban athletes for years from the primary area of their life from which they built their personal identity and income. Within MMA, punitive measures for illicit drug use must be balanced with counseling and structured support to help athletes' healthy movement back into competition and/or another occupational field. But the bottom line is, something needs to be done and done now. Bear St. Clair made the following comment on steroid use and its deleterious effects within the MMA industry:

> The idiots that are on steroids and everybody's just freaked out, you know, and just pounding each other. And they just can't accept defeat. They're never going to stop. They're getting their face bashed in. It's stupid.... Let it go. Fight another day. Have a career.

In other words, steroids may be prolonging MMA careers—violently tragic ones.

8

GENDER-BASED ATTITUDES IN THE MALE DOMINATED DOMAIN OF MIXED MARTIAL ARTS

BY DAVID MAYEDA

... the reason guys, kids fight, teenagers fight on the street most of the time is to prove themselves. They don't fight to survive. They fight to prove themselves, and if you train in the gym everyday, then you're confident. You don't have to prove yourself. I've never known a great fighter that had to tell you he was great fighter.... So you'll find that with greatness comes humility.—Chris "The Crippler" Leben

Ever seen the movie *Fight Club*? We're pretty sure most MMA fans have. If you haven't, *Fight Club* came out in 1999 and stars actors Brad Pitt and Edward Norton. The movie was based off of Chuck Palahniuk's 1997 novel, titled by the same name. *Fight Club* is far more than a simple action story. It is also a social commentary on men in the late 1990s and our ongoing, never ending gender identity crisis. Yes ladies, us men, we've got issues. To describe the novel briefly, *Fight Club* is about a man and his alter ego, Tyler Durden, who goes around recruiting average, everyday middle-class men to participate in underground fight clubs as a means of reclaiming a traditionally masculine group identity. Collectively, Durden wishes for his fight clubs to destroy the cultural consumer forces that have emasculated men in a terrorist movement he titles, "Project Mayhem."

As described by Boon (2003), Palahniuk's *Fight Club* reveals how contemporary white, middle-class men feel pressured by the cultural influences of feminism to relinquish their "old-school" masculine characteristics (e.g., being physically tough, violent, emotionally recluse, protectors of women). At the same time, men must fulfill more and more occupational roles that do not require physical prowess (e.g., computer technology, service-based jobs). Guys went through these same issues back in the early days of industrialization when we stopped working as "true men" in the farms and had to work in "wimpy" factories (Cahn, 1994). Today, serving as corporate drones, men are further emasculated by our occupational consumer culture, as we are no longer required to nurture the physical qualities that historically made men, "men." All the while, an alternative masculinity is not being suggested that would enable men to remain distinctly male.

As Palahniuk illustrates, us guys, we're at a crossroads when it comes to comprehending our gender identity, lacking the venues to prove our physical bravery and self-worth where we can embrace pain (Ta, 2006). Accompanying this gender-based confusion is the fact that violence is still celebrated in so many aspects of our society. For example, even if America's "War on Terror" is not heavily supported, larger portions of American society still support the troops who fight bravely overseas. Incessantly, blockbuster movies come out that honor a specific type of violence—that which is utilized to protect vulnerable individuals and nations—*Live Free or Die Hard*, *X-Men*, *The Bourne Ultimatum*, *300*.

But in our realistic day-to-day lives, social spaces are not available to fulfill this traditionally violent masculine identity. Such an identity may still be celebrated by the mainstream media, but being violent is simultaneously suppressed by progressive feminist movements. In fact, feminist literature strongly theorizes that the traditional male qualities of being tough, rugged, emotionally distant, and so on have been so inflexible that men are advised to burst free from our masculine prisons (Brooks, 2003). *Fight Club*, however, illustrates how many men actually feel imprisoned by feminist notions that "push" them into unfamiliar gender roles. Instead we will feel freed when we can go back to being "true men." "The rigid standards of traditional masculine behaviors are ironically liberating. They enable men to distinguish themselves, to exhibit valor, to prove their manhood, to salvage their birthright" (Boon, 2003, p. 272).

While *Fight Club* speaks to a gender identity crisis of contemporary middle- and upper-class men, a great deal of scholarly literature has examined how fighting also fulfills a gender identity for males in lower- and working-class communities, often times communities of color. Messerschmidt (1993; 1986) argues that work provides a key avenue through which men establish their gender identity as economic providers. Those of us, who feel careers via socially acceptable routes are unattainable due to the structural forces of classism and/or racism, may feel compelled to assert a "compensatory masculinity" (Pyke, 1996) through violent crime. In other words, by fighting, one can emphasize his physical masculinity, and if by engaging in crime one can acquire wealth, an occupational masculinity is also fulfilled. What *Fight Club* and the scholarly literature show is that heterosexual men from all economic levels tend to pursue a masculine ideal that Connell (1987) terms "hegemonic masculinity"—a public social status that "is characterized by heterosexuality, the subordination of women, authority, aggression, and technical knowledge" (Cavender, 1999, p. 159)—in essence, the complete "man's man." Depending on an individual male's personal circumstances, he will attempt to fulfill specific and often times multiple qualities within this hegemonic masculine ideal.

Like other physically violent sports, MMA provides a social space where predominantly male participants can fulfill this traditional, violent sense of masculinity (Messner, 1992). Previous chapters have highlighted the prominence of fathers and father figures in interviewees' lives, as well as whether or not the MMA community holds a social responsibility in addressing street violence. This chapter will further delve into mixed martial artists' perceptions of male gender identity and their relationships with MMA, specifically drawing attention to the reality that whether it be in crime-based scenarios, impromptu one-on-one fights, or underground fight clubs, too many boys and young men try to prove themselves through violence.

Masculinity in Mixed Martial Arts

Joshua Gilley loves jiu-jitsu and trains in Travis Lutter's gym down in Fort Worth, Texas. He considers himself a MMA hobbyist, has never competed in a professional MMA match and doesn't desire to do so. Why? Gilley told us in the midst of laughing, "I like my face, and I think I've got a really good nose, and I want to maintain my nose. I don't want it to look like Travis's nose." All kidding aside, by interviewing Gilley, we were able to speak with the only interviewee for this project who told us he participated in an actual underground fight club. He became part of this loosely regulated club in high school at age sixteen in Chicago, and continued to partake in it through about age twenty-two when he joined the marines. His involvement in this club stemmed from his participation in high school wrestling and conflicts that occurred between wrestling opponents from different schools. Gilley said, "… we had our own cliques in each high school, as far as our wrestling teams, and then we started settin' up stuff outside of wrestling, as far as turmoil's, having tournaments and stuff. And it went on from there." Gilley went on to explain that at first, the structured individual fights between members of different wrestling teams were serious, in the sense that the fighters were legitimately angry with one another: "Like [we] went to the parking lot to meet, and these two guys were gonna fight …"

Eventually, the staging of these fights that began from anger morphed into match-ups that were for fun. Those involved from different schools and different wrestling teams did not rival one another within their fight club. Instead, individuals were paired up to fight out of boredom and to promote excitement.

> … we kind'a got a little bit smarter about it, started holding it in more discreet locations, and kind of organizing it ourselves as far as, getting two guys and throwing 'em in a parking lot and having 'em duke it out. And we started looking at it as more as fun than when we originally did it out of anger…. As we grew out of high school, it started being more of like just something to do. So people would party Friday nights…. You know we set up underground fights on Saturday mornings and Sunday mornings.

The fight club that Gilley was involved in was not nearly as violent as the fight club depicted in Palahniuk's novel or the corresponding *Fight Club* movie. However, Gilley's stories illustrate the violent and risky behaviors that boys can organize when faced with little to do and an understanding of what is acceptable in our society for young men. Gilley said that nobody was paid or seriously hurt or injured in these fights, but we asked Gilley how he thought the growing popularity of MMA might affect these kinds of violent and dangerous activities among adolescent boys and young men today. He responded:

> I think that's something that needs to be paid attention to because kids tend to mock their surroundings, you know, whether it be video games, whether it be movies, whether it be music videos…. I think they need some kind of education as far as the responsibilities that come behind fighting, instead of just going out there recklessly, destroying somebody or trying to destroy somebody.

In fact, an article in *The Orange County Register* (Molina & Godines, 2007) titled, "Fight clubs flourishing: teenagers engaging in underground mixed martial arts raise injury, violence concerns" points out that boys in the southern California area are attempting to learn MMA on their own without any formal training or supervision. The article states, "… teenagers are taking the sport back underground by fighting in their back yards, garages and parks, say law enforcement personnel. And some have gotten injured. Last year … a boy was taken to the hospital with a head injury" (p. 1). This is a social concern the MMA community cannot ignore.

My own research (2005; 2001b) with adolescent males in Hawaii prompted one of the primary questions for this project that ended up leading to broader discussions of masculinity and gender in MMA. Gilley's previous involvement in a fight club reinforced our interest in the ways that boys and men utilize violence as a way to cure boredom and possibly build their masculinity. As so many other scholars (Phillips, 2007; Stoudt, 2006; Phillips, 2005; Messerschmidt, 2000; Mosher & Tompkins, 1998) who have conducted research with adolescent males have found, fighting is a very common activity that boys utilize to bolster a sense of machismo, even fighting with guns (Wilkinson, 2001). It is not terribly uncommon for young males to state that one way to become a man is showing others a willingness to fight, and that one's masculine image is frequently dependent upon the viewpoints of other males (Kimmel & Kaufman, 1994). With this in mind, we asked interviewees for this project what they would like to tell young males who held such attitudes, keeping in mind that they were males who trained to fight, fought professionally, and/or trained others to fight.

Jesse Juarez is a phenomenal wrestler and likely a future MMA star. He was an N.A.I.A. National Champion wrestler in college and recently won a regional MMA title. Early in our interview with the twenty-four year old Juarez, he discussed his childhood. "I had five older brothers, so I was always picked on, and I took it out on other people.... I mean every year in elementary school, I probably got suspended two or three times." Later in the interview, Juarez expanded on how his male gender development made it difficult for him to evade fighting in school and on the street when he was younger:

> There's no need to express yourself physically on another person ... I'm pretty sure your parents will teach you right from wrong, and it's hard because, you know, there's not a lot of good parents out there that [have] the time to teach their kids that.... And kids growing up, they always have to, males especially, "don't cry," you know, "hold it in, be a man about it." And society, you know, that's kind of how it is all over the U.S., so I would just let [kids] know ... you can always walk away, and I was always told to walk away, turn the cheek, but I never did, cause I wanted to prove I was tougher than the other person. It just all depends how you grew up.

Juarez expresses the difficulty that so many young males grapple with internally as they identify avenues to build their self-esteem, and further, how those internal struggles can end up being expressed physically on others. For Juarez, despite being told to walk away from fighting, the pressure of establishing a male toughness via physical fighting outweighed parental advice. And it's not as if Juarez's comments are out of the ordinary; I'm sure there's plenty of us guys who can identify with his comments. It was precisely this type of gendered pressure imposed on boys that we attempted to dissect with interviewees in this project, attaining their viewpoints as males and as mixed martial artists.

Other MMA competitors we interviewed overwhelmingly agreed with Juarez that young males needed to find healthier ways of expressing themselves and developing a sense of manhood. Nonetheless, various themes emerged that had slightly differing emphases. Quinton "Rampage" Jackson, for example was one of many interviewees who noted that in some scenarios and for many males, being able to fight in self-defense was important because fighting was inevitable in our society:

> Well, it's like this man, people been fightin' before this sport, and people still gonna be fightin' after this sport leaves. And you gotta learn how to defend yourself. That's the way I grew up, you know what I'm sayin'. I just make sure I tell kids choose your battles.… Don't fight for the wrong reasons. Just defend yourself.

Savant Young (who grew up in South Central Los Angeles, in a neighborhood similar to Jackson's) made a comparable statement, noting that people should fight only in self-defense, but also that for some males, fighting was inevitable. "Fight only if you have to. You know … you don't have to prove anything. But of course there's some kids out there and they're just born fighters, and they're gonna fight."

Finally, this "inevitability" of fighting was said by many interviewees to be related to environment, that in certain neighborhoods violence is simply more prevalent, and males commonly learned that fighting was both a normal and necessary way of life. Colin Oyama asserted this viewpoint, discussing "the way it is" in certain lower- and working-class Hawaii communities:

> I'm not saying it's right, or it's wrong.… It's a different way of life out there, whether you want to admit it or not. And those guys are gonna fight, and they're gonna be aggressive and tough. Because to survive in those neighborhoods you need those qualities or you're gonna get [run] over.

As these MMA practitioners stress, many males grow up with the perspective that fighting and violence is, if not the standard, at least commonplace enough that knowing how to adequately defend oneself is critical. Given these interviewees' profession, it is not particularly surprising to hear these opinions, and furthermore, it is not surprising that men with such perspectives would get involved in MMA later in their lives.

Other interviewees added to this topic by suggesting that traditionally violent masculine principles, while influenced by social environment, are highly misguided and can be countered constructively through the combat sports, including MMA. Dan Henderson, who hardly got into any fights as a youth, made the following point:

> Well, I mean obviously a lot of kids can't change their environment too much ... They can't move to a different area, and if that's the mentality of their environment, then go join a gym. But a lot of times it costs money to do that, so go join a wrestling team, you know, do something by nature to focus your energy in another area.... There's other avenues than just goin' out and beating up some little kid and just being the bully.

Still, most youth do not have the natural athletic ability of someone like Henderson, who wrestled in two Olympic Games and has held some of the most prestigious titles in MMA. Thus, athletics may not always be the best option for redirecting aggression, especially if coaches do not run programs in a way that builds multiple levels of self-esteem, beyond a central focus on winning. Robert Otani stated that that masculinity should never be defined in terms of violence and that masculine qualities should be aligned more with social responsibility:

> Be a man of your word. Be trustworthy. Be honest. Don't lie. I think that's being a man, not necessarily knowing how to scrap, and just because you know how to scrap doesn't mean you're a good person. You could be able to scrap and have five kids you don't take care of, and that ain't a man.

Otani's perspective was also expressed by Randy Couture:

> ... to be a real man, you stand up for what you believe in and you don't have to fight. And he knows when to turn and walk away and knows the consequences of his actions and doesn't need to go there unless his life's in danger and then it's a whole different situation.... And if this sport has done one thing, it's given me confidence to do a whole bunch of things that I never thought I'd be able to do. And I've never had to fight to do them.

Otani and Couture do highlight qualities often associated with traditional masculinity (e.g., being assertive and confident). However, these are qualities that can easily be considered positive irrespective of gender. In addition, despite being male practitioners in a violent sport, they strongly reject the cultural association of violence and masculinity.

When discussing a completely different topic, Travis Lutter also pointed out a humble view on masculinity that disrupts the typical view most people would have of mixed martial artists. After interviewer Stephen Mayeda asked Lutter if there was shame in tapping out (giving up) in a fight if one is caught in a submission hold, Lutter responded by saying:

> No, there's not.… Do I get beat in training? All the time. But if I'm not getting beat in training, then that means there's something wrong. It's like, is there any shame in losing? No … it's just my personal pride is the only thing that should be hurt. You know … it doesn't mean I'm not a man, or less of a man. That took a long time to realize though cause you put so much of your self worth into this.

Later in the interview, when asked if there's shame in crying, Lutter stated, "No, no, it's just an emotion that's coming across.… It's like me, I might not cry after a loss, but I may cry during a movie … Does that make me any less of a man? No." The diverse outlooks that many interviewees held on masculinity were far different from the stereotypical assumptions outsiders would likely hold of mixed martial artists.

In fact, a few participants interviewed even criticized us, noting that our question regarding adolescent males' propensity to build their gender identity through violence was problematic in itself. Antonio McKee (AM), who was highly conscious of social disparities and stereotypes pertinent to race and class, caught a bias in this research question, reminding us that male youth in general—not only those living in poverty—frequently utilize fighting as a means of achieving manhood, as seen in the exchange below with interviewer, David Mayeda (DM):

> DM: Most of my research is with adolescent males … and a lot of times guys will say, "For me to become a man, I gotta know how to scrap."

> AM: Well, again, you gotta look at the grounds and the mentality level of the question that you ask. You're asking a kid that's comin' up in poverty?

> DM: Yeah.

> AM: You're asking a kid that only knows how to fight, and only the strong survives. So when you ask a kid something like that, of course. Here's the catch part to it. Ask a rich kid, that's rebelling against mom and dad. They'll

give you the same answer. Now why? Is it really the way you're raised, the way you're brought up? Or is it really just a part of who you are? See, the rich kid who is brought up, he wants everything.

McKee accurately points out, as was discussed earlier in this chapter, a violent masculinity is hardly something endemic to lower-class communities, and such an association is discriminatory. McKee adds further that middle- and upper-class males who feel entitled may also view violence as a means of establishing self-esteem. As will be addressed later in this chapter, McKee brings his perspectives on youth violence into his gym with his kids' classes and non-profit organization.

Bear St. Clair also called us on this research question. He pointed out quite vividly that asserting masculinity is hardly something exclusive to young males, that males in general (regardless of age) aspire to attain multiple forms of power, and finally, that women can contribute to this traditional masculine ideal by desiring men with different types of power. St. Clair responded to our question in the following manner:

> You know what, I'm gonna take that entire statement and I'm gonna just completely pick it apart.... chuck it out the window, and I'm gonna tell you the truth. The truth is that it has nothing to do with adolescent boys, and that's actually completely structured by a bunch of people that want to be politically correct and that want to make fighting seem immature and dumb.... The reality is that everybody loves, or respects, or wants to at least be the baddest.... And all the women.... They wanna be with the one that has the most power and that's just the way it is.... And the truth is, is that it's not adolescent boys. It's everybody. Eighty year old men want to be able to kick everybody's ass in the room, because everybody wants to be the supreme alpha male, okay. And everybody's pissed off that they're not, in a way.... But tell all those people who were so nice before, come into a position of power, like maybe money.... They're gonna use it.

St. Clair reminded us that masculinity is not simply about physical violence. Hegemonic masculinity includes a variety of features that are power-based. Although it is inaccurate that "all" males seek to be the alpha male and that "all" women want to be with the most powerful men, St. Clair still raises an important point—although fighting is one way to declare masculinity, it is hardly the only way. Men in innumerable social circles attempt to acquire power over one another and over women through a wide variety of methods, of which fighting is merely one. And the perception (accurate or not) that women are drawn to this power further influences males to obtain the "alpha male" status, whether that be as the best fighter or the CEO of a major company.

Finally, almost all interviewees noted that by partaking in MMA, they were able to develop healthy relationships with other men, where violence could be practiced, but in a structured, safe, and fun environment. Over and over, interviewees stated that within their gyms, they developed some of the best friendships with their training partners, and that by practicing MMA with their friends, they were able to expel aggressive feelings. Chris Reilly, for example, pointed out the paradox that encapsulates male mixed martial artists, stating how "sweet" and "kind" so many of them are, despite holding a rage that he said was innate to men. Reilly stated, "… fighters tend to be very, very sweet people, again because … they are able to get rid of all that rage and angst that all of us men have.… they're great people to get to know and be around …"

Jason "MayheM" Miller added that his training partners are his closest friends and that the tight, physical nature of MMA practices allows training partners to enhance those friendships:

> … there's no boundary of personal space. Like you guys are wrestling. It's intimate, you know, without any sexual connotation. It's like the guys really love each other.… And that's one thing I like about the camaraderie of wrestling and fighting.… it's no big deal to grab your friend and put him in a headlock, and be like "Ha ha ha!" like a joke. My dad still does it now, and I'm twenty-five years old, and he'll still grab me in a headlock for no reason.

It should be highlighted that when Miller stated that intimacy was built "without any sexual connotation," his tone sounded as if he was merely making this clarification without any homophobic insinuations (although while in MMA gyms and around mixed martial artists in general, it was not uncommon for us to hear markers of homosexuality used jokingly to denigrate others). Returning to the issue at hand, athletes, both male and female, have frequently noted that their teams can serve as a second family. Here, Reilly and Miller speak to one of the theoretical points that Boon (2003) addresses in his analysis of *Fight Club*. MMA gyms provide a space where men can bond with other men in one of the most traditionally male activities—fighting. However, unlike the characters in *Fight Club*, Reilly suggests that through MMA participation, men can relinquish the anger and angst that men may hold (for whatever reasons), with Miller adding that the kinship developed among MMA training partners ultimately allows for healthy friendships.

In fact, I remember when interviewee Steven Saito was helping to prep me for my amateur MMA competition. After I took him down, we were rolling around furiously, and he eventually caught me in a triangle choke, forcing me to tap. Exhausted and sweating profusely, we got up to call it a night, laughing at my novice jiu-jitsu skills, or lack thereof. But it was true, the physical competition promoted a healthy friendship. Miller's observations are in line with prior ethnographic research on combat sports and male intimacy, which has found that male boxers who train together often develop extremely close, respectful, and nonviolent friendships in boxing gyms, as the gym provides a place for heterosexual men to bond without feeling threatened by emasculated influences. "The Gym is a 'safe' place to express intimacy because the textual representations of boxing as masculine and violent deter allegations of weakness or femininity" (de Garis, 2000, p. 97).

These perspectives notwithstanding, the scholarly literature argues male athletes more often have sexist attitudes and behaviors (Crosset, 2000; Benedict, 1997; Bass, 1996; Sabo, 1994) and are prone to engage in violent behaviors outside of sport (Messner, 2002). At the same time, other progressive scholarship has also reminded us that generalizations of male athletes as misogynistic and criminal can lead to racist stereotyping (Lapchick, 2000). Okay, so what do our interviews tell us about what it means to be a "MMA man?" Our conversations with MMA athletes show that within this highly masculine domain, there is promise to utilize the MMA phenomenon in socially constructive ways, where men can expand healthy relationships with each other. Additionally, the contributions interviewees provided in their discussions with us illustrate that male gender roles are hardly rigid, even in the violent world of MMA, and furthermore, that males (even those involved in MMA) are willing to talk openly about gender issues related to friendship, intimacy, crying, and adolescent safety. No, we're not kidding ourselves either. The MMA industry is just dripping with misogynistic visuals, which bluntly encourage that masculinity be built through the accumulation of muscles, aggression, and women. One only has to watch a few pre-fight interviews of MMA competitors before a fighter associates being a man with beating up his opponent. Unfortunately, the diverse viewpoints on manhood that exist among mixed martial artists are rarely spotlighted in the MMA media. In turn, young men and boys consume the only images they have available, and lose out on hearing the gendered messages that could uphold a more nonviolent society. Sam Sheridan (2007) writes that those who truly understand all that goes into fighting from a sporting standpoint "have left their egos behind, in the tough-guy sense. The pressure of proving masculinity has been removed" (p. 300). If in fact this is true—that mature, seasoned mixed martial artists respect their opponents, believe in sportsmanship, and are more interested in testing themselves than in beating down another human being, then let's see it where it needs to be seen and hear it where it needs to be heard.

Kids and Combat Sports

As the above section and other chapters exemplify, one of our primary interests is discerning how MMA's exploding popularity might affect violence in society at large, including youth violence. Would you want your children taking a class which taught them the most effective ways of fighting? I wonder how many dads just answered "yes." Well, if you want your kids to be able to choke out their classmates or drop them with a left hook, hey, you're in luck! Along with the growing popularity of MMA has come the growing number of MMA gyms that are sprouting, and in these gyms it is actually unusual if there are not classes offered specifically for kids and/or women. Sarcasm aside, we felt it was essential to talk with interviewees about the pros and cons of teaching youth various fighting disciplines. Interviewee Terrance also had a concern about how MMA's new-found popularity might impact youthful behavior, as he asked, "How is this sport gonna affect kids? They see this fighting and it's very glamorized obviously.... so I would like to see personally the fighters say things more against fighting outside of the gym." Although literature on this topic is scant, community activists have theorized that combat sports can teach children the proper values (e.g., respect, humility, responsibility) that will keep them from fighting outside of sport (Vorsino, 2006). But as this book has pointed out, MMA is the most complete fighting discipline. This coupled with MMA's immense popularity makes its appropriateness for youth a highly controversial issue, as also pointed out by Jason "MayheM" Miller: "I've thought about it a lot, cause like you know, man I love kids.... And I've thought about it a lot, like sellin' violence to the kids, you know. But man, kids are gonna imitate anything."

When we asked Travis Lutter how he felt about kids learning MMA he stated, "I'm not in favor of it at all. There's no reason for a kid to train MMA. You know, it's like, kids don't have the control. Granted, they don't hit very hard, but those gloves are really little." Lutter went on to explain that youth generally do not have the emotional maturity to safely learn all the aspects of MMA, especially when utilized in competition, where the social pressure—in particular pressure imposed by parents—is emotionally detrimental. Lutter, however, does teach classes for kids in his gym, but not focusing on the comprehensive MMA discipline. Rather, his classes for kids follow more of a traditional model in which only one discipline is taught, for example either wrestling or kickboxing, but not in combination.

Michael Frison had a slightly different viewpoint, stating that it was okay to teach children MMA but with the proper values integrated—those values that are naturally incorporated into traditional martial arts. Discussing the kids classes offered at the gym where Frison (MF) works, he stated:

> MF: We basically teach the kids MMA. We don't label it MMA. We just call it kids class. But basically we're teaching them Brazilian jiu-jitsu, wrestling, boxing, muay Thai.... They do the same things our adults do.
>
> DM (David Mayeda): And what are those values that you really promote? And how do you promote them?
>
> MF: With the children specifically?
>
> DM: Yeah.
>
> MF: Well, we have what we call a "Star Program." It's integrated into their belt ranking. So, they do things like, they have to do chores at home. They have to get good grades. They have to read a certain amount of books. If they don't, they don't get promoted. And one of the things is, a lot of the kids will do anything for the belt. And, plus just the attitude, every single day we talk about the class. We spend ten minutes of the class talking about what it is to be a martial artist. And not only what it is to be a martial artist when you're in here boxing and when you're competing, but also in your day-to-day life. You know, respect, respect for your elders. You know, just generally how to be a good person.

The discrepancy in viewpoint between Lutter and Frison was essentially representative of our interviews. Mixed martial artists we spoke with either stated that it was healthy for youth to learn specific combat sport disciplines separately (Lutter's stance), or MMA as a complete discipline (Frison's stance), but as stated in both cases, it was absolutely essential for kids classes to emphasize sportsmanship and the values taught in traditional martial arts classes, previously discussed in Chapter Six.

Mixed martial artists we spoke with discussed the benefits that youth could reap when taught combat sports properly. Paul Halme teaches kids classes in his jiu-jitsu gym. He stated that he tends to focus more on developing healthy leadership qualities among youth, and that when he sees or hears of positive change in one of his students, it's one of the more gratifying experiences for him:

... I get some kids who come in there, and I go, "Ah, I feel bad for this kid," and you know, six months later the kid's out there, just having fun and a lot more confident. The parents say the kid's doing better in school. It's really, really positive.

Halme's views are congruent with general sporting principals that claim sports build self-esteem, resiliency, positive peer relationships, and so on. Again, what makes MMA so tricky is that it is teaching the sport of fighting (or teaching one fighting discipline). Hence, whether minors are taught a specific combat sport or in full MMA form, it is critical that youth are encouraged to develop healthy social roles, conflict resolution/communication skills, and to understand the potential consequences of fighting off the mat. Said Chris Onzuka:

... especially the younger kids, the high school kids, [I] tell 'em, here, I have big expectations for you guys.... Even if I don't see it yet in the outside, I see it on the inside cause a lot of times guys just need encouragement. So why limit yourself getting a criminal record? You can work your way through college.... The way you act now is the way you act when you're gonna be an adult.

Unquestionably, when MMA instructors teach children, they hold a responsibility that goes beyond the typical sportsmanship clichés.

Given MMA's direct tie to fighting, promoters and instructors have an obligation to take the extra step and put forth structured messages for youth about not getting into fights, how to safely and realistically avoid fighting, and how they can emphasize other positive aspects of their lives that will further influence them not to fight. For example, research has shown that youth who have positive attachment to school (Wright & Fitzpatrick, 2006), positive peer groups (Ward et al., 2007; Smith et al., 2001), and consistent, positive relationships with adult family mentors (Blitstein et al., 2005; Aspy et al., 2004; Reese et al., 2000) are significantly less likely to get into fights. Consequently, MMA promoters and children's instructors in the combat sports have a heavy social obligation to *actively* encourage these types of values. Simply, getting the kids in class and off the streets for a few hours after school and on the weekends is not enough.

Antonio McKee expressed this added social obligation that MMA instructors have when working with kids. With regard strictly to combat sports training with youth, McKee said, "I let them know that hey, this is serious. This ain't no joke. You can hurt somebody." Still, McKee stressed giving back to impoverished communities and youth who need guidance through his non-profit organization, "Fight for Kids":

I get the kids that are problem kids. They love it. They just suck right to it. Why? Because I can relate to them. And by me being a mentor to them, because I can say, I been there. I've been in the streets.... I've fought all night long. That's stupid.... I have the non-profit program called Fight for Kids, and I go and I get these kids. I bring 'em into a new world. I take 'em to nice hotels. I take 'em to Disneyland and Sea World. A lot of 'em never left the hood.

McKee's philosophy involves a framework that goes well beyond typical athletic ideals. Instead, he pushes for youth to expand their understanding of community and social responsibility. Mike Onzuka pointed out an observation that ties in with McKee's points—that as jiu-jitsu instructors, he and his brother Chris often have more influence over youth than the youths' parents. Said Mike Onzuka:

… our emphasis is a little greater cause maybe the kids look up to us a lot more than they would their parents, [who] they see every single day.... So, with the little time we have, I think we have a greater impact, so I think we gotta use it to our best advantage and keep on emphasizing to these guys that, you know, look at the bigger picture. Be the bigger man and walk away.

These are the types of messages that need to be consistently built into MMA classes for kids (and adults) so that the classes are holistic in decreasing violent behavior. As McKee stresses, instructors need to be non-judgmental with youth, while also augmenting MMA instruction with "opportunities for personal development in terms of education, health, friendship, and employment" (Crabbe, 2000, p. 390). If structured in this manner, youth will learn to be more complete people, not just athletes. Research has shown that it is not athletic participation amongst males that leads to violent behaviors outside of sport, but the solitary "jock" mentality that leads to such negative behavior (Miller et al., 2006). In short, kids classes in the combat sports are especially obligated to stress developing a complete person (scholar, family member, and citizen), as opposed to just an athlete.

A final issue raised in our interviews regarding children was how youth from different socio-economic backgrounds receive MMA training. Jason Bress spoke extensively about this issue, as he has coached various combat sports in very different socio-economic communities. Bress stated that youth who live in upper-class communities often lack the discipline that they would normally get from their parents, who work too much but can afford to pawn their kids off on expensive jiu-jitsu and MMA schools (see also Chapter Six), but that in poor communities of color, youth cannot afford to take these classes. Again, Bress was referring to predominantly white, upper-class youth who take for granted their families' wealth and their families' access to what has become a fairly expensive MMA hobby. Bress went on to say that in other ethnic communities, namely different Asian American and Latino ones, that boxing is still a more popular combat sport youth are learning because it has a strong history, especially in Latino communities, and it is cheaper. Said Bress:

> … boxing will always be more dominant among Hispanics, you know kickboxing, Asians are gonna have more Tae Kwon Do. You know, they respect their stand up. So, there's, I think it (MMA) might come around in those areas, but it's gonna take a long time. You know, it's hard for them to afford! To afford jiu-jitsu, you know, these guys who teach jiu-jitsu want their, the average is $150—$200 a month. You know, it's hard for them to afford that …

Bress, who works in Southern California, was not alone in making this observation that MMA was becoming so trendy that it was not reaching youth from lower socio-economic groups who could use it as a prevention tool. Ku Lee felt the same phenomenon was happening in Hawaii. Said Lee, "… they're charging way too much now. All the kids, you know poor kids, are just fighting on the streets, while all the rich kids are fighting in high class gyms, being taught by high class fighters." Hence, in capitalizing off the increased popularity in MMA, gyms are charging rates that families in more economically distressed neighborhoods simply cannot afford.

Based on our interviews, we argue that teaching children MMA as a complete discipline is unnecessary and will not yield significant athletic benefits for youth in the future. Rather, MMA gyms should teach specific MMA disciplines (e.g., jiu-jitsu, wrestling, kickboxing) separately, allowing youth to develop those skills that will make them successful MMA practitioners later in their lives, should youth participants pursue that route. However, the full sport of MMA involves punches, kicks, and elbows to the head that definitely should not be allowed in youth sports. Youthful concussions in football and hockey are bad enough, and the chances of receiving such head trauma in MMA are not only unnecessary, but unusually risky. Teaching the proper range for strikes to the head is acceptable, as has always been allowed in traditional martial arts classes. However, allowing head strikes in youth practices and competition should not be allowed, even with full padding. And as Jason Bress and Ku Lee pointed out, there also absolutely needs to be instructional youth programs that are affordable so that youth from various demographic groups are not systematically excluded from participation.

We also asked if MMA should be incorporated as a high school sport, and with only a few exceptions, virtually all interviewees replied negatively. Quinton "Rampage" Jackson was most adamant in reflecting this viewpoint stating, "… it's still kind of like fighting. Wrestling is kind'a like fighting without punches, but MMA is fighting with punches.… it shouldn't be a high school sport at all. That's ridiculous." Other interviewees, such as Yoji Matsuo initially felt MMA might be an acceptable high school sport, but in mid-statement modified his stance, highlighting a need for major restrictions that would provide for increased safety:

> I think it would be ideal if they were to bring in MMA as a high school sport, you do it with the full gear on. Head gear, shin guards, you know gloves of course, cup. And probably no striking to the head when you're on the ground. Some restrictions so it's safe.

The types of rules and precautions Matsuo described typify amateur MMA competitions, for which both youth and adults may compete (though not against each other). Still, most interviewees felt MMA should not be integrated into high school athletics. As Bao Quach asserted, too many adolescents are simply not mature enough to safely compete in the full sport of MMA: "I don't think it would be too smart to put that in school.… People in high school are still young.… I don't think they're always smart enough to know … when enough is enough." As Quach and this chapter have underscored, young people cannot always negotiate how to responsibly separate physical power acquired in athletic venues from the street. Quach closed out his statement by saying, "some kid can probably kill some other kid on the street … you know." Amateur wrestling is certainly sufficient for high school athletics.

Attitudes on Women among Mixed Martial Arts

The final topic directly related to gender dynamics that surfaced in our interviews was the growing inclusion of female MMA competitors. To our knowledge, major MMA organizations like the UFC and IFL do not hold female MMA competitions, but female mixed martial artists are beginning to make inroads into the competitive and professional MMA world. Although we did not interview any female MMA competitors (a deliberate choice, as this may be a follow-up study), we did ask interviewees their perspectives on women's growing involvement. A few interviewees expressed viewpoints that reified stereotypical views on women—that crowds would like to see "cat fights" and that some women may be too emotional to compete in MMA. But generally speaking, women were encouraged to partake in MMA as long as they worked hard as athletes.

Jason "MayheM" Miller, for example stated that he would not want to watch women fight. "I'm just bein' honest you know.... maybe I'm just a misogynistic bastard, but I think that ya know, it doesn't interest me that much. Chicks beatin' on each other? Nah." Despite his admitted biases, Miller went on to make the following statement. "I have a good friend.... She's a freakin' Olympic-level wrestler. She's an awesome athlete.... I think it's awesome that she does [MMA]." Another interviewee who expressed gender differences relevant to his family was Savant Young. We asked interviewees if they would allow their children (or future children if they had them) to participate in MMA, both sons and daughters. Young said he very much wanted his son to get involved, but when I followed, "What about your daughter?", Young responded in his normal laughing and upbeat manner, "Um, nah, that's my little girl, and she's not gonna fight. Her little brother's gonna take care of her." But like Miller who noted a respect for work ethic regardless of sex, Young later stated of women's participation, "I'm all for it if they put in the hours like we put in the gym.... If they're not worried about getting cut ... looking like a fighter, hey, more power too them." Other MMA competitors we spoke with made similar statements, simply maintaining that if women had the athletic attributes and put in the work, they should be able to compete freely as mixed martial artists. Emanuel Newton stated, "I know some tough ass chicks that can beat the shit out of some guys ... if women want to get in there and throw down ... it's up to them ... I think women have just as much right as a man does." One the one hand, objectifying language was commonly used in reference to women (e.g., "chicks"). On the other hand, interviewees did not seem threatened at all by women's movement into the sport, although at this point, women still make up an extremely small proportion of professional MMA competitors, and therefore, would not appear to take over financial or status-based rewards.

Other areas in which interviewees noted that MMA training was useful for women were in terms of general fitness and self-defense. Tony Fryklund discussed how it was important for women to get back to their feet in a self-defense type situation, but then stated this was a critical point for anyone trying to defend themselves on the street:

> ... standup at all costs is great for women.... You don't want to be on your back. You want to be on your side. You want to get to your hip. You want to get up. These are the ways you do it. Same thing with police officers. Same

thing with children. Show 'em how to upkick. Show 'em how to do escapes from the bottom.

Fryklund's contribution here is interesting because although he immediately associated women in MMA with self-defense, he also saw self-defense via MMA training as important for people from other social groups (police officers, children) irrespective of gender. When we asked Yoji Matsuo about his opinions on women in MMA, he made a similar statement, first noting MMA training was beneficial for women as a self-defense option, but actually saw MMA's benefits on a variety of levels for both sexes:

> … it's good for women to know MMA for self-defense reasons. And I mean I think it's just a good sport to learn. It's a practical sport, and then the mental and the physical aspect of it, as I said before, that's good for anybody regardless of the sex.

In short, some interviewees we spoke with generally associated women's involvement in MMA with self-defense and fitness, but also held these beliefs to be true for males who wanted to train in MMA but not compete. And most interviewees expressed attitudes that women and girls would not be inhibited by physical weaknesses supposedly endemic to women, which historically were purported in order to make it difficult for women to progress in male dominated sports (Cahn, 1994).

A few interviewees offered additional insights that were important to women's involvement. Dan Henderson noted that the small number of women currently in MMA made it especially difficult for top-tier female competitors to find competitive training partners and attain professional competitions. Said Henderson, "… there are some women that are good fighters … there's just not that competition for them.… you get a woman that's over dominating, and she won't be able to get any fights, which has happened to a couple women that I know." Michael Frison (MF) stated that in the gym where he manages and teaches, a concerted effort is made to have men and women train together and to showcase this in all gym advertisements, as seen in the exchange below with David Mayeda (DM).

DM: Do you have women's classes specifically?

MF: No, no we don't, and that's one of the things we've done, is it's all integrated, and we do it on purpose because we think it's important. Even if you look at every one of our flyers, you know, they're (men and women) always together. And that's one of the things that we really try to promote, is men and women. And we try not to segregate and separate, and try to bring 'em together.... I think it gets away from that whole gender segregation, and that women need to have that special class, that they need to be taught differently than men, that you know, they don't want to have contact with men.... Why not? Why can't you wrestle around with a guy and work on techniques with a guy ...?

Frison brings up a very progressive perspective on gender dynamics that promotes gender equity within this MMA gym, noting that gender segregation ultimately stigmatizes women as "needing" a "special" class. Frison also stated that approximately 50 percent of the clientele at this gym were female, something we noticed when observing one of their jiu-jitsu classes.

The only potential problem that could emerge from such a perspective and policy is that the close physical nature of MMA (especially in wrestling and jiu-jitsu) could make some women feel uncomfortable when working out with men. Moreover, sexist men could covertly sexually harass women while working out with them in those particular combat sport disciplines. Thus, while the gym policies Frison brings up are absolutely progressive and empowering in theory, gyms should also provide "women's only" classes or at least have available female instructors or training partners in jiu-jitsu and wrestling classes. Randy Couture noted that women's participation in MMA is likely to continue and grow with the sport:

> I think that's gonna be the trend that's gonna continue to grow just like it has in boxing. I think girls are very dedicated and they take the sport very seriously, and women in so many avenues and in so many ways are striving for equal time and equal opportunity, so why not?

Women certainly do not garner a proportional level of attention or financial rewards in the combat sports, but as Couture notes, women's progress in boxing has slowly been increasing over the years. Considering that girls' wrestling is very popular at the high school level in some states, such as Hawaii, the MMA world should be prepared for a probable increase in women's involvement very soon.

This chapter has explored some of the ways that gender is conceptualized within the world of MMA by contemporary mixed martial artists. The conceptualizations are highly diverse and often times contradict what we would normally assume about men involved in such a violent industry. Nevertheless, MMA's violent nature cannot be denied, and it does appear to be a venue in which men can safely nurture male-male relationships without feeling that their heterosexual identity is questioned, threatened, or compromised. Knowing the ways that so many boys and young men associate their gender with violence, it is imperative that MMA organizations and gyms initiate efforts to dispute the notions that manliness is inherently associated with violent behaviors.

Additionally, although we did not investigate the topic of homophobia, it cannot be ignored in discussions on male violence. As noted in passing, it was not uncommon at all for us to overhear words like "fag," "gay," and "homo" used in MMA gyms to jokingly put down friends. Within multiple sporting circles, levels of homophobia and gay bashing can become extremely severe and contribute to a broader societal culture that accepts such discriminatory attitudes and behaviors (Pronger, 2000; Sabo, 1994). If in fact, mixed martial artists are completely secure in their masculinity, this type of discriminatory language should not even materialize. Further, MMA promoters and gym owners/manager should not tolerate such language or behavior.

Likewise, MMA organizations should not be promoting the cultural understanding that masculinity is related to violence. Although MMA organizations do not intentionally promote this cultural message, indirectly, the constant images of men competing against one another and the verbal sparring that often precedes such contests is dangerous and can surely impact male audiences to cement the association between manliness and violence. The MMA competitors interviewed for this project overwhelmingly expressed attitudes that refuted such gender-based stereotypes. However, these kinds of articulate and complex outlooks are not seen or heard by the largely male MMA audiences. It would behoove the MMA industry greatly to showcase such viewpoints, and more importantly, it is what is socially responsible. Again, the IFL has begun to take these measures, having public service announcements on their television shows that discourage street fighting, and also showing human interest stories on their athletes that offer a more complete viewpoint of their athletes' lives.

Still, it is so much more than merely saying, "Don't try this at home" or "Don't use MMA to make yourself a better street fighter." The fact that mixed martial artists in this study spoke freely, without any hesitation, about encouraging female athletes in the sport, about being able to show so-called feminine emotions, and about not bullying others, displays the rich potential MMA organizations hold in reforming our society for the better. It shows that there is potential for the MMA industry to *improve* male-female relationships, so that entitlement is based on work ethic with mutual levels of respect beyond aesthetics. It shows that young males can learn from MMA mentors that manhood is not linked to the inflexible understanding of manhood depicted in so many violent movies like *Fight Club*. But in the major promotional efforts of MMA industries, violence is highlighted to such a high degree, that these more socially important messages are virtually drowned out and forgotten all together. This gross imbalance can so easily be remedied.

9

RESPECTING AND LEARNING FROM BOXING

BY DAVID MAYEDA

I have to admit, I never really cared much for watching boxing. Like so many contemporary MMA fans, I thought boxing was a relatively boring sport. Visually, I just didn't think it was very appealing or exciting to watch two men punch each other with padded gloves, and I simply was not intrigued enough to learn the strategy involved in matches. Certainly, the few matches I caught on television never lived up to the hype embodied in movies like *Rocky*.

Despite my disregard for boxing, I was always a sports fan and felt as a young male that sports was the way to become popular and construct my social identity. Hence, I played football, ran track, and wrestled in high school. I was much better in wrestling and track than football, but wrestling was far and away my favorite. Like so many of the individuals we interviewed, I loved the one-on-one competition, and our wrestling team was very competitive. However, I decided to run track in college for two reasons. First, I always thought I had more potential as a sprinter. And secondly, at the time I thought wrestling was so physically demanding that I didn't want to experience the increased physical strain in college. I ended up loving track in college, and in hindsight I think I made the right decision.

Still, my heart had and still has a place for wrestling, and I always wondered if I would have improved in wrestling at the college level to the degree I did in track. I still get excited when I catch the N.C.A.A. National Championships for wrestling on television. Given my affinity for wrestling, boxing just never did it for me, and I'd frequently think with a little attitude towards boxers, "A world class wrestler would hammer that guy. How could he even defend a takedown?" However, as I grew older and reached graduate school, I began teaching courses in sports sociology. It was then that I came to learn the social significance that

193

boxing has not only in American sports history, but in American history as a whole. This is a history that MMA communities must also respect and never dismiss as trivial.

Boxing's Prominence in American Society

It is arguable that no other sport has had as much influence on American society as boxing. Like mixed martial arts, boxing was first stigmatized as ruthlessly barbaric, especially in the late nineteenth and early twentieth centuries, and went through the battles of reform to gain legal acceptance state-by-state. But it was not boxing's legal history that made it so significant. What makes boxing socially significant is that it evolved throughout time periods in American history when we as a nation were struggling so overtly with widespread racial injustices and inequities, and specific boxers emerged who came to symbolize the social movements of those times. Jeffrey Sammons's (1990) book, *Beyond the Ring: The Role of Boxing in American Society*, offers a masterful account of how boxers throughout the twentieth century impacted American culture.

Jack Johnson became the first African American Heavyweight Champion in 1908. After Johnson captured the Heavyweight Championship, white America went into an uproar demanding and hoping desperately that a white boxer would come along and defeat Johnson in hopes of proving African American men's assumed physical and intellectual inferiorities. Instead, the national Bureau of Investigation worked vigorously to knock Johnson down via legal procedures. Johnson's penchant for white women was the issue used to drag down Johnson, not surprising given that in those days, a black man's sexual relationship with a white woman was constructed as a crime worthy of lynching, even if the relationship was consensual. Hence, Johnson was "convicted of crossing state lines with his (white) mistress and of giving her money and presents" (Bederman, 1995, p. 4). For white men, such acts were not considered criminal, but Johnson was sentenced to one year in prison, fined $1,000, and ultimately pressured to leave the country, which he did for seven years.

As can be seen, Johnson's impact on American society was absolutely colossal. Considered the most hated man in American society, Johnson was characterized by racist white America as everything civil society should supposedly fear in black men—intellectually savvy, physically dangerous, and out to "taint" white women. Recall that in the first half of the twentieth century, America (especially the American South) was still adjusting to the abolition of slavery. The South was trying desperately to salvage the racialized structure that disempowered black communities for centuries, largely by criminalizing blacks. Of course if white men had sexual relations with black women (consensual or forced), nothing happened. Conversely, if a black man had consensual sex with a white woman, it was immediately construed as rape and justified a skyrocketing number of hideous lynchings of black men all the way up through the 1930s (Garland, 2005; Berry & Blassingame, 1982). Thus, Johnson's athletic success and flaunting of relationships with white women (even if they were primarily prostitutes), made him a political figure in American society that truly transcended sport. Johnson came to symbolize how thousands of black men dealt with the discriminatory politics of race and gender.

In the 1920s, the white Jack Dempsey reigned as the most influential boxing Heavyweight Champion, and controversy rose as to whether or not Dempsey actively refused to fight any black boxers, further exemplifying how boxing reflected the racial politics of his time. By the late 1920s, Max Schmeling came along, a German who was matched up against the African American Joe Louis in 1936. Schmeling was framed as being associated with Nazi Germany, whereas Louis was distinguished by the American press in ways opposite of Jack Johnson. Louis was inaccurately portrayed in the media as a "house slave," a quiet, patriotic black American. Schmeling defeated Louis, but shortly thereafter, Louis won the Heavyweight Title from James Braddock. Not surprisingly, black communities in the American North celebrated Louis's victory, while those in the South had to conceal their joy out of fear from white reprisals.

Then of course in the 1960s and '70s, Muhammad Ali burst into American households. The day after defeating Sonny Liston in 1964, Cassius Clay transformed into Muhammad Ali as part of the Nation of Islam. Shortly thereafter, boxing promoters tried frantically to identify African American boxers who were less politically defiant to knock Ali off his throne. But like Jack Johnson decades earlier, the American government did the dirty work, stripping Ali of his title in 1967 for draft evasion from the Vietnam War. Ali was also sentenced to five years in prison and a handed a $10,000 fine.

Considered by many as the greatest athlete in American history because of his athletic and political influence, Ali protested and was back in the ring by 1970. His future battles with Joe Frazier and George Foreman are legendary not so much for their athletic greatness, but for what Ali symbolized in terms of social justice outside of the ring, nationally and internationally. Ali criticized America on a national stage for its political contradictions, as America preached racial equality while perpetuating racial injustice both within and outside its national borders. Along with Jackie Robinson, Ali truly signified the Civil Rights Movement for black America. As Wiggins (1997) writes of Ali, conservative America was "infuriated by Ali because he exposed, for all the world to see, an America that was unwilling to honor it own precepts" (p. 215).

Over the decades, of course, there have been other athletes like those in boxing who shaped American culture and stood as symbols of the rising American minority, fighting strenuously for equality. In tennis, Althea Gibson, Arthur Ashe, Billie Jean King, and Martina Navratilova did a great deal to influence various civil rights movements. In track and field, the raised fists of John Carlos and Tommie Smith in the 1968 Olympic Games remain etched is so many of our minds, while about three decades earlier, Jesse Owens symbolized African Americans' ability to succeed in the face of Hitler and Nazi racism. In baseball, Hank Aaron represents someone who persevered through disgusting forms of racism, and of course Jackie Robinson stands as one of the great American figures who sparked the Civil Rights Movement.

Still, boxing is king is this arena where sports and American social movements mix. Certainly, the MMA world has its stars, including those competitors who a majority of fans love and those who fans love to hate. But it is unlikely there will ever be a mixed martial artist who fans despise so immensely like Jack Johnson due to his racial background and his unconcealed disliking for majority America. There will never be rivalries so deeply interwoven with racial politics that the fighters represent polarized segments of American society. And it is highly unlikely that there will ever be a mixed martial arts competitor, or any sportsperson for that matter, who can galvanize a national social movement like Muhammad Ali.

In today's day and age, where corporate sponsors often times have more influence than promoters, managers, and the athletes themselves, it is improbable that MMA competitors would give up potential dollars for the sake of a political cause. Thus, because of boxing's political history, it is unfortunate that such a rivalry has developed between MMA and boxing. Obviously, the rivalry has nothing to do with boxing's cultural influence in America. It has everything to do with which of the two combat sports is more exciting, safer, and popular among American fans. However, it is a shame that so many MMA promoters, commentators, and athletes simply dismiss boxing's relevance in our society at large.

In discussing MMA's possible overtaking of boxing, Jim Lampley—a long time boxing analyst and supporter—made the following comments on ESPN Radio:

> Boxing is a sport with a hundred-twenty year organized history. A huge institutional significance in the American sports scene. Boxing has produced

many, if not most of the critical sociopolitical heroes in the American sports landscape, and to suggest that MMA is somehow on the same level is completely specious in my view. (Cowherd, 2007).

In this regard, Lampley is unquestionably accurate, and it would behoove MMA promoters, competitors, and fans to recall that historically, boxing's influence surpassed the realm of sports, something MMA has yet to even initiate.

Where Mixed Martial Arts Can Learn from Boxing

Again, boxing and MMA pundits are still stuck throwing verbal jabs at one another in quibbles over which of the two combat sports is more exciting and dangerous. In a recent debate on ESPN (aired May 25, 2007), boxing promoter Lou DiBella said of MMA, "It's sort of like human cockfighting in my view, or pitbull fighting. Guys are elbowing each other to the heads. Guys are kneeing each other. They get into leg locks and start rolling around on the ground …" In another example, Stephen Acunto—a member of the New York State Athletic Commission and who has coached boxing—said similarly of MMA that it is not a sport and that MMA "… satiates the barbaric pleasure of people who like to see someone hurt … I think they would watch cockfighting, bullfighting, dog fighting and anything of that nature" (Siegel, 2007). Although MMA has become much more mainstreamed and accepted than it was in the mid-1990s, significant boxing advocates are still demeaning the sport in ways that remind us of Senator John McCain's comments made in years past. Conversely, as presented in Chapter Seven, MMA proponents criticize boxing as the far more dangerous sport.

Rather than engage in these diatribes, MMA communities should learn from boxing's mistakes and begin taking preventative measures to impede future tragedies. Because MMA is still in its sporting infancy, we do not know what the long term affects of the sport may have on competitors. In critiquing boxing, so many men we interviewed brought up Muhammad Ali as a tragic example of what can happen to boxers who do not know when to stop competing. However, Jason Bress argued that the adverse affects of boxing may not be much different from MMA and cautioned that we should look at the large numbers of boxers (both successful and unknown) who now live out their adulthood being punch drunk and poor because as young boxers, they were used to build up better boxers. Reminding us that historically, boxing has exploited poor ethnic minorities (Jable, 1994), Bress said:

> I see a lot of Mexican boxers where, they were thrown in at a young age, beat up, you know, especially one of my really good friends.… He works at a tire shop, you know, that's wrong. You know, makes no money. His head, he slurs. You know, he's a great, unbelievable, wonderful person—heart, soul everything, hard worker. And he has no money. He was thrown to the wolves. There was no money then. It's wrong.

Guy Mezger added the following comment, also referring to the tragic fallout of boxing's legacy in which so many of those who suffered from brain damage also turned to alcohol or other forms of substance use to cope with their problems: "… I think a lot of the athletes that suffer from pugilistic dementia are the old boxers. Almost inherently, almost every single one of them had a severe drinking problem or drug problem at the time." As so many interviewees in Chapter Seven stated, rising MMA organizations absolutely cannot fall into the boxing model that throws young fighters into the ring or cage to compete against established prospects, experienced journeymen, and champions. Using inexperienced young fighters or aged out journeymen to build up prospects is inexcusably unethical and exemplifies an industry's willingness to turn human beings into inanimate commodities for profit.

Like Bress, Antonio McKee noticed that the MMA industry is beginning to see racialized patterns emerge in which poor minorities are being exploited. McKee also noticed slightly larger numbers of poor Latino fighters now entering the MMA game, and McKee cautioned that historically, boxing has stood as an industry in which largely white audiences relished in watching African American and Latino boxers beat up on one another for entertainment.

> I don't think that black people are in a position right now to where it's gonna be obvious. I think you have a Latin market now. You know, and I might get in trouble for this stuff, but what is the greatest thing a white person would like to see? A nigga and a Mexican beatin' the shit out of each other. That's just the way it is.

Those who feel McKee's sentiments are outlandish or exaggerated should be careful to examine history. At the turn of the twentieth century, boxing was characterized racially as a black versus white sport. In the 1960s and '70s, boxing was symbolized by the black versus black prizefighters who represented different political camps. By the 1980s, boxing was characterized again racially but with a black versus Latino dimension (Early, 1995). Today, boxing and MMA are seeing a much more international influence, and pundits are predicting a greater surge in Latino fighters, specifically Mexicans, in the near future (Garcia, 2007). More importantly, as McKee went on to say, it is the minorities of color who more often tend to be poor and are drawn into MMA by the potential fame and lure of monetary wealth. Hence, cautions must be taken to insure young fighters of color and those in general who are poor that they are not misguided or exploited in their quests for fame and fortune.

The counterpoint to this argument may be that it is the fighters' responsibilities as individuals to plan for their futures and learn the risks involved in a MMA career. However, the MMA industry with its exploding popularity now sways many young fighters who grew up in poverty to aggressively shoot for the big financial payoff. And for a competitor in his early twenties who grew up with very little, a few thousand dollars for one fight may seem like a great deal of money. Some media sources (Siegel, 2007) and even some interviewees for this project claimed that MMA is becoming a middle-class sport because of costly gym fees, and in some ways this may be true. But like boxing, MMA is also acting as a magnet that attracts men living in poverty, exploiting their financial desires. Accentuating this concern, Antonio McKee made the following comments, questioning both the MMA industry and fans who sometimes perpetuate this exploitation:

> It's easier to take a man that has no dreams, and has no vision, it's very easy to throw him a pebble, and he thinks he's getting a lot. You know, cause he has nuthin'. So you know a lot of these guys that are fighters, a lot of these fighters, they come from such a poor, distressed upbringing to where there's a psychological issue in their fuckin' brain. I don't care how they want to cover it up. It takes a special person to get in a fuckin' cage and beat the shit out of somebody until there's a submission. There's no sport about that. That's sick. That's why society is now embracing it, because our society is becoming sick.

As a current MMA trainer, gym owner, and active competitor, McKee reconciles his concerns with his approach to the MMA industry, addressed previously in Chapter Eight. McKee feels there needs to be significantly more media literacy, parental monitoring of youth who watch MMA, and ethical approaches to coaching MMA with youth and young adults. Moreover, it is clear young fighters need better education so they truly know what they are getting into.

But it is not only about protecting young fighters who have fewer occupational opportunities and who are seduced by the unlikely chances of a lucrative MMA career. It is also about protecting older, poor fighters who should no longer be competing and preventing such scenarios from occurring again. Jason Bress and Guy Mezger both noted that they had successfully aged out of competing and are probably healthy, but that they still get the itch to compete. In regard to getting offers to compete Mezger told us, "… every couple of months I'll get somebody offering me a fight, and the last fight was a significant amount of money.… the problem is you never want it to be over. You want it to go on forever." Mezger then explained that as a gym owner and trainer, he is no longer reliant on fighting for supplemental income: "I was Superman for a real long time, and I'm pretty much happy being Clark Kent. I have a beautiful family. I have a beautiful life." Unfortunately, Mezger's retirement from MMA competition does not typify the lives of all older MMA competitors.

Bress spoke in reference to one of his close friends who used to be a main event level mixed martial artist. Today, his friend is too old to successfully compete and adequately protect himself, but because he is in financial need, he continues to fight in MMA cards:

> Promoters put him out there to fight. He should not be fighting any more. He should *not!* But [promoters are] lettin' all these younger kids now beat him up, because he brings in the money. And he doesn't know, and he's too broke not to fight.

Is this the legacy that the MMA community wants to see twenty years from now, with hundreds of MMA athletes trying desperately to hang on, sacrificing their bodies and minds to bring in meager paychecks because they made such little money during their youthful careers and did not plan for their futures? Given these concerns and those raised in other chapters of this book, there are a number of measures MMA promoters and organizations can begin implementing. The recommendations provided below are based off of interviews conducted for this book, as well as from Newton's (2001) "A Bill of Rights for Boxers" (p. 20–21).

Suggestions for Mixed Martial Arts Reform

A. Further Injury-based Research and Active Education

In reviewing the literature for this book, we were only able to identify one research project that documented injuries sustained by MMA competitors through medical reports (Bledsoe et al., 2006). This is understandable given that the sport is so young. The UFC has pushed for legislation in various states. They have not attempted to avert it. Likewise, the UFC and all other MMA organizations (big and small) should push for research that meticulously records any time a competitor sees a medical professional due to sustaining an injury in competition. In addition to recording the injury(ies), documentation of competitors' cognitive states (e.g., feeling groggy from a possible concussion), cause of the injury (e.g., due to punch, kick, submission hold, or combination of such), suggested treatment procedures, and follow-up results should all be recorded. These data can be used to systematically identify causal patterns of injuries and in turn make educated decisions on reform over time. Furthermore, such data can be used for "active education," meaning results of such research can be used to inform aspiring mixed martial artists of the possible dangers within MMA. These data can also be used to educate parents of adolescents and children who wish to train in combat sports since injuries occur in both training and competition and are usually underreported (Tommasone & McLeod, 2006, p. 471). Bottom line, if MMA truly is as safe as so many of its participants and advocates say, the injury data will convey their conjectures.

B. *Education on Financial Realities*

Numerous interviewees we spoke with pointed out that although it appears life as a professional mixed martial artist will be lucrative, the reality is very different for most MMA hopefuls. Even well known competitors in some of the major organizations make far less than $10,000 per fight. Keith Jardine recently defeated Chuck Liddell in a main event match on a major UFC pay-per-view fight card, and for his win he only earned $14,000 (Pishna, 2007b). Yet mixed martial artists must also pay for dietary supplements, training equipment, licensing fees, possible medical treatment, possible training fees, not to mention everyday life expenses. It is questionable as to whether or not their purses, sponsors, and possible jobs as athletic trainers can truly cover all these expenses and allow for most MMA athletes to build a savings. Essentially, mixed martial artists need to be thinking about their long term futures. How much will one's purse truly help a competitor if he is not single and has a family to care for? Additionally, there needs to be a pension plan for MMA competitors. Frank Trigg was not the only athlete we interviewed who made this suggestion. Jason Bress also felt a retirement plan was essential for mixed martial artists:

> There's nothing to retire with. None of these guys, and that's bullshit. Football has it, every other sport has it. MMA doesn't have it yet. Boxing just started getting it, you know. That's not right. We train too hard. We make too much money for these people. We need to be taken care of.

While not speaking as passionately as Bress, other interviewees expressed concerns with the small purses they are offered for competitions. Jesse Juarez said, "I don't think really they're looking out for our best interests. Everybody's out there to make money. Just like us. I don't want to fight for $500, or $1,000." But many up-and-coming mixed martial artists are. Paul Halme said of novice mixed martial artists in Texas, "Yeah, they're traveling all over the place to fight for $500 to $2,000." Jason Miller added, "There's a million other guys who are willing to fight for minimum wage, you know $2.00 and a taco all day long. You know, I can't do that. I been busting my ass too long." Moreover, there needs to be a stronger focus on short and long term financial security. Frank Trigg brought up issues young adults with families should always be aware of but too frequently are not. Speaking about the extremely high cost of living in Hawaii, Trigg said:

> Look at Hawaii. Hawaii is a perfect example. The cost of living is so high and the housing prices are off the chart. Families are a few bad weeks and few car payments away from losing their house. And it's getting worse.

It is critical that young mixed martial artists (and young adults in general) are thinking on these financial levels, as they are all a few bad fights and injuries away from no longer being able to compete. Newfield (2001) proposes the following pension system for boxers: "Any boxer who has been active for four years, or has had twenty bouts, should qualify for the system. But nobody who has taken a lot of beatings should be allowed to keep boxing just to qualify" (p. 21). Although a pension system would be difficult to establish because MMA athletes often jump from organization to organization in search of fights, a similar system needs to be set up for mixed martial artists, at least in the major organizations. All aspiring mixed martial artists—but especially those who come from impoverished backgrounds and feel MMA is their pathway to financial wealth—need to be shown meticulously and bluntly how few mixed martial artists actually secure financial prosperity that will last them past their athletic prime. Not even the biggest MMA stars have salaries commensurate with average athletes in Major League Baseball, the National Basketball Association, or the National Football League.

C. Systemic Plans for Educational Advancement

As Guy Mezger pointed out, fewer mixed martial artists in the future will begin their MMA careers with college degrees. More and more MMA hopefuls will learn their wrestling skills along with the other combat sports in MMA gyms, not collegiate wrestling programs. Of course although it helps, one does not need a college education to be successful in life, and the value placed on educational advancement varies by culture and context. Still, mixed martial artists need to be realistic about their chances of making MMA a lifelong career. They need to be developing a wider range of employable skills outside of the MMA world should their careers end prematurely for any number of reasons. After I asked Chris Reilly if most mixed martial artists are learning the necessary business skills to excel in our economy after their athletic careers are over he stated:

> What skills? No! Very few of them are, very, very few. You know, I think there are some realities, such as being a fighter is a full time job. And if you really want to compete at the top level, you don't have a lot of time to be doing other stuff. I think that it's a difficult situation in that athletic careers are short, and athletes do have a significant period of life after their competition that they're often times not well prepared for.

True, professional sports generally do not have educational advancement plans built into their organizations. However, many other professional sports draw their athletes from collegiate programs, so many of their athletes come in with at least some college education (which unfortunately, not all college athletes take seriously). Providing incentives for MMA athletes who only have high school degrees to advance their education (either in traditional universities or trade schools) is the right thing to do.

D. Mandatory Medical Insurance and Increased Health Standards

Most MMA organizations, including smaller ones, were said to provide medical insurance for competitors, which would cover any medical treatment necessary that came as a result of injuries sustained while in competition. However, numerous interviewees we spoke with said they knew of instances where promoters did not provide medical insurance of any kind. This was not said to be the norm, but it definitely happens. Flat out, this cannot happen at all. Medical insurance must always be provided to all MMA competitors, irrespective of how big or small the organization is that puts on the fight card. And of equal importance, because MMA fighters more often sustain injuries while training for their competitions, MMA organizations should provide health insurance for athletes as soon as they are under contract for a competition. Most MMA fighters do not earn enormous purses that enable them to pay for health insurance in their daily lives. Furthermore, all organizations must have fully qualified doctors present at ringside, who are competent and not simply there because they are MMA fans or friends of the promoters. Thorough pre- and post-fight examinations of fighters must also take place, which pay special attention to head injuries. The recent death of Sam Vasquez only underscores this latter concern. Although all details of Vasquez's death were not made known, including his pre-fight health (Sherdog.com, 2007a), it appears Vasquez could very well have died due to head trauma sustained during his October 2007 MMA match. At thirty-five years old, Vasquez was not a young MMA competitor. Bledsoe and colleagues (2006) found that MMA injuries increase with fighters' age. MMA promoters, matchmakers, fighters, trainers, and fans need to know which risk factors increase the probability of injury and account for those risk factors when considering matches. If preventing deaths and future rates of pugilistic dementia means banning various head strikes, then the MMA community needs to seriously consider that option.

E. Consistently Enforced Drug Testing and Education

Obviously steroids and illicit drug use are a sporting problem, not just a MMA problem. However, this does not exonerate MMA organizations and competitors from taking the proper steps to quell the problem. Some states test for drugs; some do not. Some countries mandate drug testing; others do not. Regardless, all MMA organizations should test for performance-enhancing and illicit drugs wherever they hold their fight cards. And more than just those athletes competing in championship fights should be tested. Punishments for those caught using performance-enhancing drugs do not need to be so harsh that athletes cannot make a comeback. For example, the punishments for using performance-enhancing drugs in track and field essentially end an athlete's career, as athletes can be banned for numerous years (Patrick, 2004b) or even life (Jost, 2004). Whereas, we have seen athletes in other sports such as Major League Baseball receive virtually no punishment, so there needs to be a reasonable medium. Moreover, more effective testing needs to take place for the variety of performance-enhancing drugs available, including Human Growth Hormone. Perhaps more importantly in terms of prevention, more education is obviously needed that will warn MMA competitors and young fans about the short and long term negative health hazards of using performance-enhancing drugs and other illicit substances (e.g., marijuana, ecstasy, cocaine).

F. Reformed Media Guidelines and Regulations

There is absolutely no reason that in pre-fight interviews (or any interview for that matter) a MMA competitor should say something analogous to, "I'm gonna beat his ass and make him my bitch," or "I'm gonna be the man, cut him up, and send his ass home." This type of language that correlates manhood with violence and demeans women perpetuates deleterious cultural norms. Would an owner of a National Football League or National Basketball Association team allow his/her athletes to make such public statements? There has recently been movement within the hip hop music industry to clean up misogynistic language. The same effort can and should be made in MMA. Because MMA is the scientific sport of fighting, it needs to be held to a higher standard than other sports in terms of negating societal violence. The above types of verbal messages convey the idea that it is not just acceptable, but that it is good to build one's masculinity through the violent and harmful overtaking of another. Within MMA organizations, boards should be established to discipline individuals who make such comments publicly with warnings and subsequently with fines. Board members should come from within MMA organizations and from violence-prevention associations outside of the MMA industry, including those associations that prevent violence against women.

In addition to this, MMA organizations need to begin following the IFL's lead, which has started making public service announcements that promote nonviolence. The IFL also produces diverse human interest stories on its athletes that show a completely different side of the athletes outside of the ring. In speaking with the mixed martial artists for this project, we learned how incredibly nice, open, and gentle many of them are outside of the sporting context. And even when in competition, there is not intent to injure one's opponent. More public service announcements and human interest pieces (not just those that show training regiments) must be made to showcase the true side of many of these mixed martial artists that is erased in the violent hype that sells pay-per-views. There also needs to be media outreach to fathers and older males that encourage more positive, nonviolent socialization of sons and daughters. Media pieces can encourage fathers, uncles, older brothers and so on to take their younger family members (whether they are boys and/or girls) to responsible MMA gyms for training, rather than "toughening up" their children through violent measures. No, these types of media pieces and messages may not be sexy, and yes, violence is what sells in America. But that is precisely the problem. The mixed martial arts community has so much potential to communicate healthier messages to its largely male audiences. Why not tap into that potential? Dollars are not more important than social responsibility.

G. Regulation and Monitoring of MMA Gyms

As so many interviewees noted, MMA gyms hold a vital responsibility in espousing the values that promote nonviolence. Not just in kids' classes, but in all classes, there must be formal, structured dialogue that explains why MMA training perpetuates nonviolence in society at large. For adults, this may only be necessary when a newcomer begins taking classes, and if it becomes known that an adult student is using MMA techniques in fights outside of the gym. But for youth (including children and adolescents) this means providing ongoing messages and activities that push for pro-social development (e.g., academic tutoring, having older mixed martial artists talk extensively about not using drugs and being able to walk away from fights with dignity, holding family-bonding activities and events). It is not enough for gym owners and coaches to simply tell youthful students, "Don't use drugs; don't get into fights." There must be more creative and structured lessons over time that lead to youths' positive development as responsible citizens. Gyms must also have affordable outreach programs for youth who live in lower-income communities that lack resources and carry out service projects for those communities (MMAWeekly.com, 2007b).

Finally, there needs to be better certification processes for gym owners and instructors, insuring communities that those teaching MMA are doing so in a qualified, responsible manner. MMA trainers (and MMA organizations as a whole) must be educated on injury recognition. "The most important prevention strategy is providing effective education to the athlete, as well as the coach and trainer regarding the importance of recognizing concussion and seeking appropriate and timely medical attention" (Patel, Shivdasani, & Baker, 2005, p. 681). Contrary to popular belief, a concussion is not a swelling or bruise of the brain. McKinley (2000) offers the following definition and indicators of a concussion:

> The injury generally occurs when the head either accelerates rapidly and then is stopped, or is spun rapidly. This violent shaking causes the brain cells to become depolarized and fire all their neurotransmitters at once in an unhealthy cascade, flooding the brain with chemicals and deadening certain receptors linked to learning and memory. The results often include confusion, blurred vision, memory loss, nausea and, sometimes, unconsciousness. (p. D1).

Other indicators of concussions are irritability, mood swings, balance problems, sensitivity to light, headaches, and inability to concentrate (Essoyan, 2007; Schwarz, 2007c). McKinley (2000) also notes that "after several concussions, it takes less of a blow to cause the injury and requires more time to recover" (p. D1). Again, concussions are extremely serious injuries, and their seriousness is grossly minimized in athletics. This is a tragic, grave mistake because the effects of concussions may not manifest for decades, after an athlete is no longer of value to a sporting organization. In other words, exploit the athlete now; discard him or her later. As mentioned before, a study of NFL retirees (average age of fifty-four) found that among players with no concussions, 6.6% reported depression. For those who had one or two concussions, 9.7% reported depression. And among those who had three or more concussions, the rate jumped to 20.2% (Schwarz, 2007f, p. A1)! Moreover, the earlier in childhood or adolescence one sustains a concussion, the worse its effects since children's and teenagers' brain tissue is less developed than adults' (Schwarz, 2007c). Recall that in MMA there is little shame in tapping out when caught in a submission hold. This cultural trait absolutely must be translated to signs of concussions as well, in MMA and other sports. If a MMA athlete receives a blow to the head and shows even the slightest signs of a concussion, the match should be stopped immediately, irrespective of the athlete's wishes. Trainers, coaches, doctors, fans, other athletes, and promoters must help to enforce this and shift the cultural trend which associates playing through concussions with valor to one that associates concussions with a serious possibility of lifelong depression.

H. Organized Labor Union

Again, because mixed martial artists are independent contractors and frequently switch competing in different organizations, it would be difficult to establish a unified labor union. Still, some kind of collective voice comprised of MMA athletes that speaks on their behalf should be institutionalized. Among other things, union representatives could "demand a higher minimum payment for preliminary fighters" (Newfield, 2001, p. 21), push for unified and safer rule changes, and advocate for increased health benefits and pension plans. Simply because mixed martial artists compete against each other is not an excuse that should impede a union's development. Players in the National Football League compete against each other in a violent, collision sport, and they have an effective union.

Building off point B (Education on Financial Realities), Chris Leben made some preliminary suggestions for a MMA fighters' union. After I asked Leben,

"Do you feel like fighters are getting enough education in terms of building a savings, financial planning, that kind of thing? That's a problem in all sports," he responded by saying:

> Well, being such a young sport, you know, like the NFL has pensions and all kinds of investment opportunities presented to 'em right away. Right now for us there's none of that, so the answer would be there's zero, so no. I'm all for a fighters' union…. it would have to start with a nationally-wide, sanctioned body, instead of every state having their own sanctioned body. Having one sanctioned body, and then depending on what level you're fighting at and how much money you're getting paid, there's certain percentages that go to your pension, goes to the commission and everything else.

It is essential that mixed martial artists begin a dialogue on this topic so that they can institutionalize a union right away, which could then report to a national commission. As Randy Couture mentioned in his 2007 post-resignation press conference, it will take a marquee MMA star to step up, get mixed martial artists galvanized, and begin a fighters' union (Sherdog.com, 2007b).

I. Development of a National Commission

There needs to be a national MMA commission that can enforce the above recommendations. For example, if a fight card is held in which MMA competitors are not covered by insurance, that organization should be heavily fined, even if no competitor is injured. A national commission could help standardize rules, drug testing procedures, and other precautionary medical procedures. Naturally, creating a national commission will be difficult since current MMA organizations are in competition with one another. However, perhaps a cooperative commission could be developed with representatives from some of the major organizations, medical professionals, MMA athletes and other sporting experts that would help foster ongoing improvement for the sport.

10

FIGHTING FOR ACCEPTANCE

BY DAVID MAYEDA

… there are still some ignorant people out there. Some people look at (MMA) negatively. They think of us as brutes going into the cage. I want everyone to understand what we do and that it's a sport to us. I fight hard, I'm friends with all the fighters afterwards and I want to have good relationships with those guys afterwards.—The late Jeremy Williams, former MMA athlete with the IFL (Jeffrey & Franck, 2007, p. 107).

To this day I have never had a puff of a cigarette or a hit of marijuana. I did hold an ecstasy tab once, and although I didn't really have an urge to take it, I remember thinking how easy it would be for someone who was just a tad more tempted to pop it in his or her mouth. I suppose you could say that was the closest I ever came to taking a hard drug. I didn't even drink my first beer until about six months after my twenty-first birthday, and I can probably count on my hands the number of times I've been sloppy drunk. When I tell people this, they usually say sarcastically, "Yeah right, whatever!" Their disbelief doesn't bother me too much. But I have to admit, if they find out I was a college athlete and consequently feel even more adamantly that I must have used drugs or got wildly drunk in my college days, I get a little more irked. So just because I was a college athlete, I was supposed to be some uncontrolled party animal? I can only imagine what the assumptions would be had I been able to play college football.

Yes, there are a lot of problems that surface from the sports world. We have already covered many of them in previous chapters. Conversely, athletes also endure unfair labeling. A study conducted by Simons and colleagues (2007) found that university faculty and students often look upon student-athletes from virtually all sports and both genders as "dumb jocks." In addition to collecting survey data, this study reported interview findings. One African American female basketball player said, "(The) Professor asked the student athletes to stand on the first day of class and said, 'These are the people who will probably drop this class.'" A white male swimmer was quoted as saying, "In a big, class (400 people). Before test professor said, 'It's an easy test. Even athletes can pass.'" (p. 251). Prior research confirms that university faculty tend to stereotype athletes as academically inferior, including those athletes participating in non-revenue producing sports (e.g., swimming, track and field, water polo; Baucom & Lantz, 2001).

Thus in this chapter, we examine issues pertinent to MMA from a different angle, documenting the ways that mixed martial artists feel classified in society as men with no depth, intelligence, or emotion—unless that emotion is anger. Likewise in this chapter, interviewees discuss how they struggle to gain respect as legitimate athletes, rather than be tagged as undisciplined barroom brawlers.

Mixed Martial Arts as a Legitimate Sport, in its Infancy

It is important to remember that although predecessors like Bruce Lee practiced and experimented with MMA many years ago, MMA was not institutionalized in the United States until 1993. Therefore, it has only been in existence at a formal level for fourteen years. During this short time span (especially in the mid-1990s), there have been big, nasty, barroom brawlers step into the octagon and find success. Tank Abbott epitomizes this genre of fighters who did not train in the MMA as mixed martial artists do today, but still gained widespread notoriety. Regrettably, Abbott also stands as the image many critics point to when demeaning contemporary mixed martial artists, arguing that they are little more than undisciplined and poorly conditioned street fighters.

This is a bit odd given that MMA has seen numerous world class athletes from traditional sports compete in the cage or ring over the years. As noted, we were fortunate to interview some of these athletes—Dan Henderson, Randy Couture, and Frank Trigg, all of whom wrestled at a world class level, with Henderson making two Olympic teams. In addition, current MMA star Matt Lindland was an Olympic silver medalist in wrestling and former MMA competitor Kevin Jackson won wrestling Olympic gold. One would think that with those types of credentials from a more accepted sport, there would be more respect in defining MMA as a legitimate sport, in particular because the afore mentioned athletes do not win all their MMA matches.

But it is not just wrestling. World class practitioners in Tae Kwon Do, boxing, kickboxing, judo, and jiu-jitsu have transitioned to make careers in MMA, some successful, some not. Part of the problem is that outside of boxing, these sports have never been terribly popular in the United States. Recently, former NFL wide receiver Johnnie Morton made his MMA debut, unfortunately for him, not in the most auspicious manner. In any case, the issue is not necessarily the lack of high profile athletes moving into MMA. The more critical issue is the visualized violence that remains etched in people's minds, stemming largely from the early days of the UFC when rules were fewer and at which time many competitors did not know how to defend themselves from an opponent who was proficient in an unfamiliar fighting discipline, thereby leaving themselves open to be victims of unmitigated blows and/or submission holds. Again, the early days of MMA made the sport appear very unsportsmanlike and hazardous, with competitors identified by casual spectators more as street fighters than as professional athletes. Allan Goes said that today, there needs to be more movement in actively shifting this identity, and that the IFL was trying to accomplish this linguistically:

> … they don't even call themselves "fighters." They call themselves professional athletes. Professional athlete, then that's very important to change this conception of the view people has towards mixed martial arts. Then, my goal is to help with this. People change their mind to this because many organizations still showing just the violence of the martial arts, but they don't show the beauty, the finesse, the technique, what is behind, what is the athlete to be there what they go through.

Thus from a professional and social constructivist point of view, Goes saw identity politics as critical in the drive to gain athletic recognition and respect.

Colin Oyama discussed how throughout the years, mixed martial artists have evolved, not only in terms of learning a variety of combat sports, but also in terms of their overall athleticism, which has helped in attaining sporting recognition and respect:

> … the quality of athletes that are coming now to fight just changed. It went from the old UFC, where you had all kinds of guys in there, to like, hey man, this guy's a two time world Greco-Roman champion, or whatever. That's when you gotta figure out, you can't just drink a beer and go and fight you know? You gotta change your attitude about it …

As Oyama asserts, within today's larger MMA organizations, many of the athletes were elite competitors in other combat sports before making the MMA transition. However, because those sports do not compensate well, they are turning to MMA as a means to carry on their craft and make some money, especially if they are still in their athletic prime. Additionally, in today's MMA scene, it is unrealistic to compete if one is not properly trained as a complete athlete.

Related to this, a number of interviewees discussed the concern that MMA was still trying to move past the ongoing analogy that as mixed martial artists, they were merely pawns in "human cockfights." Savant Young (SY) and JJ Ambrose (JA) discussed feeling typecast as non-athletes and the need for public education that shows public audiences the athletic dedication that goes into high level MMA training.

> SY: ... a lot of people think it's just a cockfight. You know, they really think we just get in there, and we hate each other after the fight, or we just want to hurt each other, or we don't train at this full-time. You know, we do this just like any other athlete. You know, this is a full-time gig, and we definitely want to ... be respected as professional athletes. Cause I mean, that's what we are.

> JA: Yeah, most definitely. A lot of people think, I mean, it's not like boxing or anything. I mean, there's so many skills, other skills involved, you know. You never get the same fight twice. People just gotta see it, it's a sport now you know. It's not just a fight. Education definitely needs to be improved.

Young and Ambrose were not alone in their unease about the way society labels their craft as a primitive, undisciplined clash of brutes who do not follow a regimented athletic training agenda. Among many other interviewees, Jason Miller added that it takes a tremendous amount of structured dedication, preparation, and planning of one's training sessions and diet in order to compete successfully at the top MMA levels. Likening the training in MMA to any other sport, Miller said, "I think the amount of discipline it takes to be good at fighting is the same as any other sport ..." Miller then explained his pre-fight training patterns, which included two training sessions per day, three to four days consecutively, and then a day off to let his body heal and recover:

> I try to be as scientific as possible about my training. Say that the guy that I'm fighting is good at takin' the back and choking me. I'll get on all fours and let a guy get on my back, and "Go!" And then try and get out. You know, try to break it down to specifics. Or, if I have to take a guy down, and the guy's a good boxer, I'll have a good boxer come in or a good boxer-wrestler guy, and I'll try to take him down. You know, while he's throwin' blows at me.

Thus, at the higher MMA levels where athletes could study video tape of future opponents, there was increased strategy and preparation involved that augmented disciplined training and dietary patterns. In short, strategic athletic preparation was modeled in similar fashion to virtually any other sport.

Interviewees did feel it was important to note that there are different professional levels within MMA. Just as there are different professional levels in football (e.g., the National Football League, Arena Football, semi-pro football) and baseball (e.g., Major League Baseball and the different levels within the minor leagues), there are different level organizations in MMA. At the time we conducted most of our interviews, Pride FC was still in existence. Therefore, it and the UFC (and to a lesser degree the IFL) were said by almost all interviewees to be the elite MMA organizations, with a good portion of their athletes deserving status on par with athletes from Major League Baseball, the National Hockey League, the National Basketball Association, and so on.

Frank Trigg, who has competed in many MMA organizations including the UFC and Pride FC, felt that attaining athletic respect was achieved when other mainstreamed professional athletes acknowledged mixed martial artists as athletes. Said Trigg:

> What matters is when other professional athletes are respecting me as an athlete, to be respected by peers. And I'm seeing more of that happening. Like Kobe Bryant or Kevin Garnett will invite me to their party, and I'm supposed to be like the guy, the fighter guy who is there. Or a baseball player will walk across a room to come and say hi to me. Then I know I am being respected by my peers, by other professional athletes. That is what is important to me.

Trigg also defined MMA as a "working man's sport," because even to this day there is not a great deal of money to made in MMA relative to America's most popular professional sports, and therefore, America's best athletes tend to pursue athletic careers in football, basketball, and baseball.

However, we also ran into discussions over how one defines "athleticism." For example, Travis Lutter suggested that critics who question MMA's status as an athletic endeavor should also examine other sports and their physical requirements, stating:

> … racing a car around a track, is that sport? I mean those guys' heart rates aren't going nearly as high as mine. Is golf a sport? What constitutes a sport? (MMA's) something competitive, and we're training. We train like athletes.

> We are athletes. So I would guess we are a sport. But do I think racquet ball or table tennis is a sport? Ya know, yeah, I mean I guess.

Other interviewees, such as Guy Mezger, agreed with Lutter in stating that athleticism needed to be defined before one could constitute what was and was not a sport, although Mezger's opinion on golf was slightly different from Lutter's. Said Mezger:

> … let's define what I think a sport is. It has to have athletic ability in it. Okay, golf is a wonderful activity … but it's not athletic. It's a skill oriented thing.… I don't consider walking the green an athletic challenge. But again, it's not that I don't like golf. I don't consider it a sport.

Thus, in defending their own profession as a legitimate sport, interviewees not only wanted to illustrate the detailed training strategies and methods they followed, but they also questioned why society would provide other sports with sporting legitimacy even if cardiovascular conditioning was not seriously required.

Randy Couture felt that there was significant movement in mixed martial artists being accepted as mainstreamed athletes. Couture felt that much of this movement had to do with the improvement in rules and approachability of many mixed martial artists. I asked Couture, "Do you feel like you guys are becoming accepted and respected as athletes now with the growth …" Couture jumped in:

> I believe we are. You know I believe with the new organization, as long as the UFC is run with regulation and unifying rules and addressing the fighter safety issues. And I think we as athletes have gained some credibility in our approach and techniques and discipline and all the things that go into making one of these fighters. And the fact that we as professional athletes are so approachable for the fans and the public has gone a long way to establishing us as real athletes and giving us credibility in the sports world. There's still a push back. It's still misunderstood to some extent. You know, you don't see us on ESPN on any kind of basis.

We interviewed Couture on September 26, 2006. About six months later, MMA made its ESPN SportsCenter debut when Matt Serra upset Georges St. Pierre to win the UFC Welterweight Title. Still, it seems MMA is fighting an unfair uphill battle, being criticized as particularly unsafe when other highly dangerous, but immensely popular sports get a bye.

Just days after Quinton "Rampage" Jackson and Dan Henderson's UFC unification title bout held in London, England (September 8, 2007), the British Medical Association (BMA) associated MMA with boxing, denouncing MMA and calling for a complete ban on the sport (British Medical Association, September 11, 2007). Perhaps it would not make sense for the BMA to speak out against the National Football League (NFL), except that the BMA did not have any reservations about NFL Europe before it was discontinued or about the Miami Dolphins and New York Giants playing in London's Wembley Stadium during the 2007 season. And note that on September 9, just days before the BMA's statement denouncing MMA, Kevin Everett, a tight end with the Buffalo Bills sustained a life-threatening spinal cord injury, which almost left him completely paralyzed from the neck down. Darin Goo raised this near tragedy in his interview and said of pro football, "If you have two highly athletic two hundred pound guys running full speed at each other and smashing heads, I mean, there's gonna be some serious damage." Thankfully, Everett has shown miraculous signs of improvement (Wawrow, 2007), but where was the BMA's criticism of American football? Then the following NFL Sunday, Detroit Lions' quarterback Jon Kitna sustained a concussion during the first half of a game against the Minnesota Vikings. Kitna showed signs of full recovery at half time and was cleared to play in the second half. Said Kitna, "I have no headaches, no symptoms, no lingering effects. But that was the worst my head ever felt, and the worse my memory was in the second quarter. Yet, after halftime there was nothing" (Lage, 2007). Despite Kitna's recovery, there was absolutely no critique in the media or by the BMA of Kitna being allowed back into a professional football game after sustaining a concussion! Rather, Kitna's valor was celebrated, and this system which allows players who have sustained a concussion to return to collision competition was completely empowered. MMA may not be completely safe, but the criticism directed towards the MMA industry hardly seems fair. What's more, the unfair criticism gets directed to those individuals within the MMA industry.

"... there's this image that we have, that we're not good people ..."—Guy Mezger

Despite MMA's movement to be accepted in some circles as a legitimate sport, mixed martial artists we spoke with felt they were still viewed by others as deviant thugs, who lacked the social, intellectual, and emotional capabilities that could contribute to a civil society. In a recent interview with the magazine *MMA*

Worldwide, Quinton Jackson discussed how he is stereotyped by staff at one of his children's schools:

> … one of my kid's teachers, I think she's new; she gets on my damn nerves! I think she knows I'm a fighter and that's why she wants me to come in all the damn time for conferences … If my boy's good, why does she want to meet me?.… I went to one parent-teacher conference and since I'm a single parent, you have to go some sometimes. She had everybody up in there like the principal, a security guard, a psychiatrist … I was like whoa, hold on!.… Then she had the gym teacher and a video camera in there too and I felt like they were going to evaluate me. I guess it's because there's not that many black kids at that school or something, and I'm one of the youngest parents.… They were asking all these personal questions about my house and I was like, "It's none of their damn business what goes on in my house!" (Villarreal, 2007, p. 19).

Accounts of these types of stories were told again and again by the men we spoke with, and this was not normally a topic we had to kick off as interviewers. Rather, interviewees initiated discussions that described how they were stereotyped as mixed martial artists, or more aptly, were labeled as dangerous and violent menaces to society.

Jackson's description of being discriminated against by his child's school staff is not unique by any means. Guy Mezger provided us with a very similar story in which school parents provided the pressure. He began by contextualizing his story, stating that his entire professional life has been characterized as apologetic. He commonly feels the need to apologize to those who are unfamiliar with MMA for being involved in the industry as a competitor, trainer, and now matchmaker. Said Mezger, "… my whole life as a professional athlete has had to be somewhat apologetic … because the misnomer is that these guys are idiots, not smart, or violent … when people find out you're a fighter, especially a cage fighter." Mezger spent seven years in Japan, and at one point he was flying to New York every Thursday to talk with young school children about life in Japan. Things were going fine, that is until some parents discovered Mezger's profession as a mixed martial artist:

> I was doing it for free and fun because I enjoy working with children, and so I would fly up to New York every Thursday. I'd teach Thursday, Friday class on Japan, and then some of the parents found out what I did, and they were like, they didn't want the cage fighter teaching their kid. So I ended up calling these parents, and they actually had a "parent-cage fighter meeting" in order for me to do this so they could realize what kind of person that I am.

Imagine the positive enthusiasm parents would have shown had Mezger been a high-profile professional athlete in football, hockey, boxing, or another more mainstreamed contact or collision sport. MMA hobbyist, Darin Goo says he is often apprehensive about discussing his fitness hobby because of people's perceptions of MMA. Said Goo, "I usually don't bring it up ... people have preconceived notions of people who participate in (MMA), so unless they're interested in the sport, I'll talk about it with them, but otherwise I don't talk about it with most people." The negative connotations associated with MMA are understandable due to the marketing strategies and lack of rules that distinguished the early days of the UFC and perhaps due to an inaccurate association with tough man contests. However, these rigid labels that still pervade are based purely on stereotypes and pigeonhole mixed martial artists to an extremely narrow definition. Thus, even when mixed martial artists attempt to contribute in positive ways to society, they are questioned and typecast in deleterious manners.

Other interviewees expressed discontent in being labeled by critics who have not spent any serious amount of time with them and simply base their opinions on the minimal amount of competitive footage they have seen on television or video. Savant Young was one person who asserted this viewpoint, stating:

> If you haven't actually seen what we go through to do it, as opposed to just watching the fight and judging it, seeing our lifestyle and how we have to be a team, and help each other out, learn doing it, then don't say nuthin' about it, 'till you come take a class. Cause you're just generalizing, and that's just like any other stereotypical thing you could say if you don't know nuthin' about it.

Interestingly enough, as we were carrying out this project, we were surprised by the number of interviewees who continued inviting us to spend time with them. They invited us to watch and/or partake in their training practices, have meals with them, meet their friends, and so on. And these were not just interviewees in our hometown of Hawaii. This included interviewees who we had just met while in California, Texas, and Las Vegas. It seemed we were not just engaging interviewees in the interviews, but they were also engaging us, so that we could have an opportunity to get to know them on multiple levels and see them as complete people, not just as mixed martial arts athletes.

Mike Onzuka, for example, went so far as to invite those who stereotype mixed martial artists to spend time with them and take the systematic steps one would normally take to become educated in something before making a knee-jerk assessment:

> I would say come to an event, because most of the guys don't come to an event. Watch the event and sit by someone who's educated already, who can explain what's happening. Number two, go to these guys' schools and watch these guys train, yeah. And then after those two things, then you make an assessment, are these guys athletes or are they animals?

Interviewees we spoke with essentially felt that they and other mixed martial artists were tagged by others as "animals" even though critics had never made any serious efforts to research the sport or get to know those individuals involved at a substantive level. Mike Onzuka went on to say that true, some of the athletes in MMA did have problems in the past, as bullies or as those who frequently got into fights (as described in Chapter Four), but that MMA was a key factor, which helped to reform their harmful attitudes and behaviors. Onzuka suggested:

> … actually talk to some fighters to see, I mean they'll tell you their past. They'll tell you how the sport has changed their lives for the better. These guys are really nice guys, really humble guys…. Are they the rough and tumble bullies that you remember in high school that used to beat up guys? They're far from that. Maybe they were that in high school, but now, they're far from it now just because of the sport, mixed martial arts.

As presented in Chapters Six and Eight, despite many people's assumptions about the combat sports, they can be used effectively to decrease societal violence, as long as they are coached properly. Nevertheless, the prevailing stereotype is that mixed martial artists are concerned about fighting and fighting only. Dustin Phan said of this perception, "I think it's just ignorance. I think a little education, we've seen goes a long way. I think this is one of those situations where it's easy just to point fingers and call names."

Other interviewees explained that the stereotype of mixed martial artists as incessantly violent persisted in part because of the ongoing visual images that emerge in contemporary MMA competitions. Unlike nearly all other sports, MMA competitions are allowed to continue even when bleeding is quite excessive. In fact, the only reason MMA matches are stopped due to blood is if bleeding impairs a competitor's vision. And as interviewees expressed in Chapter Seven, bleeding is fairly common because of the allowance of elbow strikes in most MMA competitions. Michael Frison made this observation, explaining why he feels critics continue to degrade MMA athletes: "I mean, it's a new sport, and it's coming from an uneducated viewpoint, and I think the main reason that they say that is the blood. So it looks bad." Jason Miller also explained how bleeding in MMA matches causes new viewers to cringe and maintain negative images of the sport and its athletes. Said Miller:

> The blood is the main thing. Like to me, I get cut open on top of my head. I'm like "No big deal, it's okay." But when people who've never seen blood, they're like, "Oh! He's bleeding!" And I understand that, and I'm not mad at those people for that …

Again, athletes from the combat sports interpret physical injuries in completely different ways than most of the general populace (Curry & Strauss, 1994). But simply because someone competes in a sport where cuts are somewhat common, does that instantaneously make him or her a bad person, a dangerous person on the street or in the home? Have rigorous studies been conducted which show distinct correlations between mixed martial artists and arrest records since their involvement in MMA, or studies that compare arrest records or self-reported violent behavior before and after their involvement in MMA? If not, then it is inappropriate to jump to the conclusion that a majority of those who compete or train in MMA are societal threats. True, mixed martial artists have gotten into trouble and have admitted to putting themselves in troublesome situations, but people from what other professions have not?

Hopefully with increased and improved education on MMA, critics will approach their scrutiny of mixed martial artists after being more informed, but critics should also be more responsible before making offhand assumptions about people from any social group, including mixed martial artists. Unfortunately, it is likely that mixed martial artists will continue having to cope with detrimental labeling, as the media strategies used by so many MMA organizations tend to highlight unmitigated violence and immature behavior over sport-based athleticism and social responsibility.

Perspectives on Media Portrayals and *The Ultimate Fighter*

Something Robert Otani seemed particularly adamant about conveying was that mixed martial artists are a very misunderstood group and that the media did an excellent job in perpetuating this societal misunderstanding:

> You gotta do some research before you plaque something, because you see the cage and the way they promote it to the American audience is that's just what they want, and that's just entertainment. But when you scratch beneath the surface and look into it, you know these guys … these MMA athletes, a lot of them are great guys, and they're nice people.… I think it's just, it's entertain-

ment. It's to promote. You see the cage. You see the blood. You see the little gloves and the violence and the brutality of it, but when you look at it, it's an art, and it's a sport, and it's, I really don't think it's what it's cracked up to be as far as that image that's portrayed by the media.

Like Otani, many of the other men we interviewed felt that the dominant MMA media forces created an inaccurate perception of mixed martial artists. Because the UFC's reality show *The Ultimate Fighter* (*TUF*) was such an instrumental catalyst in sparking MMA's recent popularity in the United States, we asked interviewees if they felt the reality show was good for the sport. Interviewees generally felt the reality show was great for the sport, because if it was not for *TUF*, the sport would not have grown as much as it has in the past two years. As Dan Henderson mentioned, "… that's probably the one biggest thing that has helped the sport the most. You know, obviously there's been a lot of steady growth along the way, but that pretty much catapulted it into the mainstream." At the same time, a good portion of interviewees had reservations about how the reality show cemented poor images of MMA competitors.

Very quickly, *TUF* is a UFC-produced reality show in which sixteen aspiring mixed martial artists are divided into two teams, each of which is coached or guided by a premier UFC star. In the first season, the opposing coaches were Randy Couture and Chuck Liddell, men who have competed against each other three times in MMA, but hold no animosity towards one another. In some seasons, coaches have been chosen who have personal grudges. In season three, rivals Ken Shamrock and Tito Ortiz were opposing coaches. In season five, B.J. Penn and Jens Pulver were the two coaches, and in season six, coaches Matt Hughes and Matt Serra opposed one another. In each of these latter three examples, the season culminated with the coaches facing off in an individual MMA match (the Hughes-Serra match is currently pending). In these cases where the two opposing coaches already have a rivalry, drama is clearly constructed into the "reality" show.

TUF takes place each season in Las Vegas. The sixteen participants face off in periodic individual MMA matches, aired weekly on Spike TV. A member of one team faces off against another team member until only two participants remain. Those two finalists face off on a bigger UFC fight card, with the winner earning a lucrative UFC contract. During the competition, all sixteen participants must live in one house. They are not allowed to communicate with their friends or loved ones; neither internet access nor cell phones are allowed. They cannot have reading material other than *The Bible*. They essentially live MMA day in and day out, only leaving the house to workout at the UFC training facility. We were fortunate to interview Anthony "The Crush" Torres, a participant on season two of *TUF*. Torres appreciated being on *TUF* immensely and felt he learned a great deal from it. However, he said the experience also made him appreciate what he had back home, where he said he had more "balance" between training and the other critical facets in his life:

> When I was on *TUF II*, it wasn't, you know, when you were over there away, cut off from the whole outside world, you realize that, wow we're over here, we can't watch TV, we can't talk to our loved ones, we don't have our loved ones by us. We're there for six weeks and when we come home, you appreciate your loved ones. You appreciate everything you have. Your close friends, your family, your training partners. I've kept them closer to me since.

In short, like all reality shows, *TUF* is by no means absolute reality. It was and is reality in some ways (e.g., showing some of the laborious and intricate training approaches mixed martial artists utilize). In other ways, it does not depict the men's realistic lives, as they are separated from the outside world. Moreover, because the participants are separated from others, they are forced to live during the contest in a bachelor society—a constructed "reality" that historically has never yielded positive outcomes. Interviewee Terrance said of his own experience working on a fishing boat with seven other men for six weeks:

> I was on a boat for like six weeks, and tensions were so high with the people in close quarters like that. You have no outlet.... tensions on the boat were really high. There were several cases where guys were close to goin' like this (knocks his fists together).

On the *TUF* show, not only were contestants expected to knock fists in formal competition, they were also driven to knock heads in isolated, confined quarters. Still, there is no denying the show's impact on the MMA industry.

Interviewees knew that *TUF* (just finishing its sixth season) gripped the minds of young men, women, and children across America and vaulted MMA into conventional, middle-class households. *TUF IV* winner Travis Lutter said to us, "… it's bringing in the mainstream public to the sport." Talk about mainstream public—Paul Halme mentioned how his mother still has reservations of MMA, but nonetheless became somewhat of a fan as a result of watching Lutter progress on *TUF IV*: "My mom doesn't like it, thinks it's too violent, but she's a huge fan of Travis's and watches him, you know, all the time on TV."

Other interviewees also noticed that because of *TUF*, the most unlikely MMA fans are now surfacing. Chris Onzuka explained how *TUF* has completely revamped MMA's demographic fan-base.

> … *The Ultimate Fighter* show is just a perfect example of how huge this can get. [In the past, MMA] was kind of a very clicky thing, where you had to be kind of a freak to get into it, almost a bloodlust kind of thing…. Now you have housewives talking about … all these guys. And people are really getting to know these fighters.

As will be detailed later, the *TUF* reality show episodes are dripping with drama. This has drawn in a more diverse viewership and fan-base (male and female) that is attracted to drama-driven reality shows in general, along with those fans who are interested in the more athletic dimensions of MMA.

A coach on the first season of *TUF*, Randy Couture explained to us how the reality show has dispelled some myths of MMA, showcasing for viewers the multifaceted training regiments that one must go through to become a successful mixed martial artist:

> I think the TV show, the first season of *The Ultimate Fighter* really changed the landscape for everybody. A lot of the misconceptions that the general public had about who we are and what we do kind of went out the window when they got to see a reality TV version of what goes into being an ultimate fighter. And in a lot of ways it was the perfect vehicle for getting that message across.

By watching the reality show, viewers witnessed how hard the athletes had to work. Viewers saw the physical and emotional struggles MMA practitioners endured during their training. They learned MMA moves, and simply learned about MMA in general. The show opened up new viewers' eyes to the rules enforced in MMA, how much power the referee had in ending competitions, and how most competitors displayed gracious sportsmanship before and after competitions. Nolan Hong also felt *TUF* helped to educate new fans about some of the details involved in MMA. Hong noted that by propelling MMA into America's sporting mainstream, *TUF* could help to decrease street violence:

> … when (fans) see *The Ultimate Fighter*, the reality show, and they explain what goes into being a fighter, what goes into the strategy of fighting, what goes into the different training techniques and stuff. Then they can respect it as a sport, and then realize that they … either want to train, and keep it out of

the street, or they don't want to get into altercation in the street because they know how tough it is.

Hence, interviewees felt the *TUF* show helped immensely in defining MMA as a structured sport, rather than a brutish fight where two unprepared men who despised each other were thrown into a ring or octagon to duke it out. And by further classifying MMA strictly within a sporting context, interviewees hoped *TUF* would discourage viewers from associating MMA with street violence and other negative social connotations.

However, almost all interviewees who had watched the *TUF* show had mixed feelings about it. Again, there were overwhelmingly positive feelings about how the show has made MMA so popular and subsequently increased business for MMA gyms. On the other hand, like all reality shows, the *TUF* show constructed drama and in turn reaffirmed some of the violent stereotypes of mixed martial artists. After asking Jason Miller, "Do you feel that *The Ultimate Fighter* is good for the sport?", he responded, "Yea, why not? It gives a semi-realistic view of what we gotta go through aside from like the ass grabbin' …" Miller's viewpoint of the show being "semi-realistic" and cluttered with activities unrelated to MMA training was indicative of other interviewees' feelings. Michael Frison explained some of the pros and cons that he saw emanating from *TUF*, which painted an unfair and lopsided picture of most of the participants:

> I think pros, it's definitely opened it up to a whole new audience. There's a lot more females, a lot more mainstream people. But like any reality show, the cons are they only show the drama.… They do things specifically to capture moments that don't really display the guys' real attitude, or real demeanor.

With sixteen young men confined to one house where there is virtually nothing to do, and with those sixteen men competing against each other in a combat sport for a lucrative contract, one can only expect drama to fly and be captured by the cameras.

We were also fortunate to interview Chris Leben, one of the more unforgettable contestants on season one of *TUF*. Though he appreciates his *TUF* experience immensely, Leben stated that the tension which builds in the *TUF* house is unbelievably high. When mixed martial artists are prepping for competitions, they normally find it useful emotionally to get away from their training environments from time to time. While filming *TUF*, the contestants cannot do this, and the drama that emits from this tension is utilized to build dramatic storylines that do not always paint the entire picture. Said Leben of the collective tension that builds among the MMA fighters:

> There's no escaping from it. Normally if you got a fight coming up, you know you can hang out watch a movie with your girlfriend or whatever, something to get your mind off it.... if all you can do is sit in a house with a bunch of other guys who think they can kick your ass that you're gonna have to fight, and that tension's always there, I mean you can imagine the affect that plays on you after several weeks. It's just building and building and building. You can't watch TV. You can't read a book. You can't talk to your mom. You can't call your little sis, or you don't know how anybody's doing. You know, you don't know if the world's gone to war. I mean you got no clue in that house of what's going on.

Leben also mentioned that the storyline surrounding him cast him as "being immature and being an asshole to maturing more." Leben further explained, "I've always also been loud, I've also liked to drink too much, I've also always liked to play practical jokes." Still, Leben also noted that the *TUF* experience did not necessarily mature him: "I've always been, believe it or not, a nice guy. I've always been a great guy to train with. I've always been willing to help people out." Thus if anything, the *TUF* experience inflated one part of Leben's personality that was shown on television, while failing to show other sides that existed before the show even began.

Notably, the *TUF* season that had the least amount of drama and participant conflict was season *IV* (dubbed "*The Comeback*"), in which older UFC veterans were selected as participants. Aside from a few verbal quibbles and in-house pranks, there were essentially no major disputes between participants, certainly none that led to intense arguments or fights. In the other seasons, not only did some of the coaches get into heated arguments, but participants fought and/or ridiculed each other in extremely demeaning ways. Tony Fryklund also commented on the *TUF* production, stating that it encourages conflict and drama by creating an environment that is anything but reality:

> They're showing this crap in the house. That's not a reality show cause they don't have a TV.... They're making it a difficult situation. A reality show is to see, some days my girlfriend might come with me. But on other days, she's got a lot of other shit she's doing. But reality is, in a reality show, if you come over to a gym to watch people train, there is a TV. They can go home and do what they want to do.

Instead of portraying realism in the life of mixed martial artists, the *TUF* show followed the contemporary reality television approach, scripting competitive scenarios that would provoke problems between the show's competitors—something most, if not all reality television shows attempt (Jagodozinki, 2003). As Guy Mezger noted on the whole reality show craze, "... of course you have to understand reality shows really aren't reality. It's just unscripted."

While not training and with nothing to do in the *TUF* house, show participants frequently got into heated disputes, had food fights, ruined furniture, and verbally and physically demeaned one another. Some participants, in extreme examples of "bravado," attempted to run through walls; others got drunk. Then on season *V*, two participants got into a heated fight that was clearly far more dangerous than a competition in the ring or octagon. To begin with, both of the men who fought had consumed a fair amount of alcohol just before fighting. Moreover, they were fighting on concrete surfaces. Both participants were kicked off the show by Dana White, along with a third participant who was egging on the fight. Since then, none of those participants have been on UFC cards. White also gave a verbal tongue lashing to the entire cast, stating that their behavior (including the bystanders who did nothing to stop the fight) reaffirmed the negative images of MMA that he has been attempting to dispel for years.

Still, the *TUF* show in itself generates the broad notion that mixed martial artists are at best immature and at worst, impulsive hot-heads, who if they do not fight physically on the street, are prone to instigate verbal wars in a heartbeat and intimidate others with their physical capabilities. Said Yoji Matuso in a laconic tone of the *TUF* reality show, "... watching the show, like *The Ultimate Fighter*, they present the fighters as somebody who's immature. You know I think it kind of reinforces that stereotype that I think people have about MMA as a sport." Guy Mezger was able to reconcile the positive and negative outcomes of the *TUF* show, summarizing the mainstreamed attention it has brought about for the MMA industry, but wishing the presentation of MMA athletes was very different:

> They did a really good job to spark the big wave of mixed martial arts, but the problem with it is it showed these guys, a lot of immature guys, a lot of ridiculous stuff ... And so I was a little disappointed in that because I think if you look at these guys, you think these guys are a bunch of malcontents, and there's a part of us that sympathizes and thinks it's funny. You know what I mean? It's sort of like the show, *Jackass*. There's a part of us that can't help but laugh at *Jackass*, but you wouldn't want to invite any of those guys to your house.... that's kind of what *The Ultimate Fighter* did, is it brought a tremen-

dous amount of focus on it, but it didn't really portray the guys for the most part as that great of guys, or that bright of guys.

In short, the foremost media force that served as an outreach instrument for MMA ended up being a double-edged sword for the MMA industry as a whole. The UFC has worked and continues to work vigorously to define MMA as a sport in which its athletes are professionals who act professionally. *TUF* created literally millions of new MMA fans (including myself). This massive increase in the fan-base enabled the MMA industry as a whole to grow. New MMA organizations came forward and old ones became more popular. Gyms were able to jump on the bang wagon, increasing their membership by teaching different disciplines within MMA and full fledged MMA classes. And MMA athletes were able to make a little more money for their competitions.

Unfortunately, as demonstrated in Chapter Seven, violence is what sells in American households. Truth be told, violence sells globally, but in the United States there appears to be an especially strong hunger. The *TUF* show capitalized off this cultural desire by constructing an environment in which young men would compete verbally for the spotlight and physically, for a contract with little else to occupy their time. Given these conditions, the behaviors displayed on *TUF* cannot be too surprising. Not all participants behaved in ways that perpetuated stereotypes. In fact, two of the men we interviewed who were part of the *TUF* series, Travis Lutter and Anthony Torres, were two of the calmest and mature participants in any of the series (as shown on camera). Lutter did have one verbal altercation with another participant, but relative to other occurrences on the show, it was extremely mild and never escalated.

Torres talked with us about his mild demeanor on the show, mentioning that some of his friends said he should have made more waves and gotten more attention to help push his MMA career. However, Torres felt it was more important to take the *TUF* experience as an opportunity to see how he measured up against other nationally-based talent, learn, and grow as a competitor. Regrettably, even though Lutter won *TUF IV*, he and Torres are two of the least memorable *TUF* participants. For example, Darin Goo was disappointed with Lutter's lack of air time on *TUF IV*:

> I remember Travis Lutter won season *IV*, and I was disappointed cause you never got to see him! I mean the guy was submitting or dominating all his opponents … all three matches, and he'd get a few words here and there. But you really don't get to know him because he wasn't causing trouble. It's kind of unfortunate.

Instead, Goo said the primary view audience's saw of mixed martial artists was of "belligerent crazy people." Thus, what interviewees were most concerned with was that the most memorable parts of *TUF* were not just the athletes who ended up becoming successful mixed martial artists, but also those moments that made audiences shake their heads and laugh, but ultimately think what Guy Mezger stated: "… you wouldn't want to invite any of those guys to your house."

Don't Jump to Conclusions

I have been around athletes almost my entire life—male and female, and from all levels, the little leagues up through the professional ranks. Like other former athletes and scholars who examine sports as an academic interest, I have witnessed exploitation, racism, sexism, corruption, and homophobia. I have heard teammates talk about the immeasurable pressure they feel when expected to perform beyond their physical and mental capabilities and felt that pressure myself. I have had coaches, opponents and teammates try (sometimes successfully) to intimidate me. A high school football player I once coached told me that an angry parent from an opposing team got in his face, saying he was going to get blindsided on the field. Later in the game after a play had ended and the whistle had blown, out of nowhere, he was de-cleated; this was in freshman high school football. I have heard former football players boast of how they would punch fallen running backs underneath the pile during games.

I have a friend who has had seven knee surgeries, but she continues to play basketball. Speaking of knee problems, this book's photographer tore his ACL at age fifteen playing football. Another friend tells me he sees flashing lights out of the corners of his eyes every five minutes or so; he assumes it's because he's taken his share of blows to the head, having been involved in the combat sports and martial arts almost all his life. He has not even reached his thirty's. And I continue to run, lift weights, and periodically test my old wrestling skills, despite having chronic pain in my upper back and right knee.

Yet I love sports. It is so blatantly clear that there is a dirty underbelly of athletics, but there is an opposite side of that coin. In sport there lies a beauty lined with hope (Lapchick, 1996) and a political power that is limitless. I have made and maintained some of my best friendships through sports, ex-teammates and friends who accept me for my imperfections and who are incredible, positive people. Likewise, in carrying out this project, we have met gentle, compassionate, responsible, intelligent, and unselfish men who completely disrupt the principal MMA stereotype. I have gotten to know some of these men as friends, and I am proud to say that, not because it's "cool" to have MMA athletes as friends, but because they are straight up great guys. Yes, we also met hot-heads who would probably love to violently prove their mettle on the street if it were legal, but it is safe to say these men were not the majority, and most of the men we interviewed fell far away from this latter description.

Actually, it amazes me that in this day and age when most people know it is inappropriate to pre-judge others based purely on their background that this still happens, and happens quite frequently. There were many times when I was actually apprehensive to tell professional colleagues that I was working on this project because of the negative stigma associated with MMA and my personal fear that other professors would roll their eyes thinking, "There goes Professor Mayeda wasting his time on a ridiculous topic." But the fact is, there is nothing to be ashamed of in studying the MMA phenomenon, befriending mixed martial artists, or being one yourself (as a hobbyist, coach, or competitor). The shame comes in knowing that these men, and an increasing number of women, are caught fighting for acceptance in a society that already values violence but fails to look beyond the violent nature of this sport when judging the individuals within. We need to remember that as individuals and people from different social groups, we tend to interpret situations differently. At one point in my interview with Antonio McKee, he was describing a corporate lifestyle and comparing it to his own. McKee described a hypothetical corporate working environment, but one that is indisputably real:

> You come to work, and you let Bob in there tell you what to do, and dock your hours, work the shit out of you, forty to sixty to eighty hours a week sometimes for $18.00 an hour. How do you do that? That's crazy to me. So, when you're able to understand the person, maybe then you can understand what the person does. A lot of times people don't understand people, but they want to judge.

Towards the tail-end of my interview with McKee, we were joking around about movies, and I said to him, "Man, you're crazy." McKee (AM) then threw the academic and corporate working environment he described previously right back at me. At the time, I was working well over sixty hours a week as an Assistant Research Professor at the University of Hawaii, making a little over $45,000 a year on an eleven-month contract.

AM: I want you to know what crazy to me is. Crazy is a guy like you ... how many years have you sacrificed in school?

DM (David Mayeda): Just post high school?

AM: Okay, how many years?

DM: Thirteen.

AM: Okay, to me, that's crazy. Cause I've been in business (owning and operating a gym) for three years, and not that I'm bigger or better than you, but I probably make more money than you in six months than you've made in the last three years. Now I do about $40–50,000 a month out of this gym.

DM: Yeah, I make about $45,000 a year.

AM: Okay, now crazy to me, is a man that took thirteen years of his life and set it on the shelf only to make $45,000. That's no fuckin' money. You can't even raise a real family like that!…. That's crazy! Accepting that, that's crazy. Me, I'm going after it. I want it.

DM: Well, that's what I do, that's what I know.

AM: That's because you're crazy. That's what you chose to limit yourself to. You know what, thirteen years is a long time man, that's a long time to not have. You have been taught the structured system, and it's conditioned you to be the way that you are. The only way you're gonna make it is to break away from what you're doing and write your book and publish these things.

It took me a little while to realize, but McKee was right on. Not that being a professor is something I wanted or want to give up. Still, McKee did express a different yet very valid point of view. The fact is, although we all have individual agency to make personal choices, we are also conditioned by our environments, and our varying backgrounds and experiences influence how we perceive the world differently.

People judge mixed martial artists and their sport of choice with the snap of a finger, indiscriminately marking them as crazy, barbaric, unintelligent lunatics. Often times, this image is fortified by the media and individual mixed martial artists' comments and behaviors. But more often, competitors within the MMA industry think and behave in ways that resemble the rest of society. And within this society, MMA, more than any other sport, has the potential to decrease and prevent street violence. If anything, we should be pressuring the MMA industry for reform so that its combatants are protected and circulating the proper values to its rapidly growing audiences.

11

CONCLUSION

BY DAVID MAYEDA

My Pre-fight Thoughts

Throughout this text, I have been alluding briefly to my entry into a small amateur, pseudo-MMA competition, so I thought I should write a bit about it here. This definitely was not an endeavor I wanted to pursue full time, but at the suggestion of Dave Ching and numerous friends who knew I was working on this project, I made some time to play a little bit of the MMA game. My competition took place in Honolulu on November 18, 2007 at a small event called, "The Quest for Champions 2007 Martial Arts Tournament." They had sport pankration competitions for youth, ages four through fifteen, divided into eight different age and weight categories. Adult competitors could compete in two types of competitions—submission grappling and sport pankration. Both competitions had weight classes and were held in tournament style where winners move on until a "champion" was crowned.

I decided to enter both competitions. Submission grappling is essentially a fusion of amateur wrestling and jiu-jitsu, so no striking is involved. Due to my high school wrestling background, I felt much more comfortable going into this portion of the tournament. Still, it had been sixteen years since I had last competed in wrestling, at an Orange County All Stars high school dual meet. Now about two weeks away from my thirty-fifth birthday, I would be far older than my competitors, who on average would probably be ten years or more my junior. Prior to this competition, I had only participated in four jiu-jitsu seminars, but during the two months going into this competition, Steven Saito, Nolan Hong, and our other friend, Travis Ewing, had been teaching me some very basic jiu-jitsu and boxing skills on Wednesday nights. It was as if I was cramming for a big final exam in college. My training partners were doing their best to build onto my old wrestling skills, teaching me a few basic submission moves that I could try to apply on my opponents once I wrestled them down.

Quite frankly, my biggest concern was not the competition itself. It was the possibility of facing my friend and training partner, Steven, since we were both planning to enter the 162-pound division. Based strictly on my limited experience, I should have entered at the novice level, but I decided to test myself and enter the intermediate division. Steven was entering at the advanced level, but sometimes at these small competitions, they combine different experience and/or weight classes to get an adequate number of competitors in one pool for the tournament or just so an entrant can have a match. Thus, there was no guarantee Steven and I would not meet. He knew my style, and I knew his. If we met, I would take him down, and the match would end with me either out-pointing him or with him submitting me. We both knew this.

The sport pankration competition freaked me out even more. For this competition, adult competitors could punch and kick opponents to the legs, body, and head. Luckily for me, competitors could also go for takedowns, allowing me to "ground and pound" my opponents if I was able to take them down, or "sprawl and brawl" if they unsuccessfully tried to take me down. On the ground, no strikes to the head would be allowed, and competitors were not allowed to strike with elbows or knees at any time. Furthermore, competitors in this competition were required to wear the standard MMA gear (MMA gloves, mouthpiece, and cup), as well as shin guards and headgear for added protection. Clearly, this was not full MMA.

These watered down MMA conditions notwithstanding, I was still awkward, especially while trying to box from the standing position. Our game plan was for me to go for an overhand right punch to my opponent's head, which would carry my momentum into a double-leg takedown. As we practiced this series of moves, I can't tell you how many dozens of ways I threw the punch incorrectly and exposed myself to counter strikes. Boxing and kickboxing were just not my game. When Nolan and Steven would teach me defensive strategies to various kicks and punches, I felt utterly off-balance and two steps behind.

Moreover, philosophically, I disliked boxing and kickboxing. I did not really mind hurting someone in submission grappling. At most, I was planning to grind my forehead, chin, or forearm into my opponents' heads or faces if given the opportunity, perhaps choke someone out, or tweak their arms in some way to force a submission. Sure, these moves would hurt my opponents if I could apply them, but only while in competition. Immediately afterwards, nobody feels any significant pain. However, in sport pankration (or full MMA), you have to be able to hit your opponent, and honestly, I did not want to punch or kick anyone. It just was not me. Seriously, after reviewing all that literature on concussions, how could I possibly want to try kicking someone in his head? At the same time, it's like Robert Otani said when I interviewed him, "… that's the name of the game. And if you're not gonna do it, that person's gonna do it to you." I reconciled my moral dilemma by conceding that I would punch to the head, but only to set up my takedowns. I definitely did not have a true MMA mindset, and I was glad Steven was not entering the sport pankration competition.

As for my conditioning, I felt I was in good enough shape. Matches in these competitions would only be one round of three minutes (similar to high school wrestling at the freshman/sophomore level), whereas a typical MMA match is three rounds, with each round being five minutes long. My only potential problem might have been going too hard and running out of gas. I could run and do sprints forever, and in that regard, I was in good shape. Five days before fight day, I ran two miles in barely over twelve minutes and then did some light weight lifting while biting down on my mouthpiece the entire time. I walk around at about 172 pounds, and I was already down to 166. I felt fit. But I knew running shape was far different from wrestling and fighting shape, so I didn't get too cocky about my conditioning.

Mentally, I wanted to go into this competition the same way I did my senior year of high school wrestling and my junior year of collegiate track. Those were my best years in those two sports. In a nutshell, my mindset was that if I went up against anyone of equal or lesser athleticism who did not know my style, he had no chance against me; I would flat out be too fast, smart, strong, explosive, in better shape, and relentless. All that would outweigh my inexperience. If I locked horns with someone who was innately more gifted than me, I would still go after him with an equal level of aggression, and if he beat me, he would have to put out a solid, mistake-free performance, and I would earn his respect. I'm not sure if that's just a masculinity/guy thing, an athlete thing, or a little bit of both.

In any case, that was the kind of mentality I had when I raced against professionals and the top collegiate guys nationally my junior year of college. As many of the interviewees for this book mentioned, so much of athletics is mental. Others may disagree, but I believe this holds true for all sports. I was lucky to attend a camp for elite 400 meter hurdlers while in college, mainly because it was being held in Irvine, California, and I attended the University of California, Irvine. One of the speakers was Joshua Culbreath, who won a bronze medal in the 400 hurdles at the 1956 Olympic Games. I'll never forget him stating that athletic success required confidence, but the way he put it was, you had to earn the right to be confident. In other words, you had to put in the work.

Nevertheless, hard work and innate athleticism still do not automatically translate to genuine confidence and elite athletic performance. My senior year in college, I worked equally as hard as my junior year, if not harder. I was just as fast and in as good shape as the year before, but I put so much pressure on myself to qualify for the national championships that I would press during races and tighten up at the end. As the weeks went by and I continued to miss the national qualifying time, I became more and more of a head case. I was not having fun like I did the previous year. And not surprisingly, unlike my junior year, I failed to make the qualifying time for the N.C.A.A. Division I National Championships. To this day, that is the biggest regret of my life. One is supposed to improve from junior to senior year, not regress.

Maybe that is partially why I took a stab at this MMA thing, to redeem myself and reclaim that sense of accomplishment and self-worth that I lost back in 1995. Even if I was reluctant to strike an opponent, maybe this was about asserting a sense of manhood. Truthfully, I'm not entirely sure. Competing in amateur MMA-like matches is nowhere near the same as competing at the Division I college level in any sport, so what would I really gain? It is absolutely ridiculous how much importance our society places on athletics and how much athletes' identities can be wrapped up in their sporting successes and failures. We just never want it to end. Recall what Guy Mezger said: "… the problem is you never want it to be over." The thing about sports is, it is virtually impossible to reach the pinnacle of athletic greatness and end on the highest note. For the vast majority of us, there is always someone better, always a higher level, always a bigger goal, and when that unreachable goal is unattained, so many of us define our shortcomings as failure. Another former athlete turned scholar, Michael Messner (1994), puts it this way:

> … the sports pyramid I so conscientiously climbed is rigged to bring about the total failure of everyone on it: the higher one climbs up the pyramid, the farther down one must fall when one is finally, and inevitably, pushed off by bigger, better, younger players. (p. 27).

For me, failure meant not reaching the world-class competitive level as a 400 meter hurdler, and this made me define my other life's accomplishments as insignificant. Not all athletes go through these types of twisted internal battles, but I seriously doubt if I am alone in wrestling with these types of emotions, and I don't even consider myself an athlete anymore. Let me put it this way, when Frank Trigg talked about athletes having fragile egos and going through depression (Chapter Five), he did not have to expand on his statement. I knew exactly what he meant. For many athletes, once you strip down our external facades, what's left isn't much different from the average human being. So many of us deal with severe emotional problems.

Two nights before the competition, I ran a little bit and jumped rope to keep my weight down. The next day I was in good spirits. I was able to eat a healthy, hearty breakfast and drink a moderate amount of water. That night was UFC 78, so I watched it at Fighter's Corner with the gang. It would be a good way to keep loose. Nolan brought a scale to his store where we watched the pay-per-view, and I weighed 163.5 pounds, with my shorts and t-shirt on. Basically, if I didn't eat or drink until the weigh-ins the following morning, I would easily be down to 162. I would not have to workout, but I could not eat or drink much either.

Steven, on the other hand, was 171, so he decided to compete at the next weight division. A small, amateur competition like this was not worth cutting nine pounds over night. He was clearly excited for the next day, shooting around and shadow boxing in the store in between the televised matches. After the pay-per-view, I went home. I was getting really hungry. I ate a few baby carrots and a small yogurt, but did not drink anything. It's so odd how mouthwatering raw carrots and yogurt are when you're starving yourself. It wasn't terrible though. I had cut more weight in less time in high school. My brother Stephen (our photographer) could not fly out for my fights, which he was pretty bummed about because he wanted to watch and film them. But he sent me a text message saying, "I am with you in force! And the baby (his son, Zephan) is too." I was ready.

Fight Day

When I arrived at the venue, I registered and weighed in. I could not believe it. I was still 163.5 pounds. It was 9:00am, and fights were starting in one hour. I asked one of the officials if I could try and make 162, and he said yes. I was dumbfounded about being that much over weight. Steven Saito was there, but I went down to the track by myself. I ran a mile barefoot since I did not bring tennis shoes and then jumped rope for a few minutes. I had two enemies at that point. One was time, and the second was the wind. It was really breezy, and I didn't feel like I was sweating at all. The lack of shoes didn't help either.

I started jogging 400 meter repeats, and in between each one, I would jump rope for about two minutes. I was down on the track for roughly twenty-five minutes, barely breaking a sweat. I figured I should head up to the gym and check my weight since competitions were about to start. As I was walking, I started sweating significantly more. I got to the scale, took off my t-shirt and shorts, and the scale read 160.5. I had lost three pounds in water. One of the guys at the registration table joked that I might get put into a higher weight class anyways if there were not enough competitors in my division. I did not feel too tired, and I was joking around with friends about coming in overweight and then cutting too much. On a side note, since I was running barefoot, I developed a half-dollar size blister on my left big toe. It was nasty. What a ridiculous series of events.

It took an hour or so before my first competition came around. Some of my friends came to watch—Jay and Yuka Oku and their baby daughter, Ai (Jay and I played high school football together back in California), Chad Miyamoto, who is a good track buddy of mine, Jamie Miyasato, and brothers Kaniela and Donnie Ah Nee. And of course, Dave Ching was there to document my matches and offer his support. We were fooling around making humorous pre-fight interviews to kill time. Finally, they called us to compete in the submission grappling competition. They said they had indeed bumped me up from the 162 pound intermediate division to the 172 pound advanced division since I did not have an opponent. I had ran and cut those three pounds for nothing. And naturally, my opponent was Steven Saito. Everyone was joking around that they get to see us roll with each other all the time in practice.

Steven and I had a very competitive match. Nolan cornered me, and Travis cornered Steven. The match could not have been more predictable. I took him down; he tried to sink in an armbar. I escaped and took him down again; he sunk in a pretty tight triangle choke. For some reason, I did not feel in much danger, and I was able to pop my head out. I fell back into his guard, and then Steven really caught me. He tangled me in a submission hold called a gogoplata, where he wraps one of his legs over my shoulder and then pulls my head into his shin, which is planted up against my throat. It was extremely tight. At first, his shin was pressing into the side of my neck, and it wasn't too bad. But then he maneuvered his shin right into the center of my throat. I was hurting and hoping the bell would save me. Later at lunch, Steven told me he was thinking, "Tap, Dave, tap!" Somehow, I unlocked one of his feet, turned my head, and escaped. We were both standing again. Steven shot in on me, but I sprawled out and took him down one more time. I had won under these rules on points, but in a MMA match, Steven probably would have out-pointed me because of his strong submission attempts. We hugged, and walked off the mat. It was cool, everyone was happy for both of us and our all-out efforts. Jay Oku ran up to me and yelled in his normal jovial manner, "That was awesome! Dude, he almost broke your arm off!"

I had about fifteen minutes rest before my sport pankration match, and this time they had someone for me in the 162 pound intermediate division, which made me feel better about doing the morning weight cutting. Chad had told me earlier in the week, "If you fight a local guy (from Hawaii), he's going to want to stand and bang." He was right. Still, I felt okay going in. My opponent looked so much younger and smaller than me. Maybe he did not cut any weight, which made me naturally bigger, or maybe he got the raw deal and was bumped up from the 152 pound division. After we touched gloves, he drew first blood by leg kicking me in my lower left thigh. He nailed it hard. My feet went out from under me, and I fell down. I bounced right back up, but darn, he kicked me pretty good. My boxing was just awful, and I attempted the ugliest takedown ever. He peppered me with a few jabs, and I remember noticing how they did not hurt at all, but were annoying. I did attempt a meager overhand right, leading to my takedown, and I got him.

From there, I essentially controlled the match. Once we were on the ground, the referee took off our headgear. I got side control a few times, and when he attempted submissions, it was so much easier to get out of them as opposed to Steven's attempts. I remember when I was on top of him, he was punching my back, and it felt like nothing. Nolan was cornering me. Although he was yelling numerous instructions, I don't remember hearing very much. I did hear him yelling to punch the guy right down the pipe in his sternum. I landed a few of those strikes to his chest and ribs. I'm sure they did very little damage, but it felt good to land them. I tried to get in position to apply a "key lock," but it just was not happening. The match ended, and I won, again by points.

I was pretty tired and glad I did not have any more matches. I cannot imagine how mixed martial artists fight three five-minute rounds, or five five-minute rounds in championship matches. Probably the funniest part of the day was when I showed everyone my blister and all the skin that had peeled off my toe. Everyone got a kick out of watching Steven pour some kind of antiseptic over it while I winced in pain. My throat hurt a little from Steven's gogoplata, and my left thigh was pretty sore from the kick I absorbed. I am glad he landed that kick though. Obviously, it did not feel good, but it felt good to know how a leg kick feels. Still, I definitely would not want to take a bunch of those. Dave Ching told me he was proud of me for trying this new sporting endeavor. I'm pretty sure he wants me to go further and try a real MMA match, but I think I'll stop here. So that was my little pseudo-MMA experience. Was I more violent afterwards? Did I want to go get into fights at bars? No, not at all. I wanted to go eat and take a nap.

Final Thoughts

That evening after the competition, my good friend, Ilima Ramseyer, called to see if I was laid up in a hospital bed somewhere. Ilima runs a grass-roots youth program in Hawaii called God's Country Waimanalo. She is a big sports fan, but not a fan of MMA by any means. After laughing pretty hysterically at my whole weight-cutting ordeal and blistered toe, she said, "What you men do for these sports, how you hurt your bodies, is so stupid!" It was just like most of the men Dave Ching and I interviewed. I was sore, but not seriously hurt, let alone injured. Nevertheless, I could not argue with her. As athletes, especially male athletes, we engage in some pretty irrational enterprises.

In working on this project, I came to see the MMA industry in an entirely new light. In fact, Dave and I both did. The bottom line is, we also hope you walk away from this book with a new perspective on MMA and sports in general. We hope the suggestions outlined in this book influence MMA organizations in a positive way. In this book's Forward, Jason Miller offers his honest opinion, stating that as a pessimist, he does not see many of our recommendations coming to fruition. Of course we appreciate Jason's candor, but we see promise in the MMA industry and are not ready to tap out to those pessimistic viewpoints just yet.

Historically, sports have always been a site where political movements clash with as much force as opposing athletes. There is no reason MMA should be any different. Chapter Nine offers a point-by-point guide that readers can use to hold MMA organizations accountable for contributing to society in a positive way, pushing those organizations to actively promote nonviolence, responsible citizenship, and provide adequate safety provisions for MMA athletes. Whether you are a MMA competitor, promoter, coach, fan, curious observer, or concerned citizen, we hope you take the initiative and do your part to encourage these reform measures. If MMA gyms in your community offer classes for children, make certain the coaches and adult athletes are also spending significant time helping younger students to be successful scholars, to walk away from fights, and to resist negative peer pressure. Don't be a bystander; make something happen. Seek out those men and women intimately woven into the MMA industry who share your constructive concerns. You may not be able to notice them right away when you switch on your television, but trust us, they're out there, and once you start looking, they're not too hard to find.

REFERENCES

Adickes, M.S., & Stuart, M.J. (2004). Youth football injuries. *Sports Medicine, 34* (3), 201–207.

Agel, J., Arendt, E.A., & Bershadsky, B. (2005). Anterior cruciate ligament injury in National Collegiate Athletic Association basketball and soccer: a 13-year review. *American Journal of Sports Medicine, 33* (4), 524–530.

American Medical Association. (1999). *1999 Annual Meeting of the American Medical Association: Reports of the Council on Scientific Affairs.* Accessed June 11, 2007 online http://www.ama-assn.org/ama1/pub/upload/mm/443/csaa-99.pdf.

American Psychiatric Association. (1998). Psychiatric affects of media violence. *APA Online.* http://www.psych.org/psych/htdocs_info/media_violence.html.

Anderson, C. (1997). Violence in television commercials during nonviolent programming. *Journal of the American Medical Association, 278* (13), 1045–1046.

Anderson, C.A., Berkowitz, L., Donnerstein, E., Huesmann, L.R., Johnson, J.D., Linz, D., Malamuth, N.M., & Wartella, E. (2003). The influence of media violence on youth. *Psychological Science in the Public Interest, 4* (3), 81–110.

Annas, G.J. (1983). Boxing: atavistic spectacle or artistic sport? *American Journal of Public Health, 73* (7), 811–812.

Araton, H. (2007 March 28). Steroids are a stain and hard to erase. *New York Times,* p. D1, D3.

Arendt, E.A., Agel, J., & Dick, R. (1999). Anterior cruciate ligament injury patterns among collegiate men and women. *Journal of Athletic Training, 34* (2), 86–92.

Arias, C. (2007 March 27). UFC owners buy Pride Fighting Championships: Lorenzo Fertitta, Dana White and Nobuyuki Sakakibara hold conference call. *Orange County Register.* Accessed April 27, 2007 online http://www.ocregister.com.

Arritt, D. (2006 September 22). Altering the perception: many UFC fighters such as Hughes still find themselves defending the image of their sport as it tries to move into the mainstream. *Los Angeles Times,* p. D10.

Aspy, C.B., Oman, R.F., Vesely, S.K., McLeroy, K., Rodine, S., & Marshall, L. (2004). Adolescent violence: the protective effects of youth assets. *Journal of Counseling & Development, 82,* 268–276.

Associated Press. (2007 October 8). Jones returns 5 medals from Sydney Games. *The New York Times*. Accessed October 8, 2007 online http://www.nytimes.com/aponline/sports/AP-OLY-Jones-Doping.html?ref=sports.

Baker, M.M. (1998). Anterior cruciate ligament injuries in the female athlete. *Journal of Women's Health, 7* (3), 343–349.

Bass, A. (1996). How jocks view women. In R.E. Lapchick (Ed.) *Sport in society: equal opportunity or business as usual?*, pp. 110–113. Thousand Oaks, CA: Sage.

Battista, J. (2007 October 9). Concussion leaves Green's career in doubt. *The New York Times*. Accessed October 9, 2007 online http://www.nytimes.com/2007/10/09/sports/football/09dolphins.html?ref=sports.

Baucom, C., & Lantz, C.D. (2001). Faculty attitudes toward male division II student-athletes. *Journal of Sport Behavior, 24* (3), 265–276.

Bederman, G. (1995). *Manliness & Civilization: a cultural history of gender and race in the United States, 1880–1917.* Chicago: University of Chicago Press.

Benedict, J. (1997). *Public Heroes, Private Felons: Athletes and Crimes Against Women.* Boston: Northeastern University Press.

Benjamin, G.A.H., Darline, E.J., & Sales, B. (1990). The prevalence of depression, alcohol abuse, and cocaine abuse among United States lawyers. *International Journal of Law and Psychiatry, 13* (3), 233–246.

Berry, M.F., & Blassingame, J.W. (1982). *Long Memory: The Black Experience in America.* Oxford: Oxford University Press.

Birrell, S. (1989). Racial relations theories and sport: suggestions for a more critical analysis. *Sociology of Sport Journal, 6*, 212–227.

Bledsoe, G.H., Hsu, E.B., Grabowski, J.G., Brill, J.D., & Li, G. (2007). Incidence of injury in professional mixed martial arts competitions. *Journal of Sports Science and Medicine, July*, 136–142.

Bledsoe, G.H., Li, G., & Levy, F. (2005). Injury risk in professional boxing. *Southern Medical Association, 98* (10), 994–997.

Blitstein, J.L., Murray, D.M., Lytle, L.A., Birnbaum, A.S., & Perry, C.L. (2005). Predictors of violent behavior in an early adolescent cohort: similarities and differences across genders. *Health Education & Behavior, 32* (2), 175–194.

Boden, B.P., Tacchetti, R.L., Cantu, R.C., Knowles, S.B., & Mueller, F.O. (2006). Catastrophic cervical spine injuries in high school and college football players. *The American Journal of Sports Medicine, 34* (8), 1223–1232.

Boon, K.A. (2003). Men and nostalgia for violence: culture and culpability in Chuck Palahniuk's *Fight Club*. *The Journal of Men's Studies, 11* (3), 267–276.

British Medical Association. (2007 September). *Boxing: An update from the Board of Science.* Accessed September 12, 2007 online http://www.bma.org.uk/ap.nsf/Content/boxing?OpenDocument&Highligh=2,mma.

Brodesser-Akner, C. (2007 August 20). UFC grapples for respect. *Advertising Age, 78* (33), 3, 24.

Brooke, J. (2004 June 11). Japan: suicide at record high. *New York Times, 153*, p. A6.

Brophy, R.H., Barnes, R., Rodeo, S.A., & Warren, R.F. (2007). Prevalence of musculoskeletal disorders at the NFL combine—trends from 1987 to 2000. *Medicine and Science in Sports and Exercise, 39* (1), 22–27.

Brooks, G.R. (2003). Masculinity and men's mental health. *ReVision, 25* (4), 24–37.

Cain, J. (2007a October 25). Why Randy Couture left the UFC: Unappreciated. Accessed October 25, 2007 online http://www.mmaweekly.com/absolutenm/templates/dailynews.asp?articleid=4948&zoneid=13.

Cain, J. (2007b August 17). Randy Couture discusses steroids in MMA. Accessed August 18, 2007 online http://www.mmaweekly.com.

Cauce, A.M., Hiraga, U., Mason, C., Aguilar, T., Ordonez, N., & Gonzales, N. (1992). Between a rock and a hard place: social adjustment of biracial youth. In M.P.P. Root (Ed.) *Racially Mixed People in America*, pp. 207–222. London: Sage Publications.

Cahn, S.K. (1994). *Coming on strong: gender and sexuality in twentieth-century women's sport.* Boston: Harvard University Press.

Carey, J.L., Huffman, G.R., Parekh, S.G., & Sennett, B.J. (2006). Outcomes of anterior cruciate ligament injuries to running backs and wide receivers in the National Football League. *The American Journal of Sports Medicine, 34* (12), 1911–1917.

Carter, R. (2007 January 4). The brawling New York Knicks: from bad to worse to ugly. *New York Amsterdam News, 98* (2), p. 11, 31.

Cavender, G. (1999). Detecting masculinity. In J. Ferrell & N. Websdale (Eds.) *Making Trouble: Cultural Constructions of Crime, Deviance, and Control*, pp. 157–175. Hawthorne, NY: Aldine De Grangler.

Chappell, J.D., Herman, D.C., Knight, B.S., Kirkendall, D.T., Garrett, W.E., & Yu, B. (2005). Effect of fatigue on knee kinetics and kinematics in stop-jump tasks. *The American Journal of Sports Medicine, 33* (7), 1022–1029.

Charlesworth, H., & Young, K. (2004). Why English female university athletes play with pain: motivations and rationalizations. In K. Young (Ed.). *Sporting*

Bodies, Damaged Selves: Sociological Studies of Sports-Related Injuries, pp. 163–180. Boston: Elsevier.

Comstock, R.D., Knox, C., Yard, E., & Gilchrist, J. (2006). Sports-related injuries among high school athletes—United States, 2005–06 school year. *Journal of the American Medical Association*, 55, 2673–2674.

Connell, R.W. (1987). *Gender & Power*. Stanford, CA: Stanford University Press.

Couture, R. (2006). Evolution part 2: "The Natural" way. *Tapout Magazine* (15), 13.

Covassin, T., Swanik, C.B., & Sachs, M.L. (2003). Epidemiological considerations of concussions among intercollegiate athletes. *Applied Neuropsychology, 10* (1), 12–22.

Cowherd, C. (2007 May 7). *Jim Lampley discusses the De La Hoya-Mayweather fight*. ESPN Radio, "The Herd."

Crosset, T. (2000). Athletic affiliation and violence against women: toward a structural prevention project. In J. McKeay, M.A. Messner, & D. Sabo (Eds.) *Masculinities, Gender Relations, and Sport: Research on Men and Masculinities*, p. 147–161. Thousand Oaks, CA: Sage Publications.

Curry, T.J. & Strauss, R.H. (1994). A little pain never hurt anybody: a photo-essay on the normalization of sport injuries. *Sociology of Sport Journal, 11*, 195–208.

Daddario, G. (1998). *Women's Sport and Spectacle: Gendered Television Coverage and the Olympic Games*. Westport, Connecticut: Praeger.

Davidson, N. (2007 May 24). Jackson takes aim at Liddell again. Accessed May 25, 2007 online http://www.globesports.com/servlet/story/RTGAM.20070524.wsptmma24/SStory.

Davis, L.R. (1997). *The Swimsuit Issue and Sport: Hegemonic Masculinity in Sports Illustrated*. Albany: State University of New York Press.

de Garis, L. (2000). "Be a buddy to your buddy": male identity, aggression, and intimacy in a boxing gym. In J. McKeay, M.A. Messner, & D. Sabo (Eds.) *Masculinities, Gender Relations, and Sport: Research on Men and Masculinities*, p. 87–107. Thousand Oaks, CA: Sage Publications.

Delaney, J.S. (2004). Head injuries presenting to emergency departments in the United States from 1990 to 1999 for ice hockey, soccer, and football. *Clinical Journal of Sport Medicine, 14* (2), 80–87.

Dhoot, J. (2007 June). One hot fighter: sure, Gina Carano is great-looking, but she's also dedicated to fighting and sporting an undefeated record. *Ultimate Grappling*, p. 78–79, 108.

Downey, G. (2007). Producing pain: techniques and technologies in no-holds-barred fighting. *Social Studies of Science, 37* (2), 201–226.

Downey, G. (2006). The information economy in no-holds-barred fighting. In M. Fisher & G. Downey (Eds.) *Frontiers of Capital: Ethnographic Reflections on the New Economy*, pp. 108–132. Durham, NC: Duke University Press.

Drugs.com (2007 September 9). Nandrolone facts and comparisons at Drugs.com. Accessed September 9, 2007 online http://www.drugs.com.

Early, G. (1995). Hot spicks versus cool spades: three notes toward a cultural definition of prizefighting. In D.K. Wiggins (Ed.) *Sport in America: From Wicked Amusement to National Obsession*, pp. 319–334. Champaign, IL: Human Kinetics.

Essoyan, S. (2007 November 16). A rattling reality check: doctors believe concussion patients who return too soon risk greater injury. *Honolulu Star-Bulletin*, A6.

Fackelmann, K. (2004 October 7). Girls' knee injuries have later consequences. *USA Today*, p. 9D.

Federal Bureau of Investigation. (2002). *Crime in the United States 2001: Uniform Crime Reports*. Washington DC: Federal Bureau of Investigation, U.S. Department of Justice.

Fulcher, J.A. (2002). Domestic violence and the rights of women in Japan and the United States. *Human Rights: Journal of the Section of Individual Rights & Responsibilities, 29* (3), 16–17.

Garcia, C. (2007 September 27). MMA and Mexico: a matter of time. Accessed September 27, 2007 online http://www.sherdog.com/news/articles.asp?n_id=9239.

Garland, D. (2005). Penal excess and surplus meaning: public torture lynchings in twentieth-century America. *Law & Society Review, 39* (4), 793–834.

Gentry, C. (2007). Anatomy of a Warrior. *MMA Worldwide*, (3), 60–61.

Gentry, C. (2002). *No holds barred: ultimate fighting and the martial arts revolution*. Milo Books Ltd.

Gervis, M., & Dunn, N. (2004). The emotional abuse of elite child athletes by their coaches. *Child Abuse Review, 13* (3), 215–223.

Glock, A. (2007). This guy scares you?: the fastest-rising star in the world's most controversial sport, Chuck Liddell has frightened a lot of opponents—including old-school sports guys. Not bad for someone who paints his toenails. *ESPN the Magazine*, 48–56.

Gold, S. (2007a January 14). Savagery as spectacle: knockout marketing: mixed martial arts, a sport once condemned for its brutality, is riding a wave of popularity and profit but still fighting for legitimacy. *Los Angeles Times*, P. A1, A26–28.

Gold, S. (2007b January 15). Love packs a punch: two Southland fighters share their passion for mixed martial arts—and for each other. *Los Angeles Times*, P. A1, 12–13.

Goldman, A. (2007 March 1). Mixed martial arts grapping PPV. *The Honolulu Advertiser*, p. C1, C3).

Gorn, E.J. (1995). "Gouge and bite, pull hair, and scratch": the social significance of fighting in the southern backcountry. In D.K. Wiggins (Ed.) *Sport in America: From Wicked Amusement to National Obsession*, p. 35–50. Chicago: Human Kinetics.

Graham, P. (2007 March 23). Less-violent mixed martial arts a booming business. *The Honolulu Advertiser*. Accessed May 11, 2007 online http://www. honoluluadvertiser.com.

Greenberg, S. (2007 March 5). Take me out to the brawl game … *Sporting News, 231* (10), 7.

Gregory, S. (2007 July 30). It's ladies fight night. *Time, 170* (5), 40–43.

Gross, J. (2007a September 12). Cuban sees bright future for MMA. Accessed September 12, 2007 online http://www.sherdog. com/news/articles.asp?n_id=8983.

Gross, J. (2007b July 19). Dopey: CSAC releases drug testing results. Accessed July 19, 2007 online http://www.sherdog.com/news/articles.asp?n_id=8330.

Gross, J. (2007c July 19). UFC 155-lb. champion, challenger positive for steroids. Accessed July 19, 2007 online http://www.sherdog.com/news/news.asp?n_id=8333.

Hockensmith, R. (2007 July 31). White says UFC's punishment is going to intensify. *ESPN The Magazine*. Accessed August 8, 2007 online http:// www.espn.com.

Hosenball, M. (2005 May 2). Now it's the NFL's turn to answer questions. *Newsweek, 145* (18), 10.

Hospitals & Health Networks. (2006). Youth sports: a trip to the injured lists? *H&HN: Hospitals & Health Networks, 80* (9), 22–22.

Huesmann, L.R., & Taylor, L.D. (2006). The role of media violence in violent behavior. *Annual Review of Public Health, 27* (1), 393–415.

IFL Website. (2007). Accessed May 11, 2007 online http://ifl.tv/MMA-101.html.

Jable, J.T. (1994). Sport in Philadelphia's African-American community, 1865–1900. In G. Eisen & D.K. Wiggins (Eds.) *Ethnicity and Sport in North American History and Culture*, pp. 157–176. London: Praeger.

Jago, B.J. (2002). Chronicling an academic depression. *Journal of Contemporary Ethnography, 31* (1), 729–757.

Jagodozinki, J. (2003). The perversity of (real)ity TV: a symptom of our times. *Journal for the Psychoanalysis of Culture & Society, 8* (2), 320–329.

Jarret, G.J., Orwin, J.F., & Dick, R.W. (1998). Injuries in collegiate wrestling. *American Journal of Sports Medicine, 26,* 674–680.

Jeffrey, D., & Franck, L. (2007 June). Glory days: sure, there is fame and money, but what about the downsides to MMA? A there any? If so, how do fighters cope? *Ultimate Grappling,* 58–59, 106–107.

Jensen, D. (2006, May). Hollywood gets his Oscar: Shockwave 2005. *Ultimate Grappling,* 82–87.

Jones, D. (2007June). Missed opportunity: you'd think there would be nothing good about missing the weight cut for a UFC title fight, but Travis Lutter found a silver lining. *Ultimate Grappling,* 74–76.

Jost, K. (2004 July 23). Sports and drugs. *CQ Researcher, 14* (26)

Karas, M. (2007 May 25). Prized fighter: Chuck Liddell has become the face of the surging UFC, and his star power is paying off for the growing sport. *Orange County Register*. Accessed May 27, 2007 online http://www.ocregister.com/ocregister/sports/mixedmartialarts/article_1709184.php.

Katz, J. (1996). Masculinity and sports culture. In R.E. Lapchick (Ed.) *Sport in society: equal opportunity or business as usual?*, pp. 101–106. Thousand Oaks, CA: Sage.

Kelly, W. (2007). Book review of *Japan, Sport and Society: Tradition and Change in a Globalizing World. The Journal of Japanese Studies, 33* (2), 497–482.

Kerr, J.H. (2002). Issues in aggression and violence in sport: the ISSP position stand revisited. *Sport Psychologist, 16* (1), 68–78.

Kimmel, M.S., & Kaufman, M. (1994). Weekend warriors: the new men's movement. In H. Brod & M. Kaufman (Eds.) *Theorizing Masculinities,* 259–288. Newbury Park, CA: Sage.

Kochhar, T., Back, D.L., Mann, B., & Skinner, J. (2004). Risk of cervical injuries in mixed martial arts. *British Journal of Sports Medicine, 39,* 444–447.

Krauss, E. (2004). *Warriors of the Ultimate Fighting Championship.* New York: Citadel Press.

Lage, L. (2007 September 17). Lions QB Kitna said he returned from concussion thanks to "miracle." Yahoo Sports, Accessed September 17, 2007 online http://sports.yahoo.com/nfl/news.

Lance, L.M. (2005). Violence in sport: a theoretical note. *Sociological Spectrum, 25,* 213–214.

Langburt, W., Cohen, B., Akhthar, N., O'Neill, K., & Lee, J. (2001). Incidence of concussion in high school football players of Ohio and Pennsylvania. *Journal of Child Neurology, 16* (2), 83–85.

Lapchick, R.E. (2000). Crime and athletes: the new racial stereotype. *Society, 37* (3), 14–20.

Lapchick, R.E. (1996). *Sport in Society: Equal Opportunity or Business as Usual?* Thousand Oaks, CA: Sage Publications.

Lewis, R. (2006). Why haven't we banned boxing? *Neurology, 6* (23), 5–6.

Llosa, F., Wertheim, L.J., & Epstein, D. (2007 March 12). Inside the steroid sting. *Sports Illustrated, 106* (11), 62–66.

Lundberg, G.D. (1996). Blunt force violence in America—shades of gray or red: ultimate/extreme fighting. *Journal of the American Medical Association, 275* (21), 1684–1685.

Malina, R.M., Morano, P.J., Barron, M., Miller, S.J., Cumming, S.P., & Kontos, A.P. (2006). Incidence and player risk factors for injury in youth football. *Clinical Journal of Sports Medicine, 16* (3), 214–222.

Malone, E. (2007 March). Zero tolerance: Mark Kerr, who now fights naturally, acknowledges that drugs cut into the prime of his career. *Ultimate Grappling,* 56–59.

Martin, D. (2007 July 23). Drugs in MMA part 2: the numbers don't lie. Report on MMAWeekly.com. Accessed July 23, 2007.

Martin, T. (2007 April 23). Unpredictability is par for the course in UFC: Mirko "Cro Cop" Filipovic's loss proves that nothing is as it seems in mixed martial arts. *Los Angeles Times.* Accessed on latimes.com, April 27, 2007.

Mauer, M. (1999). *Race to Incarcerate: The Sentencing Project.* New York: The New Press.

Mayeda, D.T. (2005). *Reconceptualizing Risk: Adolescents in Hawaii Talk about Rebellion and Respect.* Dissertation completed for the University of Hawaii, Department of American Studies.

Mayeda, D.T. (2001a). Characterizing gender and race in the 2000 Summer Olympics: NBC's coverage of Maurice Greene, Michael Johnson, Marion Jones, and Cathy Freeman. *Social Thought & Research, 24* (1–2), 145–186.

Mayeda, D.T., Chesney-Lind, M., & Koo, J. (2001b). Talking story with Hawaii's youth: confronting violent and sexualized perceptions of ethnicity and gender. *Youth & Society, 33* (1), 99–128.

Mayeda, D.T. (1999). From model minority to economic threat: media portrayals of Major League Baseball players Hideo Nomo and Hideki Irabu. *Journal of Sport & Social Issues, 23* (2), 203–217.

McCallum, J. (2004 November 29). The ugliest game: an NBA brawl exposes the worst player and fan behavior and serves as a frightening wake-up call. *Sports Illustrated, 101* (21), 44–51.

McCallum, J., & Gelin, D. (1995 February 2). Out of joint: Women's basketball is making great strides, but it is suffering an epidemic of torn knee ligaments along they way. *Sports Illustrated, 82* (6), 44–49.

McCarthy, M. (2007 February 23). Fox Sports Net puts bet on team-based fighting. *USA Today*, p. 3C.

McCarthy, M. (2005 November 21). Networks air greatest hits selling violence, hamburgers. *USA Today*, p. 2C.

McKinley, J.C. (2000 May 12). Invisible injury: a special report: a perplexing foe takes an awful toll. *The New York Times*, p. D1.

Messerschmidt, J.W. (2000). *Nine Lives: Adolescent Masculinity, the Body, and Violence*. Boulder, CO: Westview Press.

Messerschmidt, J. (1993). *Masculinities and Crime: Critique and Reconceptualization of Theory*. Lanham: Rowman & Littlefield.

Messerschmidt, J.W. (1986). *Capitalism, Patriarchy, and Crime: Toward a Socialist Feminist Criminology*. Towata, NJ: Rowman & Littlefield.

Messner, M.A. (2002). *Taking the field: women, men and sports*. Minneapolis: University of Minnesota Press.

Messner, M.A. (1994). Indignities: a short story. In M.A. Messner & D.A. Sabo (Eds.) *Sex, Violence, & Power in Sports: Rethinking Masculinity*, pp. 16–27. Freedom, CA: The Crossing Press.

Messner, M.A. (1992). *Power at Play: Sports and the Problem of Masculinity*. Boston: Beacon Press.

Miller, K.E., Melnick, M.J., Farrell, M.P., Sabo, D.F., & Barnes, G.M. (2006). Jocks, gender, binge drinking, and adolescent violence. *Journal of Interpersonal Violence, 21* (1), 105–120.

Miller, P.B. (1998). The anatomy of scientific racism: racialist responses to black athletic achievement. *Journal of Sport History, 25* (1), 119–151.

Milton, P. (2007 October 5). Marion Jones admits steroid use. *Los Angeles Times*. Accessed October 6, 2007 online http://www.latimes.

com/sports/nationworld/wire/ats-ap_sports12oct05,1,123429.story?coll=la-ap-sports&ctrack=1&cset=true.

MMAWeekly.com. (2007a July 19). A statement from Hermes Franca about positive test. Accessed July 19, 2007 online http://www.mmaweekly.com.

MMAWeekly.com. (2007b November 22). EliteXC Fighters Show Thanks. Accessed November 22, 2007 online http://www.mmaweekly.com/absolutenm/templates/dailynews.asp?articleid=5120&zoneid=13.

MMAWeekly.com. (2006 January 10). *Official MMA Rules.* Accessed from MMAWeekly.com.

Molinda, A., & Godines, V. (2007 February 16). Fight clubs flourishing: teenagers engaging in underground mixed martial arts raise injury, violence concerns. *The Orange County Register*, p. Local 1, 3.

Monroe, R. (2007 April). Haole boy can scrap: you might think of him primarily as a grappler, but Jason "MayheM" Miller can stand and bang. *Ultimate Grappling*, 88–89, 128.

Morinaga, D. (2006 August 29). Given fighting chance, Icon makes it big. *The Honolulu Advertiser*, p. B1.

Mosher, D.L., & Tompkins, S.S. (1998). Scripting the macho man: hypermasculine socialization and ethnoculturation. *The Journal of Sex Research, 25* (1), 60–84.

Mueller, F.O. (2001). Catastrophic head injuries in high school and collegiate sports. *Journal of Athletic Training, 36* (3), 312–315.

Muscari, M. (2002). Media violence: advice for parents. *Pediatric Nursing, 28* (6), 585–591.

Nagel, M.S., Southall, R.M., & O'Toole, T. (2004). Punishment in the four major North American professional sports leagues. *International Sports Journal, 8* (2), 15–27.

Nakao, M., & Takeuchi, T. (2006). The suicide epidemic in Japan and strategies of depression screening for its prevention. *Bulletin of the World Health Organization, 84* (6), 492–493.

Navarro, M. (2006 December 29). Controversial sport and its starts kick their way toward the mainstream. *New York Times*, P. A16.

Nelson, R.B. (1995). *The stronger women get, the more men love football: sexism and the American culture of sports.* New York: Avon Books.

Newfield, J. (2001 November 12). The shame of boxing. *The Nation*, p. 13–22.

Nixon, H.L. (2004). Cultural, structural and status dimensions of pain and injury experiences in sport. In K. Young (Ed.). *Sporting Bodies, Damaged Selves: Sociological Studies of Sports-Related Injuries*, pp. 81–97. Boston: Elsevier.

Norbeck, K. (2007). Tara LaRosa: gone to the top. *MMA Worldwide*, (3) p. 48–49.

Paik, H., & Comstock, G. (1994). The effects of television violence on antisocial behavior: A meta-analysis. Communication Research, 21, 516–546.

Patel, D.R., Shivdasani, V., & Baker, R.J. (2005). Management of sport-related concussion in young athletes. *Sports Medicine, 35* (6), 671–684.

Patrick, D. (2006 August 23). Gatlin slapped with 8-year ban. *USA Today*, p. 1C.

Patrick, D. (2004a July 19). Drug cloud hangs over close of U.S. Olympic Trials. *USA Today*, p. 1C.

Patrick, D. (2004b October 20). USADA gives Harrison 4-year ban for doping. *USA Today*, p. 3C.

Pearlin, L.I. & Johnson, J.S. (1977). Marital Status, Life-Strains and Depression. *American Sociological Review, 42*, 704–715.

Pelletier, J.C. (2006). Sports related concussion and spinal injuries: the need for changing spearing rules at the National Capital Amateur Football Association. *Journal of the Canadian Chiropractic Association, 50* (3), 195–208.

Pelley, S. (2006 December 10). Mixed Martial Arts: A New Kind of Fight. *60 Minutes*.

Phillips, D.A. (2007). Punking and bullying: strategies in middle school, high school, and beyond. *Journal of Interpersonal Violence, 22* (7), 158–178.

Phillips, D.A. (2005). Reproducing normative and marginalized masculinities: adolescent male popularity and the outcast. *Nursing Inquiry, 12* (3), 219–230.

Pike, E.C.J. (2004). Risk, pain and injury: "a natural thing in rowing"? In K. Young (Ed.). *Sporting Bodies, Damaged Selves: Sociological Studies of Sports-Related Injuries*, pp. 151–162. Boston: Elsevier.

Pishna, K. (2007a July 9). UFC 73 Salaries & Attendance Figures. Accessed July 9, 2007 online http://www.mmaweekly.com.

Pishna, K. (2007b September 26). UFC 76 Salaries: Liddell earns $500,000. Accessed September 26, 2007 online http://www.mmaweekly.com.

Pope, M., & Englar-Carolson, M. (2001). Fathers and sons: the relationship between violence and masculinity. *The Family Journal, 9* (4), 367–374.

Pringle, R., & Markula, P. (2005). No pain is sane after all: a Foucauldian analysis of masculinities and men's experiences in rugby. *Sociology of Sport Journal, 22*, 472–497.

Pronger, B. (2000). Homosexuality and sport: who's winning? In J. McKay, M.A. Messner, & D. Sabo (Eds.) *Masculinities, Gender Relations, and Sport*, pp. 222–244. Thousand Oaks, CA: Sage.

Pugmire, L. (2007 May 25). Does UFC have boxing's number?: Despite success of De La Hoya-Mayweather, Ultimate Fighter Championship's White maintains mixed martial arts has surpassed the sweet science in popularity, and that Liddell-Jackson will drive the point home. *The Los Angeles Times.*

Pursell, C. (2007 August 13). UFC: today Spike TV, tomorrow the world. *Television Week, 26* (32), 3, 24.

Pyke, K. (1996). Class-based masculinities: the interdependence of gender, class, and interpersonal power. *Gender & Society, 10* (5), 527–549.

Ramirez, M., Schaffer, K.B., Shen, H., Kashani, S., & Kraus, J. (2006). Injuries to high school football athletes in California. *The American Journal of Sports Medicine, 34* (7), 1147–1158.

Real, T. (1997). *I Don't Want to Talk About It: Overcoming the Secret Legacy of Male Depression.* New York: Scribner.

Reese, L.E., Veera, E.M., Simon, T.R., & Ikeda, R.M. (2000). The role of families and care givers as risk and protective factors in preventing youth violence. *Clinical Child and Family Psychology Review, 3* (1), 61–77.

Rhoden, W.C. (2007 January 20). In the N.F.L., violence sells, but at what cost? *The New York Times, 156*, D1.

Rhoden, W.C. (2006 July 28). In this steroids era, every feat is suspect. *New York Times*, p. D1, D3.

Roberts, A., & Lafree, G. (2004). Explaining Japan's postwar violent crime trends. *Criminology, 42* (1), 179–210.

Roberts, W. (2007). Injuries in young ice-hockey players. *Clinical Journal of Sports Medicine, 17* (3), 225–226.

Ross, C.E., & Mirowsky, J. (1989). Explaining the Social Patterns of Depression: Control and Problem Solving—or Support and Talking? *Journal of Health and Social Behavior, 30*, 206–219.

Rossen, J. (2007a October 25, 2007). White addresses everything UFC. Accessed October 25, 2007 online http://www.sherdog. com/news/articles.asp?n_id=9664.

Rossen, J. (2007b July 17). Say it ain't so, Royce! Notes on a scandal. Accessed July 17, 2007 online http://www.sherdog.com/news/articles.asp?n_id=8299.

Sabo, D. (2004). The politics of sports injury: hierarchy, power, and the pain principle. In K. Young (Ed.). *Sporting Bodies, Damaged Selves: Sociological Studies of Sports-Related Injuries*, pp. 59–79. Boston: Elsevier.

Sabo, D. (1994). The politics of homophobia in sport. In M.A. Messner & D.F. Sabo (Eds.) *Sex, Violence, and Power in Sports: Rethinking Masculinity*, p. 101–112. Freedom, CA: The Crossing Press.

Sabo, D. (1994). The myth of the sexual athlete. In M.A. Messner & D.F. Sabo (Eds.) *Sex, Violence, and Power in Sports: Rethinking Masculinity*, p. 36–41. Freedom, CA: The Crossing Press.

Sammons, J.T. (1990). *Beyond the Ring: The Role of Boxing in American Society*. Chicago: University of Illinois Press.

Sandomir, R. (2007 May 25). From the edge of madness to fighting's mainstream. *The New York Times*. p. D2.

Saraceno, J. (2007 August 6). Thanks to Bonds, 755 doesn't mean what it used to. *USA Today*, p. 2C.

Scelfo, J. (2006 October 9). Blood, guts and money: don't look now, but mixed martial arts has gone mainstream, p. 50.

Schwarz, A. (2007a May 31). An answer to help clear his fog. *The New York Times*, p. D7.

Schwarz, A. (2007b June 15). Lineman, dead at 36, sheds light on brain injuries. *The New York Times*, p. D1.

Schwarz, A. (2007c September 15). Silence on concussions raises risks of injury. *The New York Times*, Accessed October 8, 2007 online http://www.nytimes.com/2007/09/15/sports/football/15concussions.html?_r=1&ref=othersports&pagewanted=all#.

Schwarz, A. (2007d June 20). Silence on concussions may block N.F.L. guidelines. *The New York Times*, p. D1.

Schwarz, A. (2007e October 2). Girls are often neglected victims of concussions. *The New York Times*, p. A1, A20.

Schwarz, A. (2007f May 31). Study of ex-N.F.L. players ties concussion to depression risk. *The New York Times*, p A1.

Sharma, P., Luscombe, K.L., & Maffulli, N. (2005). Sports injuries in children. *Trauma, 5*, 245–259.

Shelov, S., & Bar-on, M. (1995). Media violence. *Pediatrics, 95* (6), 949–951.

Sherdog.com. (2007a December 2). Update: Sam Vasquez Dead at 35. Accessed December 2, 2007 online http://www.sherdog.com/news.asp?n_id=10203.

Sherdog.com. (2007b October 26). Randy Couture talks departure from UFC. Accessed October 26, 2007 online http://www.sherdog. com/videos/videos.asp?v_id=1316.

Sheridan, S. (2007). *A Fighter's Heart: One Man's Journey Through the World of Fighting*. New York: Atlantic Monthly Press.

Shultz, D. (2004 March 21). Fighting, Not Penalties, Is Best Way to Settle the Score. *New York Times*, p. 9–9.

Siegel, R. (2007 August 24). Mixed martial arts: sport or spectacle? *National Public Radio*. Accessed August 24, 2007 online http://www.npr.org/templates/story/story.php?storyId=13901908.

Simons, H.D., Bosworth, C., Fujita, S., & Jensen, M. (2007). The athlete stigma in higher education. *College Student Journal, 41* (2), 251–273.

Smith, P., Flay, B.R., Bell, C.C., & Weissberg, R.P. (2001). The protective influence of parents and peers in violence avoidance among African-American youth. *Maternal and Child Health Journal, 5* (4), 245–252.

Stapleton, A. (2007 July 12). Cage or ring? America's top amateur boxers ponder future of fighting. *USA Today*, Accessed October 6, 2007 online http://www.usatoday.com/sports/boxing/2007-07-12-3456597157_x.htm.

Stoudt, B.G. (2006). "You're either in or you're out": school violence, peer discipline, and the (re)production of hegemonic masculinity. *Men and Masculinities, 8* (3), 273–287.

Syken, B. (2005). All the rage: ultimate fighting. *Sports Illustrated, 103* (17), 30.

Swiatkowski, J. (2007 May 21). Jackson fighting for respect. *The Orange County Register*. Accessed May 21, 2007 online http://www.ocregister.com/ocregister/sports/homepagearticle_1701651.php.

Ta, L.M. (2006). Hurt so good: *Fight Club*, masculine violence, and the crisis of capitalism. *The Journal of American Culture, 29* (3), 265–277.

Tamburro, R.F., Gordon, P.L., D'Apolito, J.P., & Howard, S.C. (2004). Unsafe and Violent Behavior in Commercials Aired During Televised Major Sporting Events. *Pediatrics, 114* (6), e694–e698.

Tanriverdi, F., Unluhizarci, K., Coksevim, B., Selcuklu, A., Casanueva, F.F., & Kelestimur, F. (2007). Kickboxing sport as a new cause of traumatic brain injury-mediated hypopituitarism. *Clinical Endocrinology, 66*, 360–366.

The New UFC Fact Sheet. (2007). Accessed May 11, 2007 online http://www.ufc.com.

Tommasone, B.A., & McLeod, T.C.V. (2006). Contact sport concussion incidence. *Journal of Athletic Training, 41* (4), 470–472.

Torg, J.S., Guille, J.T., & Jaffe, S. (2002). Injuries to the cervical spine in American football players. *The Journal of Bone and Joint Surgery, 84-A* (1), 112–122.

Toth, C., McNeil, S., & Feasby, T. (2005). Central nervous system injuries in sport and recreation. *Sports Medicine, 35* (8), 685–715.

Tynes, J.R. (2006). Performance enhancing substances. *Journal of Legal Medicine, 27* (4), 493–509.

UFC. (2007 September 11). "UFC 75 on Spike TV is the most watched UFC event in history. Accessed September 11, 2007 online http://www.ufc.com/index.cfm?fa=news.detail&gid=7748.

USA Today. (2006 December 5). Ultimate fighting wins loyalty: wide range of fans enjoy bare-fisted duels. *USA Today*, P. 01D.

Velin, B. (2007 May 25). Superstar Liddell looks to avenge loss to Jackson. *USA Today*, p. 11C.

Vernacchia, R.A., McGuire, R.T., Reardon, J.P., & Templin, D.P. (2000). Psychosocial characteristics of Olympic track and field athletes. *International Journal of Sport Psychology, 31*, 5–23.

Villarreal, A. (2007, Issue 3). Quinton: Mr. Jackson if you're nasty. *MMA Worldwide*, 17–19.

Visek, A., & Watson, J. (2005). Ice hockey players' legitimacy of aggression and professionalization of attitudes. *Sport Psychologist, 19* (2), 178–192.

Vorsino, M. (2006 October 2). Fighting for a good cause: Papakolea club quells youth conflicts with training, discipline. *Honolulu Advertiser*, B3.

Waddington, I. (2004). Sports, health and public policy. In K. Young (Ed.) *Sporting Bodies, Damaged Selves: Sociological Studies of Sports-Related Injuries*, pp. 287–307. Boston: Elsevier Ltd.

Wacquant, L. (1998). A fleshpeddler at work: power, pain, and profit in the prizefighting economy. *Theory and Society, 27*, 1–42.

Wall, J. (2005). *UFC's Ultimate Warriors: The Top 10*. Toronto, Ontario, Canada: ECW Press.

Ward, C.L., Martin, E., Theron, C., & Distiller, G.B. (2007). Factors affecting resilience in children exposed to violence. *South African Journal of Psychiatry, 37* (1), 165–187.

Wawrow, J. (2007 September 12). Everett's mom hopeful of son's recovery. *Los Angeles Times*. Accessed September 12, 2007 online http://www.latimes.com/sports/nationaworld/wire/ats-ap_sports11sep12.

Websdale, N. (2001). *Policing the Poor: From Slave Plantation to Public Housing*. Boston: Northeastern University Press.

Weisman, L. (2005 March 31). Panthers case raises concerns about naturally occurring substances. *USA Today*, p. 8C.

Wertheim, J. (2007 May 28). The new main event: the rising interest in mixed martial arts is tied to ultimate fighting, which changed its ways to gain acceptance. Now its success is changing the sports landscape. *Sport Illustrated, 106* (22), 52–60.

Wiggins, D.K. (1997). *Glory Bound: Black Athletes in a White America*. Syracuse: Syracuse University Press.

Wilkinson, D.L. (2001). Violent events and social identity: specifying the relationship between respect and masculinity in inner-city youth violence. *Sociological Studies of Children and Youth, 8*, 231–265.

Wingert, P. & Lauerman, J.F. (2000). Parents behaving badly. *Newsweek, 136* (4), 47.

Wood, W., Wong, F.Y., & Chachere, J.G. (1991). Effects of media violence on viewers' aggression in unconstrained social interaction. *Psychological Bulletin, 109*, 371–383.

Worsnop, R.L. (1991 July 26). Athletes and drugs. *CQ Researcher, 1.*

Wright, D.R., & Fitzpatrick, K.M. (2006). Violence and minority youth: the effects of risk and asset factors on fighting among African American children and adolescents. *Adolescence, 41* (162), 251–262.

Wyatt, E., & Austen, I. (2007 May 26). Danish cyclist admits doping in tour victory. *New York Times*, p. A1, B12.

Wyatt, E., Austen, I., & Macur, J. (2007 August 11). Armstrong's team goes down with cycling's image. *New York Times*, p. A1, A12.

Young, C.C. (2002). Extreme sports: injuries and medical coverage. *Current Sports Medicine Reports, 1*, 306–311.

Young, K., White, P., & McTeer, W. (1994). Body talk: male athletes reflect on sport, injury, and pain. *Sociology of Sport Journal, 11*, 175–194.

Zimmerman, F.J., Christakis, D.A., & Vander Stoep, A. (2004). Tinker, tailor, soldier, patient: work attributes and depression disparities among young adults. *Social Science & Medicine, 58* (10), 1889–1901.

978-0-595-47891-
0-595-47891-3

Printed in the United States
104795LV00005B/146/P